What a Time to Be Alive!

by the same author

What Just Happened?!

Marina Hyde

What a Time to Be Alive!

Scenes from a Strange Age

First published by Guardian Faber in 2026
Guardian Faber is an imprint of Faber & Faber Limited
The Bindery, 51 Hatton Garden
London EC1N 8HN

Guardian is a registered trademark of
Guardian News & Media Ltd,
Kings Place, 90 York Way, London N1 9GU

Typeset by Ian Bahrami
Printed and bound by CPI Group (UK) Ltd, Croydon CR0 4YY

A CIP record for this book
is available from the British Library

ISBN 978-1-78335-331-6

MIX
Paper | Supporting
responsible forestry
FSC® C013604

Printed and bound in the UK on FSC® certified paper in line with our continuing
commitment to ethical business practices, sustainability and the environment.
For further information see faber.co.uk/environmental-policy

Our authorised representative in the EU for product safety is
Easy Access System Europe, Mustamäe tee 50, 10621 Tallinn, Estonia
gpsr.requests@easproject.com

2 4 6 8 10 9 7 5 3 1

To my parents, Diana and Alastair,
with love and eternal thanks

CONTENTS

INTRODUCTION

Hello to you, dear reader – and here we go again!

My last book of columns, *What Just Happened?!*, ended in the year 2022, and in large part chronicled the political chaos that erupted with the Brexit referendum, continued with the election of Donald Trump, and swept us onwards and downwards through the pandemic. It would be nice to think that I typed the words 'THE END' and all the chaos melted away. And it would also be nice to think that we haven't had three prime ministers since then – or rather, three at the time of writing this introduction.

No, wait – I'm sorry. The paragraph you are reading right now has been inserted literally days before we printed this book, because we've just got a fourth prime minister. Our seventh in a decade. I can't think of a pathway by which even *this* number could be out of date by the time you read it, but if anyone can pull it off, the UK can.

And, of course, my apologies if something else or a range of somethings elses has happened on top of that. Something certainly happened last time round. I will never know how they did it, but just before publication of *What Just Happened?!*, the Faber publicity department somehow managed to get a certain Liz Truss elected as prime minister, conjuring a giant, vivid, experiential marketing campaign for the book. Every night on the promotional tour, I would be gabbling away about her on stage, until I realised that the audience had phones and therefore had access to more up-to-date news than me. At which point I would have to ask, 'Hang on, is she still prime minister?!' And then, of course, one night she wasn't. Even so, her failure to reckon with her reckoning means she makes a few appearances in this book, along with some of Britain's other worst exes.

But I'm getting ahead of myself, because I began to notice something else on that tour. Once we got to the Q&A section of the evenings, and indeed the Q&A sections of all the events I did over the next 18 months, the same question would crop up again and again. And that question, as we inched towards the hard cut-off of a 2024 general election and the overwhelming likelihood of a Labour government, was: 'What on earth will you find to write about when this is all over?'

Well now. Short answer: *this*. All this that follows in the coming pages. The long answer – which I gave as tactfully and sensitively as I could at the time, given the political turmoil everyone had been living through for the past few years – was to say that while it was a lovely thought that 'this' would be 'over' with the dispatch of the Tories, regretfully I didn't think it would be. I didn't think the fundamentals of Britain's decline were easy to deal with, and I didn't think the Labour leadership was any good or had any realistic idea of how to get growth, or that the Labour party was so infinitely morally superior to the Conservatives that it would be like living in some kind of serene yesteryear utopia, where you checked the news only every week or so. And when you did, it was still mostly as you left it. No one would have kidnapped a president, annexed a country or done ketamine in the White House. Equally, I didn't want to be a complete Debbie Downer, so I'd try to end my answer on an up-note, saying stuff like, 'But, you know, maybe it'll all turn out great!'

If you're watching the events of the past few years on catch-up – or simply using this book to get you up to speed – then I apologise for dropping a spoiler in here, but, hand on heart, all did not turn out great. Within months of 'the grown-ups' being in charge, quite a few people already wanted the toddlers to be given the reins again. And a whole lot more wanted wicked Uncle Nigel to have his turn instead. I find it hard not to have at least some sympathy with many of these reactions in the abstract. After years of dysfunction and desperation, people are right to think they deserve better, even if you disagree with them on how that better will come about. It's when they stop even expecting anything better that a country feels most lost.

*

Anyway: our cast of characters. At no point during the period covered by this book did I have an absolutely clear handle on who would go on to become its leading lights. Some public figures who I thought would stick around ended up lasting the equivalent of a three-episode arc (gone too soon, Rupert Murdoch's prison chaplain fiancée!). Others were unexpectedly promoted from the chorus line and ended up becoming stars. Take Lauren Sánchez. Around the time of the earliest columns in this book, Lauren was still just a 'journalist and helicopter pilot' – not Mrs Bezos, nor the recipient of multiple philanthropy awards, nor an astronaut. Or take Mark Zuckerberg. At his regular summonses to Washington, the Meta boss still apologised for things and dressed like the reluctant teenage best man at his mother's third wedding. He now thinks all previous apologies were a mistake and dresses like an Armenian who owns an adult webcam business. Or take ChatGPT, which a few years ago could have been the name of a premium-rate adult sex-line business, but is now responsible for everything from your work presentation to an unspecified number of autonomous US weapons systems.

But we don't just have those, of course; we've also got Nigel Farage, Christian Horner and Princess Di's ghost. The only sadness is that they don't all appear in the same column. We've got the difficult men of the creative industries, from misunderstood veg banterer Gregg Wallace to increasingly-clearly-understood author and 'ally' Neil Gaiman. We've got Russell Brand being baptised in the Thames by Bear Grylls. We have Fifa president Gianni Infantino, whose baddie glow-up has been as swift as it was inevitable in his endlessly rancid organisation. And in terms of landmark events in legal history, we get to relive the Gwyneth Paltrow ski massacre trial. We've got the tireless heroes of the Post Office scandal, and the tiresome villains of Silicon Valley. We have a president turning the White House lawn into an electric-car dealership ('Wow! Everything's computer!'). We have Jeffrey Epstein, a guy who, bizarrely, turned out to be one of the most consequential figures in transatlantic public life, capable of wreaking havoc from beyond his grave. We have serial nonagenarian romantic Rupert Murdoch, engaged, sundered and re-engaged inside of a year, along with Duchess Meghan, Montecito's most down-to-earth homemaker. Indeed, I have tried to curate all these delights in much the same way as Meghan might assemble a basket of lovely little hospitality supplies to be left by the bed of a semi-willing house guest.

As for the period covered by the book, let's just say the arc of history bent in pretty much every direction bar towards justice. Many of those who had been able to convince themselves that the Brexit/Trump/pandemic upheavals were some kind of blip resigned themselves to chaos and unpredictability being the norm. Or, to put it another way, we seem to be living through a period of political and social entropy, having moved from a state of something that felt more like order towards increasing instability and an agonising loss of institutional effectiveness. Having said that, this does mean that I really haven't been short of stuff to write about, so . . . swings and roundabouts for humanity.

I'm kidding, of course. But I do want to end this on a positive note, because, strange as it may seem in the circumstances, I am an optimist. *No, but really*. I do have faith that we humans can get ourselves out of a lot of the holes we're in, even if we fall into others in the process. I do truly believe there is light at the end of this tunnel. Unfortunately, the tunnel is filled with sewage – but the glimmer is there. So if you've been kind enough to tuck this book into your hazmat suit, I thank you. Hold your nose, take my rubber-gloved hand, and let's wade through it all together.

MEDIA SPECTACLES (SPECTACULAR AND OTHERWISE)

Television adhered to the decree of Duchess Meghan and allowed us to experience wonder in every moment. From the no-stakes legal maelstrom of the Gwyneth Paltrow ski trial to Princess Di's ghost hamming away furiously in *The Crown*, the possibilities of the medium were explored in dazzling fashion. *Strictly Come Dancing* continued its long stint as the prime piece of formatted entertainment across which all UK culture wars must be fought, while Saoirse Ronan failed to understand the assignment and said something interesting, unprepared and unexpected on a chat show. Ideally, it won't catch on. Speaking of things unlikely to catch on, car manufacturer Jaguar unveiled a peak woke advert precisely two weeks after the watershed moment of Donald Trump's re-election, after which you couldn't sell a single share in woke, much less a pink car with a six-figure price tag. Meanwhile, our long-time alternative royal family, the Beckhams, caught a nasty case of the Windsors.

Did Gwyneth Paltrow ski into a retired optometrist? I couldn't care less, but the farce is unmissable

28 March 2023

A starstruck lawyer, a neutrals-clad wellness guru – this has to be the lowest-stakes court battle of all time

To Park City, Utah, currently scene of one of the great pleasures of modern life: a court battle that you'd be intensely relaxed for either side to lose. Yes, it's the Gwyneth Paltrow ski massacre trial. Take your seats for a preposterously camp battle between a well-to-do retired optometrist, who says the high priestess of fanny-steaming skied into him, and Her Vajesty herself, who says he skied into her. Why is this not happening at The Hague? Sorry, but NO sense of occasion.

Before we go any further I want to make a deeply serious point. Something happened that day. Something happened on that mountain in that luxury ski resort up there in God's cathedral, and, like anyone who has watched either the plaintiff or the defendant on the stand at any length . . . I literally could not care less what it was. I mean, this is as low stakes as it gets. Asked about what had been taken from her by the events on the Deer Valley slopes, Paltrow delivered the sociopathically straight-to-meme line: 'Well, I lost half a day of skiing.' (Bear in mind this is a woman who claims that water has feelings.) For his part, Terry Sanderson's lawyer put things into perspective by declaring: 'After the crash, he's no longer charming.'

We'll come on to the charmicidal maniac/wronged wellness guru in a moment. First, a reminder that Mr Sanderson is seeking $300,000 in damages, which – to us country mice on this side of the Atlantic – feels a little eye-catching. Of course, we have only an outsider's grasp of the baroque flourishes of the US legal system, but we surely know that any citizen of that great nation making some kind of personal injury claim understands that *this is America* and asks for at least $30m just as a point of principle. Then again, having watched him, I think I'm on the verge of understanding why Mr Sanderson values his lost charm at a mere $300,000.

In reality, so well adjusted is our early-21st-century system of social capital that there are few better ways to accrue charm than from starring in the Gwyneth Paltrow ski trial. This seems to have been something once dimly grasped by Mr Sanderson, who emailed his daughters in the immediate wake of the accident with the possibly unfortunate subject line: 'I'm famous . . . at what cost?' As for whether the collision put him off skiing ever again, on Monday he revealed he 'tried not to go back', but eventually overrode himself and took several skiing trips, albeit dressed in [*slightly traumatised pause*] 'this ungodly-looking red fluorescent outfit that I bought'. Stakes, dear boy. Stakes.

Arguably Terry's most compelling proof that he suffered a brain injury is his choice of lawyer, who makes Lionel Hutz look like Cicero. At one point in the proceedings, Kristin VanOrman almost squealed: 'I am so jealous! . . . I have to wear four-inch heels just to make it to 5'5"!' 'They're very nice,' lied Gwyneth. 'You're not trained in accident reconstruction?' ran another gambit. 'Me?' asked Gwyneth. 'No.' 'Neither am I!' chortled Kristin.

A few years ago, Gwyneth stopped acting to focus on her lifestyle brand Goop, and I would be overjoyed if she now stopped that to focus on starring in court cases serving up this level of farm-to-table hilarity. 'Private security for my client wanted to bring in treats for the bailiffs for how helpful they've been,' announced her lawyer one morning. 'So, I wanted to do that transparently and see if there are any objections?' Alas, there were some objections. That basic bitch Lady Justice apparently says madam can't treat-basket her way out of this one.

But you can't keep a good wellness entrepreneur down. Every aesthetically challenging day in that hideous orange Utah legal facility, Gwyneth has swept in wearing category-five neutrals, hopefully drawn from her own brand's Courtroom Casuals line. (Though all Gwyneth's garments are made from the neck hairs of these really incredible Himalayan goats to whose sheddings a normie like you could never have access, do be reassured they WILL be lovingly ripped off in never-pill nylon and available later this year as Halloween costumes.) Just as Goop is a place where food is never eaten but instead 'grabbed' or 'reached for', so it is that one of the best things Gwyneth's website can say about any outfit is that it 'takes you effortlessly' from one part of your day to another. In this case, from pursing your lips in court to making that evening's waiter give you the résumé and achievements of every ingredient in the biodynamic salad, before pursing your lips once more and hissing: 'No, thank you, I'll just have broth.'

As for any lessons that might be drawn from this appallingly entertaining courtroom dramedy, I am afraid I can only return to an oldie but a goodie: never litigate. Never litigate unless you absolutely positively have to – and as far as anyone can see, Mr Sanderson didn't have to. We already know what Gwyneth Paltrow's like. But we now know, from Terry's own testimony, that he ordered his former girlfriend to leave him after he began his legal journey, as 'I knew she didn't buy into it . . . My interaction with my family has been difficult,' he reflected yesterday. 'Something is wrong with my essence and what I bring to the table with them.' Earlier, one of his daughters had testified that he was 'obsessed' with the trial, while another's deposition declared he was 'emotionally abusive' and 'quick to anger' before the 2016 collision. Whatever the thread count of this dirty linen, is it worth it? For anyone other than the countless mind-boggled spectators, the answer can only be . . . no.

Diana's ghost in *The Crown*? Darling, what's new? She's the hardest working spectre in showbiz

17 October 2023

Thanks to psychics and Hollywood actors, she's never wanted for work – and she'll be a real vision in Netflix's 'prestige' drama

There is spine-tingling supernatural news from *The Crown*, a TV show that takes itself considerably more seriously than the actual royal family. This has never been a programme that wears the 'prestige TV' label as lightly as have other jewels of the era, preferring instead to drag it like a 10-ton weight into every scene while some of the finest actors of their generations pretend to be things like 'sad about the news' or 'Princess Anne'.

Giggling away with a drink and a packet of crisps, I often wonder if I am its only disloyal subject. Surely not. For a long time I really couldn't believe anyone took it seriously and assumed it must be in on the joke itself – a Nicolas Cage of a show, if you will.

I can't quite decide whether this position has been bolstered or undermined by the high-camp news that the forthcoming final series is to feature the ghost of Princess Diana. According to reports – and it's not out yet, so the usual caveats – the ghost appears to both Prince Charles and the late Queen.

The Queen sees her while planning the funeral arrangements and starts crying, having been told she 'taught us what it means to be British'. To Charles, who is apparently shown sobbing over her body in a Paris morgue, Diana's ghost reportedly says: 'Thank you for how you were in the hospital. So raw, broken – and handsome.' Oooh. 'I'll take that with me. You know I loved you so much. So deeply, so painfully too. That's over now. It will be easier for everyone with me gone.' Can this genuinely be the dialogue? I certainly hope so.

Having said all that, I have kept a close eye on the appearances of Princess Di's ghost since her death. I'm not her talent agent or anything – indeed, the post-death CV I am about to showcase might cause you to wonder if she even has reputable theatrical representation in the afterlife – but once you start, patterns do begin to suggest themselves.

One of the most regular jobs Diana's ghost takes, for example, is appearing to actors who are going to play her, to communicate how completely OK she is with their decision. And, dare they hint, kind of honoured. Kristen Stewart, who was Diana in the 2021 film *Spencer*, 'felt some spooky, spiritual feelings making this movie . . . I felt there were moments where I kind of got the sign-off.' It was the same for Naomi Watts, who gave us her Diana in an eponymous 2013 film. 'There were definitely moments when I felt Diana's presence,' explained Watts. 'I found myself constantly asking for her permission to carry on . . . There was one particular moment when I felt her permission was granted.' Mmm.

Elsewhere, Diana's ghost has an eye for an occasion. Before this *Crown* booking, she most recently appeared to – or, rather, was heard by – some viewers of ITV's broadcast of the Queen's funeral. As the hearse headed out of London towards Windsor, a woman's voice could be heard saying, 'The death is irreversible – and the fact that's she's trapped . . .' before a male commentator hastily cut in. Really a very competitive booking from ITV there, who do suffer with people reflexively watching the big events on the BBC.

Speaking of big events, Diana's former psychic and 'energy healer' Simone Simmons is still able to hear her ghost – even over the sound of cash registers. 'I know a lot of people aren't going to like it,' hazarded Simmons in 2017, 'but she said we've got to vote for Brexit. Britain was great, economically and production-wise before we joined the EU. She was interested in the referendum, and suggested I vote to leave because Britain was really great before the EU.' Righto.

During Covid, Diana's ghost seems to have fallen in with an Australian anti-masker. Then, in 2018, a Japanese spiritual leader announced the deceased princess had been in touch to reveal that 'England will experience another revolution'. Also: 'I prefer Islam.'

Then again, Diana's a great lover of pubs, frequenting the England's Rose in Oxfordshire (formerly the Feathers) and several others, even if her chat tends towards the predictable. Like many with their . . . gift, is it? . . . psychics frequently reveal that she has told them that Kate is perfect, but she can't be doing with Meghan.

Not that Her Royal Spectralness is always welcome. A parson was reportedly called to Sandringham in 2001, after the servants refused to work in one chamber. 'The parson said,' wrote the *Mail*'s long-time royal correspondent Kenneth Rose in Volume II of his diaries (1979–2014), 'that the oppressive or disturbing atmosphere may have been because of Princess Diana.'

A poor show – but it must be said that workwise, the 2000s for Diana's ghost had the humiliating flavour of John Travolta's 1980s. 2003 found her appearing in a pay-per-view seance in the US. The DVD of this televisual horror show is emblazoned with the words 'BANNED IN GREAT BRITAIN', which would sadly have limited the presumably much-needed royalties available to its naturalised American presenter, former *Avengers* star Patrick Macnee. Macnee certainly looks to be thinking of the pay cheque as he watches psychics compete to get the best content from other-side Di.

For someone who in life could pick up the phone to the likes of Elton John or Liza Minnelli for a sensational gossip, it must feel a bit of a comedown having to spend eternity with only ghastly old chancers like these to natter to. Diana supposedly appears to one medium couple at the seance, who say she's 'met Mother Teresa'. (Funny way to put it, given she and Mother T met several times in life, but perhaps they'd shared a drink from the River Lethe.

Or maybe Mother T was just being standoffish about the fact that Diana's death, five days before her own, ended up completely overshadowing it.)

That seance came before the era of prestige TV, of course, meaning it was not inherently classy. Strange now to think back to that benighted time, when actual culture secretaries somehow thought they had better things to do than write to Netflix. 'I fear a generation of viewers who did not live through these events may mistake fiction for fact,' feared Oliver Dowden about the previous series of *The Crown*. For my part, I fear he is now deputy prime minister. It would be wonderful to know Diana's view on both that incidental detail and her upcoming appearance in *The Crown* – and, since she's the afterlife's greatest showbiz trouper, it surely won't be long before we find out.

One day, all matters of state will be decided through *Strictly Come Dancing*. That day seems near

15 October 2024

The Saturday-night staple is no longer just a dance show – it's a battlefield, where political fights and culture wars are waged

Within two years – maybe one – the pre-eminent mode of political discourse in our society will be things that did or didn't happen on *Strictly Come Dancing*. This imperial phase for our culture was actually predicted by Edmund Burke in a sealed section of *A Vindication of Natural Society*, viewable only by those with a pure heart and the sophisticated conviction that ballroom has always been war by other means. I think Burke also foresaw Gregg Wallace, whom we'll come to in a sec.

As you may know, the top-rated BBC Saturday-night show has once again been fitted with its 'row' suffix. The latest incident to rock *Strictly*, in the parlance of these things, concerns pro dancer Katya Jones and Wynne Evans, the guy who plays the opera singer Gio Compario in the Go.Compare adverts. And if you gave in to even a twitch of a smile at the thought of contemporary sexual politics being litigated via those proxies, then you should be immediately reclassified into that least escapable modern category: Part of the Problem. As for the problem – is it very bad to have spent two days scrutinising the footage, watching the row mushroom, studying the two separate apology videos for something the pair insist was a joke, and still be distinctly unclear on what did or didn't happen? If so, I can only apologise.

To briefly summarise, footage from Saturday shows Wynne's hand slightly creeping round Katya's waist, and her moving it back. There also seems to have been a declined high five. As mentioned, both have since posted video apologies – e-pologies, if you will – saying it was just a silly inside joke. And look, I have a huge amount of time for formal statements containing the words 'we were just messing around in the Clauditorium'. (Likewise, today's official Corporation statement about something said in a *Mrs Brown's Boys* rehearsal, which declares the BBC 'against all forms of racism' and sounds like something Derek Zoolander might have on a T-shirt.)

The *Strictly* row has drawn forth all the forces of the pre-industrial woo-woo complex. Take 'body language expert' Judi James, doyenne of this venerated science, who is somehow yet to receive the nod from the Nobel committee. Judi was on hand in the *Daily Mail* to reveal the 'true meaning' of the pair's joint apology for the joke. 'Wynne's smile looks awkward and becomes a teeth-baring gesture when he opens his mouth to try to speak,' she decrees. 'His "Yes, sorry" looks penitent and he finishes with a lip-clamp with his mouth pulled down at the corners in a denial ritual. Katya leans into the camera with her brows raised and finishes with clenched teeth.'

Not to be in a denial ritual, but . . . sorry, what? I'm certainly looking forward to Judi being let loose on the concurrent Gregg Wallace videos. The *MasterChef* host also seems to be in some kind of – yes – hot water over on-set jokes, and has consequently felt the need to set the record straight. Has he succeeded? Well, we can probably all agree that none of us would wish to have been sitting in our home study yesterday with a selfie stick while saying the words: 'These allegations were investigated by the BBC six years ago and my comments were found to be not sexual.' This sort of thing is normally the prelude to joining Substack. Then, this morning, Gregg could be found yomping across a field with that same selfie stick, revealing he was stressed but sticking to 'my healthy lifestyle choices . . . I really like a mango. I really like a pineapple. I really like a bowl of blueberries.'

Gregg has himself done *Strictly*, of course, such is the nature of light-entertainment cross-pollination. He subsequently revealed of his stint on the show: 'I was having a really tough time . . . The side of my face broke out into a rash, like cold sores but up the side of my face.' Unable to go on stage one Saturday night, he summoned a therapist to the studio – 'I got parking for her' – only for her to fix him with the words: 'Gregg Wallace, as important as you think you are, nobody gives a shit what you dance like, mate.' This wasn't the line he went with after elimination, of course, but arguably she had a point.

Yet for something meant to be a bit of fun, *Strictly* can have the flavour of some totalitarian country's state television, with its nutso apparatus of fervently expressed joy and gratitude, underpinned by beady-eyed artist chaperones and mandated apologies that typically resemble hostage videos. It is getting to the stage this season where I can almost imagine a contestant giving their minder the slip and defecting to *I'm a Celebrity* in the dead of night. Press conference on the Gold Coast airport tarmac, in which they denounce the warped ideology of the glitterball and reveal the existence of a network of tango re-education camps.

Perhaps this is one of the downsides of the post-streaming-wars world. There is just less television that people gather round at the same time now. Aside from sport, the formats that still retain the power to bring the nation together in serious numbers, live, also frequently seem to polarise it, or at least become freighted with vastly more meaning than they can possibly bear.

Strictly's unasked-for status as the show across which most culture wars must be waged increasingly reminds me of those shudder-inducing stories about battery chickens. These unfortunate creatures are intensively farmed in order to scale them up at unnatural speed, but they still cheep like chicks and have legs that are unable to support the weight of their bodies. Without wishing to call it too soon, is it just possible that a dancing show is being forced to bear too much cultural weight?

I don't expect stone-cold truths from a chat show, but Saoirse Ronan delivered one

29 October 2024

The men on Graham Norton's sofa found self-defence a hoot. I'm sure most women have found themselves in that conversation

In a development that absolutely must not catch on, something interesting has happened on a TV chat show. What a precedent: I'm desperately hoping the entertainment industry rallies around to prevent it ever happening again. We can probably count on it. The dance of all chat shows these days is almost entirely mechanised. You go on. You do your rehearsed anecdotes. The news that the late Michael Parkinson is being relaunched as an AI barely raises an eyebrow because it's all so synthetic anyway. Therefore, the moments when it isn't take on outsized significance.

As you may have guessed, we are talking about last Friday's episode of *The Graham Norton Show*, on which the *Blitz* star Saoirse Ronan appeared as a guest, alongside *Gladiator II* actors Denzel Washington and Paul Mescal and *Day of the Jackal* leading man Eddie Redmayne. We join the sofa as Redmayne is doing an anecdote about how his *Jackal* preparation involved him being trained in self-defence, in order to do what Team America would call 'his acting'. (Not how Eddie put it, obviously. And yet, the reality.) Redmayne's revelation that he was shown how to use a phone as a weapon if attacked proves quite the hoot, with Mescal riffing on the absurdity – 'Who's actually going to do that, though?' – Norton chiming in, and Denzel laughing along. Ronan is trying to say something, but she gets honked over, before managing to cut through with a line for the ages: 'That's what girls have to think about all the time.'

Oooooof. The look on the other actors' faces after Saoirse has detonated this chat-icide bomb is hilariously mesmerising, as is the sudden silence, which is split-second but also seems to last 27 years. Ronan obligingly diffuses it by provoking the audience's applause with a rallying 'Amirite, ladies?' And then everyone moves on. Well, everyone except the internet, which has been picking over the entrails ever since.

The clip itself will be familiar to any woman who has ever wondered if they can be arsed interrupting some self-styled comedy gold happening around them to say something that matters to them. As mentioned, Saoirse herself has at least one failed attempt at interjection, before waiting, as one must, and trying again – at which point the guys are having such a rip-roaring time doing their bit that initially they don't appear to realise she has opted not to respond with the time-worn improv gambit 'Yes, and . . .'.

Possibly the best part of the entire thing is the moment after, surely a shoo-in for the Best Silence Oscar. Personally I'd have liked it to have been broken by Denzel thundering, 'WHERE IS

YOUR IMPROV NOW?', but for some reason such lines desert our leading men. Caught unawares, Redmayne offers a sort of wan yas-kween nod. But the applause for Ronan is seized on as a natural break, and the conversation moves on without anyone at all discussing by far and away the most fascinating thing said on the sofa thus far.

But look, I know what you might be thinking: is all this unfair? I mean, they're only on a flipping chat show, aren't they? The trouble is that there are so few of these sorts of moments in the obsessively controlled world of contemporary showbiz that we are left with the somewhat absurd situation of twats like me remorselessly analysing this tiny clip like we're huddled in the White House situation room watching live footage of some Seal team raid on a stronghold and holding our breath for the kill order. And yet, this one proves no less satisfying each time you see it. Ladies and gentlemen – she got 'em.

No one is suggesting that the male actors and presenter involved deserve some huge backlash for this. What people are saying is that the moment was telling. When clips like this go viral, it's for a reason. For this many civilians to share them – this many female civilians, let's face it – means they instantly saw something they recognised. Most, if not absolutely all, women have been in a version of that conversation in their time, and almost all have not found the precise words to say in the moment it was happening, instead coming up with them either while stewing on the way home or two weeks later in the middle of the night (still stewing).

For the right words to be found in the moment, on primetime television, is a fantasy arguably more powerful than any of the ones the chaps are currently promoting in their movies and prestige TV projects. No offence to the Roman gladiator, former-Roman-gladiator-turned-arms-dealer and public-school assassin with whom Saoirse was sharing the sofa, but Mescal and Washington just got totally Colosseumed, while Redmayne took an absolute burn bullet to the forehead.

Even now, their publicists will be frantically workshopping reflective answers for pending interviews in which they may be asked about Ronan's point. What makes it somehow more darkly amusing is that these particular three male actors are always projected as being among the good guys of showbiz. And I'm sure they are. But what they can't do, even with all their combined decades of Acting, is think their way into the part of literally any woman, in any place, walking home after dark or going down an almost deserted route on just another day in a lifetime of knowing she could be prey. You get quite good at thinking about how boring little things like phones or keys might be able to defend you in those moments, as any woman will wearily concede. We all dream of a future without this forever hum of fear, where we too can join in the absurdist joke.

And yes, of course it was all just a joke. But consider the real-life context in which this tiny little sofa vignette occurred. We are a week off a US presidential election in which the fact that the bookies' favourite has been accused of multiple sexual assaults over multiple decades has not even been an issue. Even with my expectations adjusted to meet the times, it will never not blow my mind that we are going to get to the end of this presidential campaign and the fact that at least 26 – TWENTY-SIX – women have accused one candidate of sexual assault has not even remotely dominated the news cycle. There has not been one week or even one day in which that message has caught fire and everyone has talked of absolutely nothing else. It is just – what? – accepted? Expected? Priced in? Boring? Either way, perhaps it helps explain why many women are not in their best 'take a joke' mood right now.

Hats off to Jaguar's 'inclusive' new branding: now people of all backgrounds won't buy its cars

22 November 2024

In the aftermath of Trump's victory, the ad already looks like a period piece. But aside from that – I mean, seriously?

There are many eve-of-the-offensive conversations I would love to have been a fly on the wall for. Inside the Trojan horse, say, with that Ancient Greek SAS unit bantering the day away, before busting out for their daring small-hours raid. Or inside the Jaguar marketing department, on the night before their new rebrand, as these crack experiential troops prepared to release this week's new ad on an unsuspecting luxury car market. Picture the champagne corks popping as the socials are timed to post the video at the appointed hour. 'I hope the pre-order guys are ready for an onslaught, because we've got eight capital "D" Diverse models in category-five tulle busting out of a pink-planet lift wielding a hammer – and precisely NO cars! Let's make some sales history!'

Anyhow. Arguably it's gone slightly worse than the wooden horse, which, when you think about it, was one of the most successful high-performance vehicles in history/mythology. Sure, it was oversized, over-reliant on heritage materials and probably took corners like a supertanker – and yet, I defy you not to take your hat off. No one said urban warfare couldn't be quirky and design-led.

Back in the present day, meanwhile, marketing folklore is already building up around the Jaguar campaign, which made its debut this week to reactions ranging from vocal bemusement to vocal derision. As far as I can make out, the best this ad's defenders can come up with is that 'the internet is talking about it', which feels like one of those mad, missing-a-step start-up memes. 'It's Uber, but for socks.' 'It's Airbnb, but for salads.' 'It's SpaceX, but for a weird car you can't buy yet.'

Not that there aren't various people saying obdurately that they completely love it, even though it's obviously tired and boring and about as 'brave' as 'using your platform' at the Oscars. But the one thing we can be absolutely sure of is, not a single one of those defenders will be buying a single one of these cars. And – regrettable newsflash – selling cars *does* remain the core mission of a car company. In fact, hilariously, there aren't even any cars to buy for a while, because Jaguar will now halt output entirely for at least a year, with three new EVs not due for sale till 2026. Those will cost almost double what a current Jag does, with the firm claiming this ad announces its intention to reach younger, richer people whom it idealises as 'cash-rich, time-poor'. Hence this 'breaking away from the category tropes', which for some reason reminds me of those political activists who tell you that they don't need those old voters – they can get new, better ones.

In *Adweek*, the chief strategy officer of Interbrand was one of those going all counterintuitive, praising Jaguar for 'showing up like a creative business rather than a car manufacturer'. Hmm. This feels like praising a bottom-of-the-table team for showing up like a creative business rather than a football side.

The big question is: how on earth did this all happen? Remarkably, there is no rogue outside agency that can be blamed for going off-piste and persuading fusty old Jaguar executives – painfully aware that they are outsold six to one by their Tata Motors stablemate Land Rover – to take a last-ditch big swing. Nope, this was all done in-house.

But the main culprit is timing. Swings this big take months to be signed off, and back when the concept of this campaign was approved, it must have seemed perfectly of its moment. Various media outlets have dredged up a clip of its 'mastermind' accepting an award just one month ago, in which he announces, with a distinct air of self-congratulation, that Jaguar has established a full 15 DEI groups. Righto. There is something ludicrous about a guy who is poised to roll out cars that are going to start at a hundred grand boasting about being mega-inclusive. It reminds me of the time when Coutts debanked Nigel Farage, stating that they were 'above all' committed to being an 'inclusive organisation'. To which the only reply is: you're a private bank where people have to have at least £3m in cash savings to open a current account. WHAT ARE YOU TALKING ABOUT? Do you 'include' low-income, middle-income or even the vast majority of high-income people? Then, honestly, pipe down.

Alas, Jaguar seem to have got the piping-down memo too late, declaring this week that 'This is a reimagining that recaptures the essence of Jaguar, returning it to the values that once made it so loved, but making it relevant for a contemporary audience. We are creating Jaguar for the future, restoring its status as a brand that enriches the lives of our clients and the Jaguar community.' OK! Although, counterpoint: you're releasing a tired mess, two weeks post a Donald Trump election victory and amid the undeniable sense that there has been a vibe shift in the era of woke capitalism that has perplexed and delighted consumers for the past few years, in distinctly unequal measure. In some ways, the timing of this ad calls to mind all those Sunday newspaper columns viciously slagging off Princess Diana that – print lead-in times being what they were – appeared just as the world was waking up to news of her death. There had, to restate the point, been a vibe shift.

The effect is to render Jaguar's new ad an instant period piece. Or, to put it another way, while it might have been infinitely less iconic in terms of design, there is a sense in which that lift in the advert really has turned out to be a secret weapon. Trouble is, it's pointing the wrong way. Jaguar have Trojan-horsed themselves.

It's *With Love, Meghan* – not just a TV show but a landmark piece of art. And not in a good way

4 March 2025

A whole political and cultural era is passing, and who better than the Duchess of Sussex as a symbol of all we have left behind?

Are peonies a life philosophy? Are 'life philosophies' even philosophy? I have to hold on to the idea that they aren't, even in the face of a decade or so of Instagram blitzkrieg, most currently in the form of Duchess Meghan's new eight-part TV show, which dropped on Netflix first thing this morning. *With Love, Meghan* seems to have migrated fully formed from Mark Zuckerberg's social media platform on to Ted Sarandos's streaming service, powered by the hashtags that bypass the need for joined-up sentences, let alone thinking. Or as Her Grace explains: 'Everyone's invited to create wonder in every moment.' This is an offer not even promised by most major religions.

The mildest way to describe this show is as a ghastly artefact of a particular cultural era that recently met its apocalypse. But more on that later. To anyone who says, 'It's just meant to be fun': bullshit. Netflix reportedly paid $100m (£78m) to Prince Harry and the manic pixie-dream duchess for an overall deal, so for the streamer it's meant to make back at least a small amount of the big amount of money they lost when audiences failed to connect with the Sussex-authored documentaries about global-justice activists and polo. For Meghan, it's supposed to assist her transformation into a domestic guru. If you don't mind arching an eyebrow at the lifestyle lunacies of fellow Montecito resident Gwyneth Paltrow, then at least have some consistency and give yourself a pass on this one. This show is sensationally absurd and trite, and if you watch it, you'll know it.

Language is either category-five twee or has been reduced to non-sentient babyspeak. 'Good vibes, good hives.' 'Clean clean clean clean.' 'Single-skillet spaghetti. S–s–s. S–s–s . . .' I won't labour the 1% of the 1% mood, though someone driving through one of America's most rarefied billionaires' communities to buy a few hundred dollars' worth of flowers while telling you, 'It's the little things that count,' is obviously ridiculous. As is referring to a bucket as a 'garbage vessel'. Nor will I, 'as a woman', do more than note that you don't see successful men spending for ever on all this stuff. Zuckerberg and Sarandos presumably decided a very long time ago that part of the goal is to not even know where your kitchen is.

Of much more interest is how these Insta-perfect worlds have grabbed people by the throat and siphoned away so much of their valuable time and attention in recent years. Scrolling the platform or watching Meghan's show (they are almost identical sensory experiences), you note how much of the language is explicitly religious. Time is described as 'sacred', practices are 'rituals', people are continually feeling 'blessed', snacks are 'an offering' and the emphasis is on 'honouring' this or that. It becomes hard not to see all the flower frogs and rosemary sprigs and garbage vessels as holy kit, arranged in esoteric fashion as if to summon a form of peace. Or rather, #peace. But peace through retail, always – even if the product turns out to be you.

It's amusing to learn from publicists and Meghan herself that the duchess's artisan this-and-thats will be available in the Netflix brick-and-mortar stores opening this year. Other eras have had their epicureans or hedonists, of course, who lived and sometimes died for the ideal of simplicity or pleasure in an epic kind of way. But today's gazillion-strong influencer community has zero intellectual underpinning to it, which is why it's so often the unwitting butt of its own joke. I'm trying to picture Oscar Wilde being told that Netflix is going to sell limited-edition artisan Oscar Wilde buttonholes in its shop, and him just fainting at the obvious horror of it all.

Sorry to press an unmodernised yet perfectly adequate word into action, but of course all this stuff is perfectly *nice*. It's nice if the table is laid nicely, it's lovely if the flowers are lovely, it's caring of you to make people feel cared for, whatever that really means. (I wonder if the truly selfless tablescape actually exists – Meghan's entire MO feels desperately 'compliments to the hostess'.) As I say, it's all *nice*. But it's neither a long nor an interesting conversation; at best it should serve as a backdrop to one. And yet over the past rise-of-the-influencer decade, it seems to have *become* the conversation.

Decades often seem to be about certain things, before another, defining thing sneaks in under the radar. The 2000s seemed to be about celebrity culture and Islamist fundamentalism, but in retrospect the 2008 financial crash – both its causes and the failure to deliver justice in its aftermath – was the key event. The 10 years we have just lived through might have seemed to be about social media and what came to be summarised as woke culture. But a global fracturing was stealing in under the radar.

It certainly isn't any more. In fact, watching *With Love, Meghan* early this morning already felt like a past washing over me, so much so that I decided that maybe – and please stay with me for this hot take – maybe Meghan has made a landmark TV series after all. Immerse yourself in it for an episode or eight, and you instinctively feel that both the show and the duchess embody the age that has suddenly become bygone. And that is the exact feeling that countless people have been experiencing since this year turned – that an era is dying. Or rather, that it has already died, and suddenly. There were many others, but Meghan was as good an avatar for it as any – torn between wildly ineffective social justice activism and the narcotising retreat of the peonied table. But this is now over, and I think we can all feel it in our bones. Rest in peace/power/whatever. But godspeed to something else – something better – being born.

First it was family, now it's a feud. But even in meltdown, Brand Beckham is raking it in

15 August 2025

Brooklyn and his wife Nicola have fallen out with the rest of the multimedia-lifestyle-industrial complex. Luckily, it's all being kept very private

What is 'Brand Beckham'? I don't mean to question the very idea of a celebrity brand – far from it. In fact, part of the reason that celeb-watching phrases like 'the brand' and 'controlling the narrative' have gone completely mainstream is because of David and Victoria Beckham. So ubiquitous is the professionalisation of celebrity these days, and so media-literate is the public, that it's hard to remember just how revolutionary the Beckhams were in British culture back in the day. Twenty-five years ago, nobody except some rarefied elite publicist wanged on about narratives. But now everyone knows how to read an influencer. Almost all celebrities are regarded primarily as people who are selling something. Furthermore, people act like mis-selling a lifestyle is worse than several major financial crimes.

Anyway, back to the brand. What is the Beckham brand? Not their many specific product brands, nor the many other ones to which they lend their images for advertising. The thing I'm talking about is more like a movie star's screen persona, the unifying characteristic, the theme that permeates all their roles, the magic that fans go back for. In the case of the Beckhams, the brand is really their family. Two became six.

In the more distant past, this meant Victoria and David selling news of the pregnancies to *OK!* magazine, then selling the first baby photos and so on. In the age of Instagram, as their children have grown up, it has meant constantly tending this idyllic image by posting private family moments, having everyone show up en masse for the launch of each other's football franchises/fashion shows/face primers/food lines/50th-birthday marathons and dutifully sending daily public messages of love, support and thanks to each other across social media platforms, where others can see them. Whether it's family or business – and sometimes it isn't entirely clear where the dividing line is – it's all very much the family business.

As distilled in David's Netflix documentary – self-commissioned, naturally – the message is that no matter what triumph or disaster comes their way, the Beckham family are about each other. Any adversity is folded into their story and ends up being repurposed into (lucrative) triumph, because this is a family that sticks together, and which draws its strength from that. It's aspirational and sometimes charming. It has worked.

So what happens when a gaping hole is blown in the idyll? In some of the most eye-popping showbiz news of the summer, it has emerged beyond all doubt that one of the family – firstborn Brooklyn – wants nothing to do with the others. If the idea of a feud was plausibly deniable back when Brooklyn and his wife, Nicola Peltz, got married three years ago, it was harder to maintain when the pair didn't show up for any of David's 50th-birthday celebrations this May. It is now impossible, following Brooklyn and Nicola's decision to post to Instagram huge numbers of photos of their very recent wedding vow renewal ceremony. (Vow renewals: another part of modern celeb culture that didn't really happen before they happened in magazine buy-ups or on social media.) Details of the lavish big day? The ceremony was officiated by Nicola's billionaire father, Nelson, and she wore her mother's wedding dress. Oh, and not a single member of the Beckham family was there, and it's said they only found out about it by reading it online.

Questions abound, from various sides of the fence. To a list of occupations that already includes footballer, photographer, model, monograph author and chef, is Brooklyn adding hostage? How can the Beckhams bear the pain of rejection? Or do people really cut themselves off from highly functional families? One of Nicola's friends who attended the ceremony posted in praise of her having 'the guts to walk away' from 'a toxic family'. Victoria's own self-commissioned Netflix documentary was due to come out this autumn (executive producer: David Beckham). How on earth is it going to spin this? Anything other than four hours of open-heart soul-searching is going to look a bit 'Tractor production up in Volgograd!'

The cautionary sadness is that these questions can't really be considered invasive because they relate to a show the Beckhams have eagerly invited us to watch at every possible moment. The family has so assiduously cultivated public engagement with their internal dynamics, choosing daily to live out loud across social media, for better – but now, for worse. It feels a little much to slap the adjective 'Shakespearean' on a story that involves a guy who once included the worst picture ever taken of an elephant in a coffee-table book of his own photography (launch party held at Christie's, London), but there is certainly a tragic irony in social media, which the Beckhams have hitherto controlled so masterfully, being the place where their schisms were exposed.

They were undone by omission, given that one of the other things our first family have embodied is a complete shift in showbiz journalism. So much entertainment coverage now comes from parsing who is or isn't tagged in Instagram posts, who has stopped following who, who omitted to like this or that. And anyone can do this. It's a form of mass Kremlinology.

At the peak of their tabloid fame – or the first peak, perhaps we should say now – it became commonplace to suggest that in the modern era, the Beckhams were our real royal family. They seemed a reaction against all that old blood, that nepo privilege, that public repression of private truth. But now? Well, perhaps some of the plotlines are converging. Perhaps the House of Windsor and the House of Beckham are not so different after all.

It's a Brooklyn v. Beckham Inc. disaster: what happens when the elephant in the room goes rogue

20 January 2026

Sir David and Victoria cornered the market in selling their family's privacy for money – but there was a price to pay, and Brooklyn Peltz Beckham has just sent them the bill.

The way 2026 has started, none of us wants to see the word 'nuclear' in a headline, so on some level you have to feel glad that last night's news alerts announcing in real time that someone 'goes nuclear' and 'launches nuclear attack' related to Brooklyn Peltz Beckham. At the time of writing, the story about his Instagram broadside against his parents, David and Victoria Beckham, accusing them of treating him as a commercial prop all his life, was by far, far and away the best read on the *Guardian* website, as well as the most deeply read. Again, I'm glad this blow-up wasn't used as geopolitical cover, because if ever there was a time for Trump to invade Greenland largely unnoticed, maybe this was it.

Whoever wrote Brooklyn's intercontinental ballistic Instagram – and it wasn't the childlike authorial voice behind the regular 'I always choose you baby . . . me and you forever baby' posts to his wife – the sentiments will be his. Here's a sample: 'My family values public promotion and endorsements above all else. Brand Beckham comes first. Family "love" is decided by how much you post on social media, or how quickly you drop everything to show up and pose for a family photo opp . . .'

Wow: elephants. Brooklyn Beckham can't photograph them but he sure can address them when they're in the room. If you watched Victoria Beckham's lavishly produced Netflix documentary last October, you might have wondered why it didn't even glance at the biggest elephant in Brand Beckham's room: the clear and agonising no-contact rift with their eldest son that has been festering since last year and beyond. But most big documentaries these days aren't documentaries in the way previous practitioners of the craft might have understood the word. As her husband's was before it, Victoria's doc was a self-commissioned advertorial, on which the subject also served as executive producer. This is the haute version of the curated, public-facing existence that defines our dysfunctional age, but it trickles all the way down via fourth-tier influencers and that friend of yours who can't stop posting about her perfect life. The Beckhams, at the vanguard of celebrity culture ever since both it and they exploded in the late 1990s, are a part of how we all got here.

Before I go on, I should say I find this family rift desperately sad. I can't imagine the agony of being cut off by a child, and hope I never have to even contemplate the possibility. All parents make mistakes, and all children do too. I believe the Beckhams truly and deeply love their children, but, to adapt Logan Roy, they have made it hard for them to be serious people.

Brooklyn has been commodified since he was a foetus. The story of Victoria's pregnancy was sold by his parents. When he was born, David and Victoria sold the first pictures of him. They sold intimate looks around their home and his nursery. They sold their wedding, staying up till 3am on the night of that big day, deciding which pictures would be featured in *OK!* magazine. They sold everything – mostly, back then, to *OK!*. Its proprietor, Richard Desmond, wrote in his autobiography about spending what felt like every Friday with the young couple at Victoria's parents' house, where they would all 'plot and plan the next features we'd do'. A huge cheque was always involved, and the Beckhams wanted the limelight – all of it – so much.

But as time went on, David and Victoria acquired more sophisticated advisers, who understood the rapidly morphing potential of controlling image and brand and built a vast, diversified empire for them off the back of it. When social media came along, the Beckhams channelled their business through its pipes. As I've written here before, they were past masters at not simply turning to their children and telling them they loved them, but photographing them, tagging them and sending the message of love via social media. Alchemically lucrative – but an accident waiting to happen?

I honestly think the Beckhams are now so lost to this commercialised version of family life that they probably long ago lost the ability to comprehend how weird and potentially corrosive it is. I keep thinking of the line in *Goodfellas* where the Mafia wife Karen says, 'And after a while it got to be all normal.' And maybe there is something rather 'Family' – with a capital 'F' – about the Beckham mob. The trouble is, with families not being meritocracies, every now and then the gene pool is going to throw up a Fredo Corleone or a Christopher Moltisanti who just isn't suited to the weird life and can only play out as a liability. Again, as covered here before, it has happened a couple of times with that other deeply strange family business, the Windsors.

The Windsors, of course, don't have a choice. The Beckhams' wealth is estimated at about half a billion pounds. That is more money than even they could ever spend, and the only truly credible explanation for why they continue to live their life so remorselessly out loud is because they still crave the attention. And, realistically, because they have forgotten how else to live.

They are the unicorns of this lifestyle, but not exactly alone. Some of us have always been Instagram and Facebook refuseniks and never publicly post pictures of our lives or families or any of it. But it's not the norm, and billions of people have entirely forgivably been sucked into a world where they are the product, where they work for free for the tech lords, who successfully devalued the idea of privacy at the altar of their big lie: that 'being connected' via their networks is far more important than privacy; that it is a win for humanity; that it is social. But it isn't. Societies are in a mess. Literacy's in a mess. Young people's mental health is in a mess. The world's in far more of a mess than it was when the tech lords found it.

I see Keir Starmer's thinking about banning social media for under-16s, so maybe someone could stick an amendment on any bill, banning parents from plastering their kids all over it from the moment they're born. Maybe they can't meaningfully consent to working in Mark Zuckerberg's content mines any more than celebrity kids can meaningfully consent to being monetised by their parents. Or maybe all those ships have sailed.

As for what David and Victoria Beckham will do, David was pictured at Davos this morning. Encouraging times. But clearly they will also be locked in crisis talks, and my bet is that they'll issue a statement saying how much they love Brooklyn and always will, and something like how there will always be a place waiting for him at their family table. And I truly believe all that. As someone behind the scenes will say as the team approves it, it's *authentic*. But even that word has been corrupted, hasn't it? It has come to suggest a monetisable easy charm, an ability to make staged commercial situations seem appealing, an instinctive capability of embodying a brand or a lifestyle. We live in an age of dangerous slippage, from private to public, from living to trading, from the idea of ourselves as agents of free will to us becoming unpaid and unwitting products. Not to interrupt his brief main character moment, but Brooklyn Beckham's the least of it.

LETTUCE REMEMBER THE CONSERVATIVE PARTY

Rishi Sunak's premiership was marked by his two most recent predecessors' tireless attempts to present themselves as misunderstood victims rather than deadly perpetrators. Both Boris Johnson and Liz Truss protested their innocence from the maximum-security international lecture circuit, with Johnson occasionally flying back to the UK to attend various political disciplinary proceedings or brief that he might be persuaded back into No. 10, if people really begged – at least until Nigel Farage hit on the tactical masterstroke of naming an immigration wave after him. On 22 May 2024, Rishi Sunak stood in driving rain to announce that there would be a general election on 4 July, surprising many with the early timing. Though not certain aides and protection officers in his inner circle, who were arrested after having placed bets on a July date. The campaign went . . . poorly, with the landslide defeat opening up a leadership vacancy that was fought over by Kemi Badenoch and Robert Jenrick. Clash of the termites. Suffice to say the Conservative party was declared effectively dead – so dead, in fact, that within precisely 18 calendar months they were polling higher than Labour.

Why is British politics a raging bin fire? Don't ask the misunderstood heroes who held the torches

27 January 2023

From Truss to Johnson, former chaos-mongers are sure none of it is remotely their fault. In fact, the time is ripe for a comeback

It's encouraging to see Liz Truss hoving back into view, after a period in the wilderness only slightly longer than that endured by the OG Messiah. And, indeed, only slightly longer than her entire premiership. As one ally told the *Financial Times* this week of her abortive adventures in the public finances, 'Liz believes that the policy was right but she didn't get the political backing she needed.' Erm, does that quite cover it? Having failed to get backing from her colleagues, the markets, business, the Bank of England, the public and experts from the Institute for Fiscal Studies and beyond, Liz was arguably a full six infinity stones short of a gauntlet.

Still, it feels inevitable that another betrayal narrative should be cranking up. You can never have too many, can you? Having accidentally divested itself of various of its other manufacturing industries, the UK is now world-beating in producing betrayal narratives, with supporters of any number of the politicians who played a part in the rolling chaos of the past seven years still claiming that their standard bearer was falsely victimised by people who simply lacked their vision. British politics throws the best pity parties. Consider us the Valhalla of misunderstood heroes.

Quite why this is the default narrative of UK public life is unclear, other than the fact that the scorched-earth mess of it all has to be blamed on someone other than the people who just happened to be holding a blowtorch in the Westminster area at the time. The ranks of the betrayed grow ever larger, encompassing (but not limited to) such reverse luminaries as Truss and her chancellor Kwasi Kwarteng, Boris Johnson, Jeremy Corbyn and Nigel Farage. Acolytes of all the above believe their leaders' visions have been betrayed by someone or other in one way or another, when the reality is they were undone by such trifles as 'the voters', 'reality' and 'the consequences of their own actions'.

Alas, this is not how their various tribes continue to see it, with the preferred position being to blame someone or something else for the shortcomings. British politics has been a series of bin fires over the past few years, but the various factions would have you believe that if only their bin fire had been allowed to burn a little longer, a phoenix would have risen from it. Within our politics, taking responsibility is dead as a concept. The result is a public realm where it is always someone else's fault, and no mistakes, ever, can be conceded by operational figures.

Only in this atmosphere could 102 Conservative MPs have believed last October that it was finally time for a return for Boris Johnson, who had vacated Downing Street in disgrace a full six weeks previously, after a series of self-generated scandals that had led to apoplectic public outcry and a downfall that had required 57 ministerial resignations over not much more than 48 hours to finally shift the blockage. When he chose not to formally run in the second leadership contest last year, Johnson's supporters let it be known that his betrayers were simply not sorry enough yet for what they had done. 'Now is not the time for Boris,' one sniffed. 'They will be desperate by June next year.' Certainly wouldn't rule it out. Westminster outriders feeling wounded over what happened to Johnson are all over the place these days. On Brexit, they even seem to imagine he was betrayed by his own deal.

Then again, Brexit is perhaps the richest source for betrayal narratives, with the ground being laid almost immediately after the vote. In 2017, Nigel Farage explained that if he didn't get his perfect, shiftingly defined version of Brexit, he would 'don khaki, pick up a rifle and head for the frontlines'. In fact, he's farting out gin adverts and appearing on GB News and Cameo (where the platform describes him as 'highly responsive' to requests to say any old shit for 73 quid). But he's still finding time to assert betrayal and perpetually hints he may even feel betrayed enough to return to the frontlines – of politics – someday in the not too distant future. Which will at least allow me to attend his 37th resignation speech in due course.

Less politically successful, but feeling no less betrayed, are supporters of Jeremy Corbyn, who still blame the media for the former Labour leader's failure to win two elections, the first against the worst candidate and campaign in recent memory, and the second (by a landslide) against Boris Johnson. Perhaps betrayal is easier to swallow than the idea that the last thing on earth anyone in the red wall was doing on the doorstep was regurgitating anything some twat like me had written in the *Guardian*. (Let's face it, if newspaper commentary of any type were remotely market-moving, the columns warning people off Johnson – from left and right – might have effected something other than a massive majority in his favour in 2019.)

So now the Trussites take their place among the furiously betrayed, despite the fact that their leader left office having broken virtually every egg at her disposal, landing the UK with a vast bill and absolutely no prospect of an omelette. In fact, with nothing resembling an omelette having been served up for years now, it's possible – just possible – that the real victims of betrayal are not all these politicians, but the public.

Decision time: did habitual liar Boris Johnson tell some lies? It's going to be tense

21 March 2023

The former PM is wheeling out the old clown act to rebuff the Partygate allegations. Let's hope it's for the last time

One last heave – in all senses of the word – for Boris Johnson, Britain's worst ex, who tomorrow flops himself out in front of the privileges committee and asks it to consider an auto-satirical question: did the foremost British liar of the age tell a lie? If you want a sense of our self-respect as a nation, parliamentary investigators have spent 10 months gathering evidence on that question, while £220,000 and rising has been spent by the taxpayer on Johnson's legal defence. It is, let's face it, a long way to go to reach the conclusion, 'Lol, of course he told a lie – it's BORIS JOHNSON?!?!?!?!?'

Strip away the incidental details of this latest adventure in a career of turbo-fibbing and you are faced with a reality as old as bullshit itself. Johnson, who last told the truth during the Reagan administration – and then only accidentally – has somehow got the government to fund state-of-the-art lawyers to prove he wasn't aware of parties happening in his own house, attended by his own self, against his own rules, and in at least one case against his own laws, having gone on telly every single night to tell people that compliance to the letter of said rules and laws was a matter of life and death. Please bear this in mind if you tune in to his appearance tomorrow afternoon, along with the question: does our country have a path to dignity? Because this ain't it.

Wednesday's spectacle in the bollocksseum promises to be yet another poignantly belated cautionary tale. Most sightings of

Johnson since he was dragged out of office have served as a sobering reminder that, having been politically roofied by him, this really was the man we let be prime minister for three years. Despite raking in millions in the past few months, Johnson still dresses like he buys his outfits in 10kg sacks printed with the words 'ASSORTED CLOTHES'. Far from being winsome, the famous hair increasingly tends towards the 'specialist' end of the unkempt spectrum. As he runs down his sixth decade, Johnson is one pair of Reactolite glasses short of looking like something off the beast wing at HMP Full Sutton.

Having submitted his supposedly 'explosive' defence dossier yesterday, 48 hours before his scheduled appearance, the ex-PM and his team were outraged that it wasn't rushed immediately into publication by the privileges committee – the sort of affront that gives off huge Norma Desmond energy. Our star has simply failed to grasp that he isn't in the priority lane any more and that people will get around to him when they get around to him, and not before.

That hotly defensive defence dossier has now been published, and the overwhelming feeling is . . . stop whining and wanging on and weaselling out. You were the actual prime minister – man up. Johnson has lied so much and for so long and in such varied arenas that he presumably doesn't even know he's doing it any more. In many ways, the true disappointment is that his lawyer, David Pannick, has not advised him to go with a plea of diminished responsibility.

Admittedly, Johnson's delusions are shared, albeit by fewer and fewer people. There remains a rump Westminster fandom that still believes there's a superior version of his prime ministership back there, if only the suits would release it – a sort of Snyder cut of governing. There isn't. We all lived through the reality. Though significantly dwindled in number, these fans are no less toxic than they were. You might have noted one of them pre-emptively referring to Wednesday's hearing as an 'organised lynching' – a way of putting it that suggests we can look forward to Nadine Dorries storming the committee room while singing 'Strange Fruit'.

Naturally, anyone can see why Johnson's sense that his political career is not yet over remains so incredibly powerful: it is, quite simply, the only thing in which he has ever truly believed. You know this hearing really matters to him because he isn't even on holiday for it. Do recall that last October's fall of Liz Truss was the only time in his entire political career that Johnson returned home from holiday for a crisis – and how telling that it was a crisis in someone else's leadership, and consequently an opportunity for him. As London mayor, he carried on with his American road trip while his city rioted. As prime minister, he skipped multiple Cobra meetings at the start of Covid to focus on his Shakespeare book/divorce/lack of focus. Later, he couldn't be arsed returning from some Scottish yurt-based break to deal with the exams crisis. So tomorrow's date with destiny exposes the tragically serious reality that the clown act seeks to keep hidden: he is still in pursuit of the only job in which he has ever made sense to himself.

And yet, this pursuit feels decidedly doomed these days, vibes-wise. Whereas last October a comeback seemed at least a possibility (however lunatic), Johnson now feels inescapably yesterday's man. You can't quite put your finger on exactly why, but the air has gone out of it all. Of course, he'll have his close-up tomorrow, and his memoirs will give him a few more when they're published. But the phrase that was always used to give him licence – 'that's just Boris' – now sounds bored and dismissive. Oh, that's just Boris. That's just Boris, just another clapped-out warlord living in Knightsbridge, trying to make his father a consul or give a horse a peerage or something. You know what he's like – and the caravan has moved on.

Are Tory MPs as deluded as Boris Johnson? It's a tough act to follow, but they're doing their best

16 June 2023

Why accept responsibility for enabling their old boss when they could carry on his grand tradition of denial and avoidance?

Carrie Johnson recently confirmed that she is expecting her third child, and I wish her stamina. At one point I also had three children under the age of three and a half, and I can confirm that's quite a handful. However, at least I was not also married to a toddler at the time.

The Johnson household will soon effectively contain four babies of various sizes, with the 58-year-old one currently going through what Nanny might call 'a difficult stage'. He will be 59 on Monday, the very day parliament debates and votes on the damning privileges committee report that found he misled it. Unfortunately, the ex-prime ministerial nappy has already been filled, and the pram screamingly emptied of all toys. Or, as Johnson put it to an aide last summer, hours before the resignation of 57 (FIFTY-SEVEN) ministers finally forced him to quit: 'dignity is a grossly overrated commodity'. Takes an overrated commodity to know one, I guess.

From ambushed by cake, then, to ambushed by snakes – why do these annual misfortunes dog Boris Johnson? At least, as predicted, other career options are already available. Courtesy of the *Daily Mail*, Johnson has just accepted the position of 'newspaper columnist', an extremely silly job, which in large part involves implying you'd do it better, if only they'd give you a turn running the country. As far as Boris Johnson is concerned, surely we have tested the central premise of that one to destruction.

Anyway, back to the destruction. The Conservative party is at war with itself, public servants have been subject to a campaign of intimidation at the highest level and the inquiry into the government's error-prone and at times calamitous handling of Covid is just beginning. Cut to black and the screen caption 'Four years earlier'.

Four years earlier; it is summertime, and a man called Rishi Sunak is himself writing a newspaper column, which appears in *The Times*, beneath the headline 'The Tories Are in Deep Peril. Only Boris Johnson Can Save Us'. And it's certainly all there – the notion that Johnson has 'instant credibility', is 'one of life's optimists' and has 'policies underpinned by values'. To the country's problems, Mr Sunak writes, 'there really is only one logical answer: Boris Johnson'.

Flash-forward 18 months from then, and Johnson's government is rolling out a hard-hitting new advertising campaign. A very ill-looking woman in an oxygen mask is staring despairingly into the camera. 'Look her in the eyes,' reads the caption, 'and tell her you never bend the rules.'

Now skip forward again to Thursday, which Johnson spent howling about his 'expulsion on trumped-up charges'. The only thing that is Trumped-up is him. All populists secretly hate their people, and Johnson was the same. But he also came to secretly fear them, which is why he didn't have the balls to face them at the ballot box during any recall byelection. And why, a few turns of the wheel ago, he pulled out of running formally in the contest to replace Liz Truss, having initially thought he'd found the only thing worth returning from one of his many ligger holidays for.

Via these strategies of avoidance and denial, Johnson persuades himself that he is actually adored by the country. In fact, last summer, he was booed by crowds on the steps of St Paul's as he arrived for the late Queen's platinum jubilee service, just as he had been booed by crowds at the cricket and would soon be booed by crowds on Whitehall clamouring for his departure from Downing Street.

It's not that his implosion could have been predicted; it's that it was. That's the thing with fatal flaws – you know at the start how it's going to end. For all Johnson's splashy manoeuvrings, the focus now must be on the Tory MPs who should have known this. Right up to this present moment, Johnson didn't just lie – he lied about the lies he had told, and he lied about the lies that he had not yet told but had every intention of telling. Having explicitly denigrated the terms 'witch hunt' and 'kangaroo court' to the committee, these were precisely the phrases he deployed when he didn't like the way it was going.

Johnson can dish it out but never take it. He himself ended the careers of those who didn't suck up to him, without a second of remorse. He expelled 21 Conservative MPs for the crime of opposing him on a no-deal Brexit, including two former chancellors and his hero Winston Churchill's grandson. Those who refused to return to his heel were barred from standing in the next election – not for lying to parliament, but for telling it the truth about the danger of crashing out of the EU without a deal. This week, his supporters threatened to deselect MPs who voted for the report on Monday.

Yet having banked their aggression, Johnson has now called them off, telling them not to vote against the report after all. Sorry, but that sort of get-out shouldn't do. Tory MPs need to stop running and face up to what their party enabled, and at least make some profoundly belated attempt to acknowledge that and do the right thing. The parliamentary Conservative party in the majority showed appalling judgment on Johnson, despite mountains of indications that it would turn out badly. It failed to understand the vital flaws not simply in Johnson's criminally overhyped 'oven-ready deal', but in human character itself. People don't change; they just become more exaggerated versions of themselves in one way or another, and anyone who couldn't see that Boris Johnson would end up behaving like Boris Johnson, to the vast detriment of the country and its democratic institutions, is too stupid and naive to be in politics. Monday is the time for Conservative MPs to turn up and find some backbone and self-respect – and if they still can't, to accept that they, too, are in the wrong job.

Sunak seems convinced that who dares wins. Spoiler alert: sometimes they lose really badly

24 May 2024

A drowned-rat PM, a blank-page contender and a frit Farage refusing to stand – all in the first 48 hours. Are you not entertained?

Even in a year of largely lacklustre summer movies, you have to accept the reality that Rishi Sunak has scheduled his general election against the release of *Beverly Hills Cop 4*. Coming back again, you say? Same old hapless colleagues? Straight to streaming? Whether the public really craves a fourth consecutive outing for previously beloved franchise *The Conservative Government* is not altogether unclear: audience tracking suggests the IP is knackered and people want to see this one about as much as they wanted to see the *Cats* movie. At least in that they were able to VFX out the arseholes.

But look, stay with the PM on this one! And please note, we're already into the phase of election berserkery in which you can always find a sympathetic party thinker to tell you that, actually, the bad thing you just saw with your own eyes will play so, so well where it matters. 'Rishi did not look like someone who is ready to compromise, and I think that's really good,' judged the *Mail*'s Sarah Vine of his election announcement. 'I thought his vibe was really good.' Mm-hmm.

Literally no obvious setback is resistant to this treatment. Word of advice, and sorry if I sound like Lee Twatwater: if you are ever in a position where you're explaining that, actually, there are election points and respect to be earned from looking sad and droning on while your Gentleminion suit gets trashed by rain, YOU HAVE ALREADY LOST THAT ELECTION. The prime minister looked like a guy who doesn't even need to leave a note saying there is no money. Rishi Sunak is waterlogged.

Or, as Michael Gove apparently told him in the emergency cabinet meeting earlier that day: 'Who dares wins. You dared, and you will win.' Collectors of moments when Michael Gove just says any old deadpan shit for a laugh are going to have a huge cataloguing exercise on their hands in the coming weeks. I myself have a memory palace full of such treasures, which I plan to open to the public on 5 July.

Happily, as well as that emergency cabinet meeting, the surprise election news also forced a huge number of emergency podcasts. I sometimes wonder if political podcasts are to our era what Vietnam movies were to the American late 1970s: a chance to reflect elegiacally, and indeed lucratively, on how sad and pointless it all was. Indeed, the sheer number of frontline politicians who could lose their seats might lead to a flood of future buddypod franchises. Plus a light-hearted perils-of-modern-dating one hosted by the current defence secretary. Working title: 'On the Sh-Apps'.

In terms of what we have immediately lost, though, the government has explained that its asylum removal flights to Rwanda will not take off until after the election. Have they scuttled their own flagship, or is the Rwanda scheme so badly holed it would have sunk anyway? Truly the *Bismarck* of policies (the ship, not the statesman). Likewise for Sunak's proposed legislation to ban smoking for young people, which – if memory serves – was supposed to be his legacy project, but now seems to have been ditched in order to hold an election the very day his younger daughter's school term ends, presumably permitting a near-immediate getaway should he also pull off the historic twofer of losing his seat.

Forgive the suggestion of election spoilers – and despite polling maestro John Curtice giving Labour a 99% chance of victory – I think we have to pretend that it is at least possible that Sunak could pull off history's most unlikely political comeback. But at this stage I would settle for Westminster's snippiest interviewee merely pulling off a conversational comeback.

That said, the titchy tetchy does say he wants to have no fewer than six TV debates with the Labour leader, one every week. Rishi Sunak v. Keir Starmer – arguably the least watchable limited series you could possibly come up with. And I watched *She-Hulk: Attorney at Law*, so that means something. Starmer's yours-to-lose position in the polls is allied with both his natural caution and the ancestral psychic pall of pulling on the Labour shirt to play in a general election. So the next few weeks will be like watching a very buttoned-up man try not to have an accident.

As for Nigel Farage, what a surprise to learn that he will be present but not involved in Reform's election campaign. Farage loves his country, but he loves American TV money more, and the prospect that his orange friend might say one throwaway thing about him on one third-tier stage on one night of the US election campaign is simply too much of a draw for this terminal beta, who – let's not forget – conceded, then unconceded, then reconceded, then re-unconceded during the night of the 2016 EU referendum. Many people do actually prefer to forget that, of course, so doubtless we'll still have to listen to Nigel when he pitches back up after the election to save the Conservative party, or something.

Ultimately, after the past few years, the one thing most of the country can agree on is that the quality of politics and politicians needs to get so much better. Yet for all the already evident stage management of the campaigns, it should be noted that the Conservatives are currently short of 93 prospective candidates, while about 100 Labour ones have yet to be unveiled. All parties are scrambling to fill the gaps. I hate to rain buckets on anyone's parade, but . . . is this really the recipe for a return to high-calibre politics?

Are Tories bent on scoring own goals? Alleged election betting shows real dedication

20 June 2024

Tory party campaign director's leave of absence over alleged bet hands Labour the perfect metaphor

Break out the comedy air quotes, because Tony Lee, the Conservative party's director of campaigning, has taken a 'leave of absence'. A development to which one's immediate response is: wait, this Conservative campaign has a director??? Does he work in the snuff genre? If not, this is surely the *Heaven's Gate* of general election campaigns – and you have to remember that that fabled cinematic flop collapsed not simply an entire genre (the western), nor simply an entire legacy movie studio (United Artists), but the entire promise-filled era of film-making known as the New Hollywood.

Righto: metaphors. In the weeks leading up to Rishi Sunak's general election announcement, you would think the one thing the party that had been in charge for the past 14 years wasn't short of was metaphors. Britain was now a country whose own excrement was literally lapping at its shores. Britain was now a country whose prime minister travelled from central London to Manchester to announce that the government's flagship central London to Manchester rail project would no longer be going to Manchester – or, indeed, to central London. The list went on. Say what you will about recent administrations, but you absolutely could not question the Conservatives' commitment to creating their own metaphors. It was quite possibly our last manufacturing success story.

Which brings us to the revelation that two Tory parliamentary candidates are under investigation by the Gambling Commission for placing bets on the election date before it was formally announced by Sunak.

Last week, the *Guardian* revealed that Sunak's closest parliamentary aide, Craig Williams, had placed a £100 bet on the date. Yesterday evening, the BBC revealed that a police officer in Sunak's protection detail had been arrested and suspended over an election-timing bet. Hours later, the BBC revealed that a second Conservative candidate, named as Bristol North West hopeful Laura Saunders, was also being probed for allegedly placing a bet on the election date. Then, this morning, the Beeb revealed that someone else – oh, do look, it's campaigns director Tony Lee himself! – was being looked into over an alleged bet related to the timing of the election.

Please take a moment to create a fantasy scenario as to how on earth this hugely unfortunate series of events occurred. Did someone – perhaps the director of Conservative campaigns – take a look at the party's prospects and spot a gap in the metaphor market? Did Tony Lee issue some form of APB, perhaps along the lines of: 'Guys, we can see that Labour is short of just one metaphor – specifically, something to illustrate the idea that we gambled with the country to enrich ourselves. For the love of God, can anyone help them out?' I want to say: look, if you want a job doing, etc. But I think that legally, I am required to say: if allegedly you want an alleged job allegedly doing, etc.

As for what, precisely, we're dealing with – you always see the bookies' publicists press-releasing odds on things like the next election date or who killed a *Coronation Street* character or something. When I worked on this paper's Diary column, we'd sometimes ring those PRs and claim we wanted to place a bet on these supposed markets, in the interest of seeing if they actually existed in the real world or were just a publicity trick. There would always be an incredible amount of waffle in reply. The fact is, the bookmakers watch these novelty markets incredibly closely as they are so vulnerable to punters with inside information. So what is being alleged here is not just irregular betting but intense stupidity.

How many stupids are there? By lunch, the Conservative campaign's HQ had issued a statement saying, 'It wouldn't be proper to comment,' adding that they had been contacted about 'a small number of individuals'. Why not say three? Oh, man – it's not more than three . . . is it?

This was not a question answered by the various Conservatives on the campaign trail today. Touring the breakfast studios was Michael Gove, who regretted being unable to discuss an ongoing investigation, before waltzing onwards and breezing of the party's electoral prospects, 'We're not in Fergie time yet!'

Once again, we can only salute a senior politician's unique understanding of football terminology. But in the interests of accuracy: Michael, it would be good for the Conservatives if you *were* in Fergie time, because it would mean that you might be about to pull off an astonishing late-stage winner, with the clock controversially running on till you did. An alternative analogy for this particular general election campaign might be the infamous Nigerian match in which Akurba FC lost 79–0 to Plateau United Feeders, with the Feeders scoring a goal every 37 seconds in the second half. The Nigerian Football Federation called it 'a mind-boggling show of shame'. And lifetime bans ensued.

Elsewhere, Jeremy Hunt already seemed to be on the memoir circuit. This morning, the guy who is still actually chancellor of the exchequer told a story to something called the *Times* CEO Summit – big campaigning stop, apparently – about how he got his job. 'I got that rather unexpected call from Liz Truss asking me to be chancellor,' reflected Hunt. 'Which I thought was a hoax and refused to take the call and could not imagine any situation ever where Liz Truss would actually ask me to be chancellor, so that was a bit surreal, and then in that first week literally I'm picking the entire mini-budget!'

Sorry – is it not still the election? Why is he reminding people of this lunacy? Is there a point at which play becomes so remarkably atrocious that it could even amount to alleged election-throwing? Perhaps the Nigerian Football Federation could investigate.

Sunak axed, the cast eviscerated: at last, it's the Tories' season finale

5 July 2024

It was worthy of a TV special. Truss, Rees-Mogg, Shapps, Liam Fox: so many erased after 14 years of dystopian soap opera. And not a moist eye in the house

Well, if you're just joining us, the nation has delivered an all-night victim impact statement. Labour has won a landslide and the Conservatives have suffered their worst-ever general election result. Keir Starmer – the prime minister – has promised 'national renewal . . . to fight until you believe again'. Liz Truss has failed to save South West Norfolk, let alone 'the west'. That is the big picture (if not the whole picture, with turnout and Labour's share of the vote notably low). Meanwhile, it's incredible to think that only a short while ago we thought we'd eradicated measles and Nigel Farage. Both have now been brought back, largely by the same people.

But look, after the 3am to 7am shift, no one will be able to say the right doesn't do comedy. There were moments worthy of entire Netflix specials, as in sports halls and community centres various Dickensian grotesques were ushered into their Christmas future, live on stage. Alas, it was going to take more than buying the Cratchits a turkey to get out of this one. Jacob Rees-Mogg heard his fate standing next to a candidate wearing a baked-bean balaclava. He'll be crying into Nanny's starched bosom today. Committed sewage apologist Thérèse Coffey was pumped into the sea in Suffolk Coastal. Andrea Jenkyns had the middle finger given to her by the voters of Leeds South West and Morley. In Welwyn Hatfield, Grant Shapps chanted 'supermajority' five times into the mirror, and then it came for him.

Then again, Michael Portillo losing his seat was supposedly 1997's big moment. So perhaps the question is: in two years' time, which current hate figure will be presenting a cosy travelogue on Europe's most picturesque illegal migration routes? Alternatively, do remember that one person's onstage humiliation is another person's milk round for directorships in the arms trade.

Speaking of absolute weapons, hat twat George Galloway wimped out of his own count in Rochdale, presumably out of fatigability. He lost to Labour. There was jubilation for the Lib Dems, who finished not a million miles behind 'the natural party of government', and for the Greens, who won all four of their target seats. The SNP can now squeeze its MPs round the flip-down dining table of a motorhome. Referendum arguments may move to Northern Ireland, with Sinn Féin now that nation's largest Westminster party.

As for Reform . . . Farage won in Clacton, a constituency for which he will now have to hold surgeries, presumably by Zoom link from his hot desk in the US presidential colon. Or, as he put it in his victory speech: 'This is the first steps of something that is going to stun all of you' – at least confirming his political abattoir will be bolt-gunning its victims unconscious first. Farage is the horror version of *Inside Out*, where Mendacity is only just holding off Racism at the control console. His cultural hinterland extends to a single *Goodbye, Mr Chips* DVD he got free with the *Sunday*

Times in 2008, and the idea that this hollow chancer should still be one of the most significant politicians of the age says everything about the age.

Anyway, back to the Conservatives' four-hour *in memoriam* reel. Penny Mordaunt, Jonathan Gullis, Michael Fabricant, Gillian Keegan, Steve Baker, Alex Chalk, Johnny Mercer, Michelle Donelan, Victoria Prentis, Liam Fox, Mark Harper . . . all out, along with many more. So many cabinet ministers fell that the ones who live may actually develop survivor guilt. It's currently unclear how gruesome things will be among the extant Conservatives in this post-apocalyptic world. As a fictional president once wondered of Dr Strangelove, will the living not end up envying the dead? Far from it, Strangelove reassures him, forcing down an involuntary Nazi salute. What will abound is a spirit of bold curiosity for the adventure ahead!

Speaking of which, 13th fairy Suella Braverman finally turned up, holding on in Fareham and cooing, 'I am sorry that my party didn't listen to you. The Conservative party has let you down.' Expect to see her humbly attempting to disembowel fellow survivors Jeremy Hunt and James Cleverly in the forthcoming trial-by-combat for what convention demands we style as 'the soul of the Conservative party'.

At his count, Rishi Sunak explained he'd already conceded the election in a congratulatory call to Keir Starmer, adding, 'I take responsibility for the loss.' In Downing Street, he confirmed he would be standing down as Tory leader in some sort of due course, stressing, 'I have heard your anger.' Then, instead of yet another speech straight from the Tortured Prime Minister's Department, this one offered humility and magnanimity, as well as a pointed reminder of the positive (and fragile?) progress that saw him become the UK's first British-Asian prime minister. What a contrast to the relentless negativity of his past six weeks. Sunak's campaign was conducted like a gender-reveal party, where the device that's meant to release the puff of blue smoke accidentally functions as a pipe bomb and burns the house down.

It also closed out several years of mind-boggling chaos, dysfunction and national decline. They won't be playing anything from this album on the Conservative party's *Eras* tour. The Tories have cycled through five prime ministers over the past eight years, to the point where they were recently found going through the rubbish, pulling the first guy back out, thinking, 'Actually, he doesn't look half bad now,' and making him foreign secretary. This is the behaviour of addicts.

Not that they have the monopoly on erraticism. Any dispassionate view of these results suggests the fabled post-Brexit 'realignment' is more of a dealignment, the huge sweeping gains of this or that political moment able to be reversed in previously unthinkable time spans. Volatility might now be our defining electoral characteristic, and a rise in sectarian politics cannot and should not be ignored. Because, hey, what's the worst that can happen with that one? Meanwhile, many people who derided the simplistic 'Get Brexit Done' slogan in 2019 have pretended not to notice that the winner here went out under the even more gnomic banner of 'Change'.

Yet, in the wider global context, what a win. One summer evening in 1914, the foreign secretary, Edward Grey, famously remarked: 'The lamps are going out all over Europe.' In our own times, a darkening has recently felt near at hand, as hard- or extreme-right parties have gained ground across the continent, to say nothing of the US. But here – in this country, in this moment – a different direction has been taken. That matters today, and anyone not on the wingnut fringes who hopes to avoid those gathering shadows should wish Keir Starmer good luck with his task. For plenty who would snuff out the lamps are also rising – increasingly, they walk among us.

It was Badenoch v. Jenrick on GB News. And if that sounds bad, watching it was worse

18 October 2024

Each had an hour to show why they are the future – at least until the next Tory debacle means another leadership contest.

Distressingly, the GB News stream I watched the Conservative leadership hustings on kept glitching out, meaning every time I went back in I had to watch the exact same ads for a blood pressure monitor and some body horror thing about draining ankle fluid. You hear a lot about 'no-go zones' on GB News; on this evidence, the channel is a no-go zone for advertisers seeking to reach the coveted 18–34 demographic. But look, let's open the door to our walk-in bath and let the waters of the contest rise around us.

And you have to say that this week the race to be the person regicided by the Tory party in two years' time has certainly warmed up. It is now almost tepid. The choice is between Kemi 'I'm an engineer' Badenoch and Ozempic survivor Robert Jenrick, a would-be populist who on Wednesday had to be told live on air – the day after it happened – who the new England football manager was. Sort your life out, Jenrick.

Anyway . . . the debate, in which the candidates did not actually debate. In front of a truly overwhelmingly male audience of rank-and-file party members, Jenrick went first. He acquires principles like planning controversies, so it's always mildly intriguing to see what he's flogging this time out. Some Frankenstein catchphrases, certainly. He would like Britain 'to be the grammar school of the western world'. Pressed on Nigel Farage, he explained, 'I want to retire him.' (Well, that's not hard. Farage retires every two years. It's the chronic unretiring we need to focus on.) If Jenrick were the party leader and there were an election tomorrow, 'We would be in a hung parliament. So before we begin the task of turning this around, we would be in a dramatically better position.' So tempting. Years of legislative paralysis caused by the Conservative party's nutso trips down constitutional rabbit holes could be followed by some more legislative paralysis.

Physically, the look Jenrick seems to be going for is the Wolverhampton JD Vance. Speaking of whom . . . on the basis of having obsessively compared past and present Google Images of Jenrick during the boring bits of last night's broadcast (all of it), I am 49% floating the theory that he has started wearing eyeliner for public appearances. If he disagrees, then . . . what is it wannabe edgelords like him always say? Oh yep – 'Debate me. You've never debated anyone like me.' Debate me about eyeliner, Rob. I'll take all comers.

As for Badenoch, she affects smiley warmth but her vibe is very much Ministry of Magic hardliner who's been parachuted in to the Tory leadership contest. It's her way or the highway, children – and if you don't think everything said in the 1922 Committee isn't going straight back to Cornelius Fudge, then more fool you. That said, aspects of Badenoch's pitch are genuinely surreal. At one point she defended herself against charges of being awol in the discourse by saying she only went 'on media' when she has something to say. Suggesting that over the past few weeks, she just hasn't had anything much to say. Then again, Badenoch is running on an amusingly original platform of having no policies. As she tantalisingly put it last night: 'I have great policy ideas, but I don't believe that what's in my head is going to get us out of the mess we are in.' Righto. The tactic would appear to be something of a missed opportunity, given that, unlike Jenrick, she does seem to believe in something other than saying literally any old shit if it will help you ascend a quarter of a millimetre further up the greasy pole.

Asked to name his favourite recent Conservative prime minister, Jenrick couldn't pick one, saying only, 'I served in the government of each of the last five of them.' And that's the banter era right there, an unwitting reminder of the pure chaos his party has put the nation through. Chaos for which Jenrick seems to have been present, yet not involved. 'When I was minister for immigration,' he said at one point, 'I saw things that made me angry.' Please, guys, give him the chance to say, 'When I was prime minister, I saw things that made me angry.' In the meantime, try this tack in your job and see how you get on. When I was typing this column, I saw sentences that made me angry, but seriously, what could I do?

In terms of the wider context, Badenoch's day had already been enlivened by an intervention by Jurassic Tory backbencher Christopher Chope, who explained he was voting for Jenrick because 'much as I like Kemi, I think she's preoccupied with her own children . . . Kemi spends a lot of time with her family, which I don't resent at all.' Ironically, Chope is a man who so many people desperately wish would spend more time with his family. I do actually resent the fact that he doesn't. Yet bear in mind that despite a 29.8-percentage-point swing against him at the recent general election, he still has a very healthy 7,455 majority. Great job, Christchurch!

I guess diehards gonna diehard; indeed, anyone still a member of the Conservative party these days may be considered so diehard they are potentially undead. Yet the odds and the polls still suggest Badenoch appeals more than Jenrick to the metaphorical Christchurch of it all. Perhaps any wavering member could decide on the basis of the biggest whopper told on stage on Thursday night: Jenrick saying, 'My values have never changed,' or Badenoch's claim that 'I don't like fighting. I don't look for fights.' Either way, not long to go now. The deadline for voting? Why, Halloween, of course.

One stock seems truly doomed this week: if you hold any Kemi Badenoch, accept my condolences

11 April 2025

Hard to know if her leadership is sheer ineptitude or an act of artistic expression. This week, humiliated by Nigel Farage. Next week, who can tell?

It's intriguing to watch the Conservative party treating next month's local elections in England like a movie in which it has a secret cameo. Please don't spoil the surprise for the fans! But yes, it turns out it is actually in this film. Who knew? For all of Labour's many upsets since it came to power, it doesn't feel as though a single one has been skilfully turned in the Tories' favour. Conservative leader Kemi Badenoch is very, very bad – so bad that you can't even be bothered to come up with anything other than a will-this-do nickname for her. Kemi Very Badenoch.

More often than not since KVB beat Robert Jenrick in the leadership equivalent of Argentina v. West Germany, she has seemed to be running the party like a performance art project you really wouldn't want to see. Sorry – that's obviously a tautology. We can just say 'like a performance art project'. For almost six months now, Badenoch has made a huge deal of the fact that she quite deliberately doesn't have any policies, instead repeatedly promising the 'biggest policy renewal programme in 50 years'. Given the minuscule amount that has actually emerged, I'm afraid my ears can now only rearrange that declaration into 'I will come up with some policies in about 50 years.'

Instead of policies, Badenoch has bandwagons, whose drivers regard her as an unwanted ride-hitcher. She's sort of hiding in the bike rack of the bandwagon, or possibly beneath the bandwagon, clinging on to its chassis. Eventually, her presence becomes detected, and those pushing for new or different grooming gang inquiries note she's suddenly noisily on board. Which is odd, considering that Rishi Sunak's government could only be arsed to implement very few of the last inquiry's recommendations – and that the role of women and equalities minister in that government was held by one Kemi Badenoch.

But leaving aside her policy (singular?) for a while, this week Very Badenoch could be found on the airwaves, declaring that the Tories were open to making deals with Reform UK on local councils. 'I have categorically said that I'm not doing deals with Reform,' she said, going on to effectively list several examples of ways the Tories could do deals with Reform at local level. What has brought on this logical collapse? According to Kemi, 'When someone says they want to destroy you, you don't invite them into your house and ask to do a deal.' But also, you sometimes do, because 'You don't get to have a rerun of an election at a local level.' Do you get to have reruns of elections at a national level? If not, what is she on about? AGAIN?

This is a rhetorical inquiry that appeared to be shared by Nigel Farage, who lost no time in playing a similar hand rather better. Farage won't do a deal, until he will, but unlike Badenoch, he did remember that what you're supposed to do when asked these types of questions is explain why the other lot would be an absolutely terrible choice to vote for.

But look, Badenoch has other idiosyncratic ways of rallying her troops, launching her party's local elections campaign on Thursday by explaining to members that if you map the 2024 general election results on to the local council seats being contested, 'we lose almost every single one'. Thanks for dialling in, Braveheart. Thus far, the sole point Kemi seems to have taken in the campaign is down to *BBC Breakfast*'s ludicrous decision to try to shame her for not having watched *Adolescence* – a crime that is fast becoming on a par with not having cried in the street when Princess Di died. That said, back in real life, we can scientifically estimate that her *Adolescence* retort is worth about a 0.0001% swing in Broxtowe.

Alas, away from her safe space – minor culture-war skirmishes and posting on X – Badenoch tends to come off as incredibly poorly prepared, given to relying on a set of about four assumptions in the absence of that preparation, and consequently can only be regarded as terminally out of her depth.

This may well be the conclusion of various donors, with a *Times* story on Thursday ascribing a drop in donations to the Conservatives to concerns over her leadership. It certainly features some eye-catching quotes from big donors. 'It's a bit like a new Tesla,' decided one. 'Do you really want to put your money in it until you see if it's actually going to get to the end of the road?' Tesla! If there's one stock that the Tory leader would prefer not to be equated with right now, our anonymous friend may well have alighted upon it. Even so, that flight of fancy was a lot more appealing than another big Tory donor, who confirmed the withholding of funds from the Badenoch-led iteration of the party by explaining affectlessly: 'My lot are waiting for evidence that their money will actually buy influence.' I suppose it's quite bracing to hear people talking openly about the purchase of political influence, even if they won't put their name to it (yet).

All of which suggests we might as well brace for another summer of Conservative attempts to bloodlet. As the grasshopper rubs its legs, so the Tory party sharpens its axe. Really, very little suggests the onset of long balmy days like the unmistakable desire to throw open the windows, and then to throw a leader out of one.

Mirror, mirror on the wall, who is the biggest patriot of them all? It is I, Robert Jenrick

26 August 2025

When I gaze deep into my own eyes, what do I see? An iron-willed, crime-crushing flag-raiser whose ascent to the Tory leadership is surely inevitable

I wake up early – earlier than Nigel Farage. Not drinking as much as him helps. But look, no shade. As I keep telling interviewers, I admire Nigel's longevity. He can keep going for ever, can't he, aged whatever-he-is and with that lifestyle, which makes his biological age only a couple of months more than Joe Biden's was last summer. I'm a huge fan.

Then it's a pacy run round the constituency, or one of the nicer bits of London or Herefordshire, if I'm at one of my other houses. If I spot a lamp post that hasn't been flagged, I make a mental note to go mental at the team. By next week I want to be photographed St Georgeing anything over 10 foot: wind turbines, 5G masts, the giraffes at London Zoo. Then we stick it on the socials. Run me up the flagpole and see who salutes me.

Breakfast is typically a full English yoghurt and whichever type of coffee doesn't constitute taking the wrong side in the culture war. I previously took Ozempic, but I didn't inhale. What people see now is the result of me, personally, taking a stand. I had the discipline to control my northern border – my mouth – rather than letting it be a soft touch for marauding doughnuts or foreign pastries that should quite reasonably have sought refuge somewhere safe but weak, like within France or James Cleverly. As I survey myself in the mirror, I'm incredibly proud of the fact that I went so much further than one in, one out. Far more crap now leaves my gob than goes into it. That's down to the same iron will that I would bring to the leadership of the Conservative party.

Not that there's a vacancy. Kemi's doing a great job. Certainly, a job. A part-time job, some would say. I'm sure she's exhausted herself quite enough for one week with her *Sunday Times* interview. Of course, they asked her about everyone saying I was soon to be leader of the Tory party, and she said, 'I think even Rob himself finds it distressing.' Bless her. But what she needs to remember is that I'm much, much stronger than that.

Then it's straight into the Range Rover and off to work, unless I'm doing a video in a tube station. I'm getting incredible feedback for my videos from people who would previously have given me a wedgie. Having said that, last week I saw the most problematic thing I've seen on a phone since Richard Desmond showed me his property development idea at a Conservative fundraiser and I personally greenlit it. This time, though, it's on my phone, and it's a video posted by Chris Philp, in which he says he got threatened with a knife at the migrant camp in Calais. I immediately texted Chris: 'Who do you think you are – MrBeast?' Got the cryface emoji back, so had to press it. 'Seriously, mate, who do you think you are???'

Reaching the office, I discover another big shipment of flags has arrived from Temu. I ignored last week's message from the Department for Business that I am personally increasing the trade deficit with China: patriotism is bigger than all that stuff. I may not buy British but I certainly fly British. One of the team has left out a print-out of the recent ConservativeHome popularity ranking, which I topped. That's a nice touch – if you want to work with me, you need to be committed to the project. I like to joke that it's the law, and I know because I used to be justice secretary. Well, secretary to the justice secretary, but yeah. Same difference.

The morning is spent publicly complaining about things we either didn't fix or made worse when in office, but I don't see contradictions. Some might say I was one of the public faces of the campaign to lock people up during the pandemic. But they forget I actually twice freestyled the rules – so what did I really believe? Honestly, I'm embarrassed for people who keep bringing up past versions of Robert Jenrick. It's like talking about Peter Parker before he was bitten by the radioactive spider, or the Hulk before he gets the gamma dose. Seriously, if Marvel did shadow ministers . . .

Mid-morning, the team will sit with me for my telly time. Unfortunately, today we switched on, and Farage was unveiling a plan for mass deportations. According to Nigel, who looked tired, he's going to deport all immigrants who arrived here illegally. Hundreds of thousands of people, and if they don't agree immediately, then they'll be imprisoned at military sites, before being expelled. I'm stunned. That is genuinely horrible – for me. 'Why didn't any of you lot think of that?' I scream at the team. 'How am I supposed to outflank him on immigration if he keeps advancing his army? He's halfway across the Polish border by now!' There's a short silence. 'You could deport all immigrants,' says one. 'Except your wife,' says another. 'You could,' says a third, 'think of a tougher and more eye-catching name for the internment camps.' 'Like what?' I snap. But they all look at their shoes. That's the trouble with this generation – no concentration.

The afternoon is taken up with the standard work of a modern MP and public servant: running through tweet ideas and workshopping a banterious text to JD Vance. After that, I power the Range Rover home for dinner as a father of daughters. When Nigel's tucking in to the post-prandials, I'm tucking myself in. We all need a hinterland, as I tweet just before falling asleep.

It's Tory conference: Boriswave goodbye to a deluded party on its way to electoral annihilation

7 October 2025

When both Reform and the Liberal Democrats are eating your lunch, and even Nadine Dorries has abandoned ship, it might just be time to call it

Spare a thought for the Conservative party. It's hard believing in meritocracy, yet finding yourself polling at 15%. It's even harder having wanged on mercilessly for decades about natural selection, yet now constantly finding yourself appearing in the same sentence as the phrase 'facing extinction'.

And it's harder still to find polling guru John Curtice doing panels at your conference in which he outlines the route back to even the same time zone as being in contention. 'You've got to get yourself back to base camp,' Curtice explained in one mild-mannered drive-by on Sunday. 'At the moment you frankly can't even see the Himalayas.' Given the well-documented traffic issues on Everest these days, we have to face the possibility that more people have reached the summit of the world's highest mountain this year than have joined the Conservative party.

To the party's gathering in Manchester, then, where the leadership of Kemi Badenoch continues to come off as a performance art piece entitled *All Fall Down*. It's not so much a conference as one of those soap montages that signal the death of a character. By the time Robert Jenrick went on stage at midday, holding up a judge's wig like a sock puppet and promising to 'take our country back' (again), 20 councillors had defected to Reform since breakfast. The conference is so mad and sad that it features an exhibition of Margaret Thatcher's clothes, which various Tory ugly sisters and brothers have been metaphorically trying to squeeze themselves into ever since the party ousted her a full 34 years ago. After this many failed impostors, it's just possible they should smash the glass slipper and get on the apps instead.

Begging the party to swipe right – quite a bit further right – we have Jenrick, the endlessly metamorphic shadow justice secretary who's had more eras than Taylor Swift. If you felt a seismic straining in the north-west this week, that was Jenrick desperately trying not to do an Andy Burnham and cast this conference as The Official Launch Party of a Showboy. Here, he's been at pains to suggest, he's just one of the team, just a humble fledgling content creator, as at home in the world of short-form video as he is halfway up a lamp post in a tight polo, carrying a six-pack of made-in-China St George flags.

Regrettably – or, as far as he's concerned, fortunately – some recorded comments of Jenrick's from a Conservative association dinner back in March were leaked to the *Guardian*, in which he lamented a visit to Handsworth in Birmingham, where he 'didn't see another white face'. A few sentences further on, Jenrick stated that 'It's not about the colour of your skin or your faith,' which gave Badenoch the leeway to defend him this morning, although she did explain: 'I don't think this is where the debate should be, about how many faces people see on the street and what they look like.'

I'm sure she doesn't. Then again, Badenoch is a master of this kind of insouciantly robotic understatement, apparently telling a meeting of Conservative association chiefs a couple of days ago that the party's poll ratings are 'not where I want us to be'. Which reminds me that John Curtice had a few other truth bombs to drop. 'The Liberal Democrat vote is now much more geographically concentrated than your vote,' he informed Tories at his conference event, 'and the electoral system is now treating you like it treated the Liberal Democrats. And so although the Liberal Democrats are just behind you in the polls, they are going to almost undoubtedly win more seats than you.' Oof.

It must be said that this wasn't the vibe you'd have got from shadow chancellor Mel Stride's speech. 'Let's face it,' claimed Mel hilariously, 'we're the only party that gets it.' Nkay. Go on. 'And that means we have to face some hard truths to which other parties turn a blind eye.' By way of an example, he announced that the Conservatives would slash the civil service to 2016 levels. And yet, where was the hard truth – namely, that the civil service has ballooned since then because of all the extra stuff it's had to do since Brexit, the Conservative party triumph with the world's longest list of small print?

Still, there has been the odd bright spot. Unable to accept that the lethal force of the term 'Boriswave' is going to permanently do for him, the undead Boris Johnson has spent recent days mounting embarrassing rearguard actions against his own policies. On Monday, he could be found popping up in frantically casual fashion to say he 'went far too fast' on net zero, and that he personally 'got carried away'. Of course, of course. Ever since Reform started saying 'Boriswave' every five seconds, Johnson appears to have shed devotees at a quite alarmingly fast rate. Nigel Farage is his political Mounjaro. Even Johnson's most devoted superfan, Nadine Dorries, has been seduced. She'll still love him and everything, but it must be tough for Boris to face up to the fact that Nadine has defected to a party whose biggest diss literally has his name in it.

Elsewhere, the Tory leadership prefers instead to suggest the party eating its lunch is touting policies that fall apart under scrutiny. As Badenoch whined this week: 'Reform is saying stuff because it hasn't thought it all through.' Well, yes. In time-honoured tradition, they are just saying some shit to get elected. Which is, let's actually face it, a little something they learned from their predecessors. More than anyone else on the political spectrum, the most recent iteration of the Conservative party popularised the idea that actions did not have consequences, that cake could be both had and eaten, and that there were no trade-offs on the route to what Badenoch was this week still calling 'the sunlit uplands'.

If only Labour had absorbed these lessons. Yet incredibly, after having had to live through the post-2016 convulsions alongside the rest of us, Keir Starmer and Rachel Reeves failed to realise that their own bullshit would also not survive contact with the reality of government. As was pointed out at the time, Starmer and Reeves sought power by making ridiculous promises about what they wouldn't have to do, either because they were hopelessly naive or just hopeless. They are now reaping that particular whirlwind, which will reach maximum intensity on the Enhanced Fujita scale with next month's budget.

Thus, it increasingly feels as though cautionary tales are this country's only remaining manufacturing success story. Jenrick's speech today ended with him gibbering: 'I can feel Britain's fortunes turning.' We all can. Perhaps the kindest way of putting it is that the Conservative party is part of the new 'left behind'.

JUSTICE IN THE POST

Despite being the most widespread miscarriage of justice in British legal history, the Post Office scandal remained a niche interest for the news media and consequently a closed book to most British people. All that changed in the very early days of 2024, when ITV aired its drama *Mr Bates vs the Post Office* and public anger erupted. A lot of politicians were appalled that it had taken a TV show, of all things, to advocate so eloquently for justice for the victims. Quite right. Surely that should have been the job of much more important entities – e.g. politicians? By the time former Post Office CEO Paula Vennells finally broke cover at the public inquiry, the story was box office. But as so many wronged subpostmasters continued to wonder: were criminal investigations and prison just for the little people?

Hundreds of lives ruined. Not a single person held to account. And still: silence on the Post Office scandal

2 May 2023

Horrific detail piles on horrific detail as the inquiry rumbles on, barely noticed by those for whom this injustice is seemingly not sexy enough

I can't help suspecting that former Post Office chief executive Paula Vennells might have been more publicly vilified if she'd done a bad tweet, rather than merely presided over a company during the most widespread miscarriage of justice in British history.

Forgive the return to this furrow, but no matter how often they are restated (far from often enough), the details of the Post Office scandal are so incredible as to be almost literally impossible to believe. Put as sparsely as possible, 736 subpostmasters and subpostmistresses were prosecuted for theft, fraud and false accounting in their branches between 2000 and 2014, yet they had done nothing wrong, The fault was with a new computer system designed by Fujitsu and forced on to them by Post Office management – a system that the top brass allegedly knew was faulty.

The individual stories are horrific. People's lives were ruined; at least four took their own lives. Many were imprisoned, including a teenager. Tech was trusted over humans with unblemished records. As things stand, more than a year into the belated inquiry, not a single person has been held to legal account, from Vennells to the managerial class of the Post Office to Fujitsu to the civil servants responsible for oversight. Instead, Vennells got a CBE, and the rest of the anonymous boss class doubtless joined her in failing upwards on the gravy train.

The grim saga rumbles on with comparatively little coverage, given its scale and significance. It was arguably ever thus, with all the big beats of this story broken by the likes of Rebecca Thomson at *Computer Weekly*, the journalist Nick Wallis, *Private Eye* and the victims themselves, such as Alan Bates. *The Times* is currently running an excellent series of articles on where we are now, which has revealed that 59 of the victims have died before the end of the inquiry, while some were allocated only £1,000 in legal aid. The Post Office has spent £100m on City lawyers.

But you have to wonder whether the Post Office story is somehow not sexy enough for much of a chatterati who prefer their scandals to unfold over a feverish day on Elon Musk's platform, and not in unloved inquiry rooms and the anguished testimonies of the likes of Seema Misra, locked up on her son's 10th birthday in a 'horrendous' jail, where, among many other horrors, she discovered a prisoner who had taken their own life. Seema was pregnant when she was jailed and gave birth to her second child while wearing an electronic tag. And hers is just one of hundreds of victim stories so mind-boggling and frequently tragic that you cannot believe they happened to those most quietly emblematic of local public servants, the British subpostmaster and subpostmistress.

Alas, the Post Office scandal has never truly seemed to stir the souls of those who regard a day spent online dragging this or that user as activism well spent. This feels symptomatic of a wider issue with what we classify as a campaigning victory these days. The key stages of the Post Office scandal have had far less coverage and garnered far fewer social media clicks than various comments by, say, Jeremy Clarkson or Gary Lineker. I appreciate it is far, far more difficult to 'cancel' the iniquitous systems that led to the Post Office horror than it is to 'cancel' someone in public life who you think has said something unacceptable – but it does very much need doing. The fault of systems is far, far more important than the fault of individuals, however much easier it might be to yank down a single person.

Getting caught up in endless cycles of 'calling out' might work to punish individuals for their individual infractions, but it doesn't change the bigger, more significant problems, and anyone who thinks it does is kidding themselves. Or allowing themselves to be kidded by people who have a vested interest in them not changing things. I know some politicians and certain pundits bang on disparagingly about the 'woke mind virus' or whatever, but I often think they must be secretly thrilled with the virtue games of recent times. It really couldn't suit them more. How much better to have people sidelined into endless 24- or 48-hour online meltdowns, in which they are either pitted against one another litigating the narcissism of small differences – the dream! – or obsessing about one person's transgressions and leaving iniquitous and dysfunctional systems free to sail on regardless.

Some of this is thought to be generational, and I have nothing but sympathy for the generations that come after mine, who have been shut out of so much of what they are entitled to and which most of those who criticise them simply took for granted. My theory is that if you give people absolutely no economic power, they will use what little power they have to lash out in one way or another, and it's pretty hard to blame them for that. The disputed thing that some people call 'cancel culture' is an example of it, and if capitalism's elders and supposed betters really cared so much about stopping it, perhaps they'd think about giving younger people a stake in capitalism, instead of expecting them to abide by a set of rules of a game in which they are not even allowed to be player characters.

It might be nice to think otherwise, but I don't believe that getting angry on Twitter particularly helps anyone other than Elon Musk, or that sitting in judgment on every passing infraction is anything other than a hiding to nothing. It is not effecting change; it is the illusion of effecting change. It is exactly the sort of looking-the-wrong-way that allowed the Post Office scandal to happen – and if we keep doing it, the people who really run things will keep on getting away with it.

We have seen heroes emerge from the Post Office scandal. Now focus on the villains

2 January 2024

Ministers feigned shock, while executives pointed fingers at others, but gradually the truth is coming out. The public anger is working

It's a week since ITV's *Mr Bates vs the Post Office* aired, and can you hear that sound? Can you feel the gathering thunder of politicians' hooves, as the herd suddenly migrates towards the great plains of looking busy, of seeming outraged, of suddenly giving a toss?

'Everyone has been shocked by watching what they have done over the past few days,' declared Rishi Sunak on Sunday, acting for all the world like he had found out about the most widespread miscarriage of justice in British legal history from a TV programme. Which he didn't. Of the pursuit of more than 900 innocent subpostmasters, some of whom were jailed, and the ruined lives of many more, the prime minister explained: 'Obviously, it's something that happened in the '90s.' Which it isn't. Prosecutions of innocent postmasters happened up until 2015, with the coalition government in place for the years in which the Post Office allegedly mounted a full-scale cover-up of the injustice it continued to mete out. Former Post Office CEO Paula Vennells was awarded a CBE in 2019. Which is also not in the '90s. And, just as I was writing this, she's only gone and handed it back.

The Post Office scandal is about two things. First, the ease with which corporate executives were able to pursue, demonise and destroy completely innocent people, particularly using the justification that technology should always be trusted over humans. And second, the ease with which those bigwigs have been able to escape any accountability themselves for doing something far, far worse than anything they wrongly accused their most junior underlings of. They escaped it for decades, and are still escaping it. It is not just Vennells who has questions to answer far beyond the issue of that CBE. There is a whole host of senior figures from the Post Office, Royal Mail and Fujitsu (which supplied and maintained the Horizon system) who were involved in or stood by the long-term policy of pursuing and privately prosecuting postmasters, as well as successive ministers from the Gordon Brown administration onwards who were made aware of the problems and either didn't really listen or chose to believe the Post Office. These are all people we should be furiously keen to hear more from.

Not for them the maximum-security prisons, the social ostracisation, the bankruptcies, the mental and physical breakdowns, the giving birth wearing an electronic tag. Ministers come and go, but the executives failed upwards. The upper tiers of business in this country seem almost impossible to be cast out from. One simply moves on lucratively elsewhere. A certain status of person in our society can be imprisoned for theft (or for non-theft, as it would turn out), yet for actions that led to the most widespread miscarriage of justice in British legal history, to the ruination of hundreds of lives – well, not one person ever has even been charged. In a lot of cases, they seem to have been promoted.

At last, one of our many successive governments looks like it is going to do something serious about the compensation and overturned convictions part of the subpostmasters story – but only because it can see the nation demands it. One thing we shouldn't have any truck with is people complaining that it took a TV drama to bring the issue to outraged national consciousness. I've been in touch over the past couple of days with several people who are either involved in this story or produced the earliest journalism on it, and you won't find a single one of them begrudging the way the scandal has finally gone nuclear. They are simply thrilled that somehow, anyhow, we might be moving closer to resolution for the victims. Forgive me – the surviving victims.

Some thought ITV booking Nigel Farage for *I'm a Celebrity* would have a huge impact on public life. In fact, it won't affect where he goes now, one way or the other – that path was already set. But the ITV drama department's decision to commission *Mr Bates vs the Post Office* is far more significant, and it will be one of those rare TV dramas that has a massive and measurable social impact. The story now leads the news in the mainstream media every single day. Many people found out about it for the first time after watching the programme; many more only registered the scale and scandal of it after having seen this complex tale of computer systems and accounting dramatically rendered. That is public service broadcasting at its best and most powerful.

Those hungry to learn more are directed to the public inquiry happening right now, to which the Post Office has repeatedly failed to hand over evidence. From Thursday, the inquiry will hear testimony from a series of those who worked for Fujitsu. Or will it? Last summer, on the eve of a crucial evidence session from a former Fujitsu engineer, the Post Office suddenly found 4,767 documents it had neglected to disclose, so the witness's appearance was dramatically called off. There are frequently multiple significant documents that lawyers believe the Post Office and Fujitsu are not disclosing, as well as other evidence.

Also last summer, unbelievably, it emerged that the current CEO of the Post Office had actually run a bonus scheme to reward executives for cooperating with the inquiry – surely their most basic civic and moral duty. This was at the same time that 81-year-old former subpostmaster Francis Duff finally received £330,000 compensation for having lost everything during the scandal – only for the official receiver (part of the Department for Business) to immediately claw back £322,000 of it to cover bankruptcy and owed income tax. He couldn't afford to heat his home last winter.

Meanwhile, I keep reading that the Post Office has been compensating victims (however slowly or, in many cases, not at all). In fact, two years ago, the Post Office asked the government to step in to pay the bill or else it would be insolvent. The government agreed. So the entity compensating victims has largely been the taxpayer. Us. Again, bit weird to think that the then chancellor Rishi Sunak affects to have learned about the story from the telly last week, but there you are. Fujitsu has not paid a penny in compensation, instead picking up billions of pounds of further government contracts, and continuing to do so.

Finally (for now), I will say that the Post Office scandal has hundreds of human tragedies at its heart, but it is not a natural disaster. These types of victims exist because there are perpetrators, and unless those involved are held to account, we will continue to present as a society with one rule and endless get-outs for executives and quite another for the little people. The inquiry continues. The story continues. Stay angry, and keep watching.

Rev. Vennells wept but couldn't remember much about sending innocent subpostmasters to jail. All so long ago

22 May 2024

As the former Post Office CEO faced the inquiry and her victims, she said 'sorry' a lot. About what? It was never really clear

The former Post Office CEO Paula Vennells would like the victims of the most widespread miscarriage of justice in British legal history to know that she hasn't actually done anything deliberately wrong, and that she honestly doesn't understand how all this has happened. I guess she's asking all the jailed and wrongly convicted subpostmasters to try to imagine being swept up in a Kafkaesque nightmare of undue blame. So . . . please add the murder of irony to her notional future charge sheet.

To Aldwych House in London, then, where Paula produced tears in time for the lunchtime bulletins and reprised them for the section in which her emails seemingly found her on a fishing expedition for other 'contributory factors' that might have caused an appallingly persecuted subpostmaster to take his own life. More on that horror show later. For now, let's just say Vennells currently 'can't recall' more about the Post Office than you'd expect a tenuously engaged CEO on 700 grand a year ever to have known.

Vennells was sworn in on the Bible with a beatific smile. Trying to recall the last time I saw that unsettlingly detached expression, I realised it was being worn by Liz Truss the day she sat in the Commons listening to her emergency chancellor, Jeremy Hunt, dismantle her entire economic programme in a dispatch-box drive-by.

Pressed early by the inquiry's Jason Beer KC how on earth she hadn't known what was going on, Paula explained: 'I was too trusting.' Barely a quarter of an hour later, this humblebrag had done a complete 180, as she said: 'I was sometimes criticised at team development events for being too curious.' Was she? At one stage, Vennells had even been unaware that her organisation employed a team of about 100 enforcers driving private prosecutions. I'm reminded of those people who worked for Bernie Madoff on the 18th and 19th floors of his office and somehow didn't realise he and a crack unit were running the world's biggest Ponzi scheme on the 17th.

By the way, when you exit the lift on the fifth floor of Aldwych House, a sign points you in one direction for the infected blood inquiry and in another for the Post Office Horizon IT inquiry. British officialdom's supremely arrogant lack of curiosity: destroying lives since British officialdom began. But as chair Brian Langstaff's immensely powerful report into the infected blood scandal proved earlier this week, these walls can really talk.

Today, they were hearing the testimony of an absolutely key figure in the Post Office scandal, one who hasn't uttered a word on it in public for almost 10 years, much to the anguish of the many subpostmasters packing the room to finally get a bit more clarity on how their lives were, y'know, ruined by the organisation she ran. Huge numbers of people, once told they were the only ones having problems with Horizon, were in the inquiry room, from Alan Bates to Jo Hamilton to all the other victims who have become accidental public figures. In the breaks you could hear many of them exchanging their takes on Paula. 'No contrition.' 'Very corporate.'

Memorable exchanges were also available in the evidence. Take the texts between Paula and the former Royal Mail CEO Moya Greene from earlier this year, which were projected excruciatingly on the big screen and read like dialogue in a bad daytime detective drama. 'I think you knew,' Greene typed to Vennells. 'How could you not have known? . . . I can't support you now after what I have learned.' Paula explained to the inquiry that her obliviousness was something to do with the lack of 'corporate memory' about the birth of the Horizon system. Alas, Beer – and forgive the slide into legalese – simply didn't have time for this shit, replying: 'How come we've been able to find it out just by asking for the documents?'

Oof. Top takeout? Paula Vennells is sorry in an incredibly passive-voice sort of way. She is sorry 'that that was the case', sorry 'that it can be read like that', sorry 'for all that the subpostmasters and their families have suffered'. But who made it the case? Who wrote it like that? Who caused the subpostmasters and their families to suffer? Come on, St Paula, put your finger on it.

It's absolutely wild that Vennells was reportedly the current Archbishop of Canterbury's personal pick for Bishop of London, the third most important position in the entire Church of England.

Justin Welby has certainly mastered the passive voice himself, declaring recently that 'more questions should have been asked' about Vennells. Yes! By you! 'My faith does not write the [Post Office] strategy,' declared Vennells in one breezy interview from her early years as the organisation's CEO. 'What my faith does is motivate me around how I deliver it.' Righto.

Watching Vennells today, I found her a wholly inadequate holy inadequate and kept wondering what was really going on beneath the mandated contrition. Maybe she still hangs on to the secret conviction that subpostmasters were actually on the take or being led into temptation, as one of her emails put it in a weirdo echo of the Lord's Prayer.

Speaking of living her values, we must return, heartbreakingly, to the suicide of Martin Griffiths. Despite having been the victim of an armed robbery at his branch, Griffiths was deemed partly culpable for it, as well as being relentlessly pursued over a shortfall caused by Horizon. On the afternoon of the day Martin walked deliberately into the path of an oncoming bus, Alan Bates wrote a witheringly furious email to Vennells and others informing them about Martin's desperate action, judging of this institutional 'thuggery' that the Post Office 'got him in the end'.

He quoted Martin's family's own email to him: 'May God forgive them.' That very evening, Vennells was on the Post Office's internal email, pointing out that there were 'usually several contributory factors' to suicide and 'accusations of blame were unhelpful'. Within days she was asking for 'background' on Griffiths and any previous mental health problems or potential family issues – presumably any and all speculative causes other than 'hounded to death by the Post Office'.

It's easy, when you hear this level of corporate psychopathy, to think this inquiry was always an inevitability. But it wasn't. This was a way of operating that Vennells and the organisation she ran got away with for so long because people couldn't or wouldn't believe what the victims were saying. You have to keep reminding yourself of this, even when you're sitting in the middle of it.

And then, in the loos during one of the breaks, you suddenly find yourself washing your hands next to someone played by Monica Dolan in the highest-rating, most history-making TV drama of the entire year. Funny – not to say extraordinary – how things turn out. Suffice to say, the inquiry continues.

Innocent subpostmasters went to jail, but now it is clear: the Post Office's boss class belong there instead

8 July 2025

You thought it couldn't get any worse, but the most widespread miscarriage of justice in British legal history just got wider

Millie Castleton was eight when her subpostmaster father was falsely accused of theft by the Post Office. Immediately, her family were branded as thieves and liars. She moved school, where she became the target of bullying for her father's 'theft'. The verbal abuse was followed by physical attacks. Meanwhile, racked by stress, Millie's mother developed epilepsy, and Millie began sleeping with her so as to be on hand when she suffered seizures. The child became depressed and self-loathing, feeling like 'a burden' to her family. She won a place at university but developed anorexia and could not continue.

In her absolute gut-punch of a statement to Sir Wyn Williams's Post Office Horizon IT inquiry, the first volume of whose report dropped on Tuesday morning, Millie wrote: 'I fought. I tried. I am better for it . . . That nagging voice in my head still says ugly things sometimes. It still tells me that my past and my family's struggle will define me, that it will be a branding on my skin forever . . . I'm 26 and am very conscious that I may never be able to fully commit to natural trust. But my family is still fighting. I'm still fighting, as are many hundreds still involved in the Post Office trial.'

How does every one of these stories feel like the saddest thing you've ever heard? How did Millie's father, an entirely innocent man, end up hounded into homelessness and a £310,000 'debt' to the Post Office? How in the ever-living Fujitsu does Lee Castleton still not have justice nearly two decades on?

That story is just one case highlighted in the first volume of the report, with Williams calling the human impact of the Post Office scandal 'profoundly disturbing'. Other takeouts? The most widespread miscarriage of justice in British legal history just got wider. We used to think that 900 innocent subpostmasters were convicted after the Post Office pursued them for branch shortfalls – shortfalls that were not actually down to theft, but to a computer system that the Post Office and its developer, Fujitsu, knew was faulty. Today, we learned there were, in fact, approximately 1,000 convictions. At least 10,000 victims are eligible for compensation, and that number is rising.

And there have been even more tragic numerical upticks. It was previously thought that six victims of the Horizon scandal had taken their own lives; today, we learned it was at least 13. A further 59 victims contemplated suicide at various points in their ordeal, and 10 of those actively attempted to take their own lives. At least one was admitted to a mental health facility on more than one occasion. Many self-harmed. Many say they began to abuse alcohol.

Some numbers haven't changed, though: the tally of people charged for ruining this many thousands of lives still stands at precisely zero.

That blame side of matters will be addressed in the next phase of Williams's report, and a significant police investigation is already under way. But the inquiry chair wanted to use this first volume to urgently catalyse the 'full, fair and prompt' redress the government keeps saying is due to victims. In fact, he's very keen that the government should spell out what full and fair redress means. Ideally by, like, yesterday – but, in the absence of that, ASAFP. That's not Sir Wyn's abbreviation, I should stress, but it's very much the vibe of this compelling report, given the number of victims still to be compensated by any one of the four redress schemes. Of these, three are run by the government, and one by the Post Office. The Post Office! That feels totally normal – like appointing the wolf as loss adjuster for the three little pigs' house insurance claims.

Yet even at this first stage, Williams was clear that these thousands of individual horror stories were not the result of some kind of antagonist-free natural disaster. They happened because *there were perpetrators*. Someone blew thousands of houses down. His report states that all of these people and their wider families are to be regarded as victims of 'wholly unacceptable behaviour perpetrated by a number of individuals employed by and/or associated with the Post Office and Fujitsu'.

Indeed, a notable feature of today's report is how many of the victims had begged for help when their Horizon terminals started showing weird shortfalls. One postmistress had made 256 calls to the helpdesk about Horizon problems. She would later be incarcerated and denied contact with her daughter on the latter's 18th birthday. Her daughter died the following year. I have to say that even selecting which glimpses of suffering to include in this column feels disrespectful to all the others; the fact is that every single one is a tragedy whose ripples can only be guessed at. Small wonder Williams recommended that close family members affected by this are also compensated.

And so to another of those families. The facts of Harjinder Butoy's story are modern, but its emotional dynamics feel like something straight out of a Thomas Hardy novel. Here was a man in the prime of his life, with a thriving small business that was established with a loan from his brother. Then, a twist of fate . . . and the descent is dizzyingly rapid. The total loss of reputation, a court case, imprisonment. His shame – the shame of an innocent man – reported in newspapers, from the *Daily Telegraph* to the *Punjab Times*. Harjinder's whole family were sucked into the vortex of his misfortune: his wife was left homeless and penniless with their three young children; his brother's loan could never be repaid; his parents gave everything to try to ameliorate his situation, though everything wasn't enough. Mr Butoy spent longer in prison than any other victim of the Post Office scandal, and 14 years passed between his suspension and his conviction being quashed. His bankruptcy dogged him for a decade or more, his mental health has been destroyed, and he has not been able to find work since leaving prison.

It feels impossible not to think of Harjinder's fall in counterpoint to the seemingly unstoppable rise of senior executives at Fujitsu, and most particularly at the Post Office, where the boss class secured bonuses, directorships and – who knows? – maybe even a few places in hell.

Harjinder broke a long silence on the eve of this report's publication. 'I just want everyone to know the impact, what's happened to us all,' he said. 'But I also need someone to be punished and let them go to prison and feel like what we've been through.' Quite so. But do 'someones' like that go to prison, or is it only people like Harjinder Butoy who do? That is the key question that remains, and no country where the little people pay for the sins of the bigwigs should ever consider itself properly civilised. Compensation should be full and fair – but so should justice.

NO DRAMA STARMER

Keir Starmer's general election victory in July 2024 was amusingly hailed as the return of the grown-ups. Can you get buried by your own landslide? If so, it took about two months for Starmer to find himself up to his neck. From rows over expensive freebies to accidentally echoing Enoch Powell, the prime minister swiftly became marginally less popular than Ebola. Delusional or dishonest promises on tax during the general election campaign predictably came back to bite his chancellor, Rachel Reeves, whose tears in the House of Commons might have been about something personal but came to symbolise something universal: a perception that the government was already very tired and emotional. Could Labour turn to regicide, channelling the same bungling bloodlust the Tories had spent the past decade delighting us all with? Why, I rather think they could.

Take it on trust, Britain's politicians beg voters. Trouble is, we all know they're lying

28 June 2024

Will the return to 'boring' politics make all of Britain's problems magically disappear? If you believe that, I have a bridge to sell you

'We're not pitching you a new Netflix series,' intoned Labour's shadow business secretary, Jonathan Reynolds, this week. 'We're not putting on politics as entertainment.' And certainly, absolutely no one could accuse the extremely likely next government of that. The thing about a new Netflix series, of course, is that the streamer will want to have an absolutely nailed-down idea of how much it is going to cost and how it will be funded before it gets the green light. Weirdly, you have to do this if you are pitching *Is It Cake?*, but not if you are seeking to run the world's sixth-largest economy. This means it's possible that the thing the frontrunner party tells you is the manifesto is not actually a manifesto, but something else. Cake, maybe. Is it cake?

'We want to return to serious government,' Reynolds continued loftily, 'to effective policy and to politics as public service, not as pantomime.' Right. One of the things we've heard for some time now is ordinary people saying they just want politics to be boring again – which is understandable, but always feels rather cargo-cultish. It is as though the fact that politics was boring back in the good times logically means that the good times can be restored by somehow making politics boring. I . . . don't think it works like that. Without wishing to unleash any spoilers for the season ahead, the UK faces huge and deepening problems – and anyone who tells you they can be fixed by 'boring politics' is selling something.

A number of sales pitches are available. If populism is claiming there are simple answers to complex problems, then pretty much every manifesto offered this election is a populist one. For my money, the most ominous thing that happened this week was the underplayed Institute for Fiscal Studies slapdown of another Labour frontbencher, this time Nick Thomas-Symonds, who had told an interviewer: 'We've also been open, always, that we may open the books and discover that the situation is even worse than it is at the moment.'

Ah, 'the books'. Please, not 'the books'. Just as it was not accurate for Margaret Thatcher to pretend that the public finances were entirely analogous to a housewife's budget, so it is not accurate to try to flog people the idea that the United Kingdom is a small business that the Labour party is apparently about to buy, sight unseen, while hoping it doesn't find any nasty surprises in 'the books' or perhaps under 'the bonnet'.

But listen, don't take it from me. Take it from the IFS director, Paul Johnson. 'Oh dear, oh dear,' he responded to Thomas-Symonds's comment. 'The old "we may open the books and discover the situation is even worse . . ." The books are wide open, fully transparent. That really won't wash . . .' It was Johnson's familiarity with the books, in fact, that led his organisation to issue rebukes to both Labour and the Conservatives for claiming their manifesto policies could be funded by extremely 'trivial' cuts to services or tax rises, when the reality is that they will require far more significant tax rises or cuts, likely both. One of these sins of omission is going to matter, and it isn't the Conservative one.

During this campaign, no politician has said the plain fact: this country will soon not be able to afford even its current 'lifestyle' (if I may deploy some mirthless air quotes), let alone the one to which Labour rightly aspires. The received wisdom is that Theresa May once told the truth during a campaign – justifying what was immediately branded her 'dementia tax' – and tanked the election.

It was, as always, more complicated than that, but it still passed immediately into strategy folklore. The British people's appetite for fantasy was again held to be insatiable, and without any side effects.

As they draw to a close, then, the past 14 years of Conservative government can be characterised as an era when evasion as a presentational device became evasion as a policy position. Successive governments simply haven't told the hard truths or done the hard work the country has needed. Nothing big has been done, except in the endless rabbit holes of constitutional politics the Conservatives have led us down. And those big things have only made matters worse.

Meanwhile, during that same period, there has also been just the vaguest sense that British people don't like politicians lying to them. Lying is one of those things that undermines trust across the board, not just in the team that's doing it. It was the same with Partygate, with MPs' expenses and with the current election gambling scandal. Going further back, it was the same with the Iraq war. These things undermine trust in ALL politicians, and by extension in the democratic process, and if that's unfair because one side was worse than the others, then feel free to go house to house explaining to normal people that they're looking at it all wrong.

In the end, Keir Starmer's Labour is asking an electorate whose trust in politicians is already the lowest it has ever been to take something on trust. And even his detractors should wish him luck and hope that things can only get better – the country deserves it. Reality being what it is, though, people may come to resent the deliberate evasions of the would-be government sooner rather than later. Maybe the moment of reckoning can be covered up or put off by some more evasions – 'the books'. But if that fails, and the next government is left having to explain reality to an even less trusting electorate, then what can it say? Sorry, but ours were the good type of untruths? Let's hope the public will understand, or the transfer of power will simply be a transfer of anger.

With the best glasses donor money can buy, surely Starmer can see that this week has been a total disaster

20 September 2024

When the only recent PM to have worse approval ratings is Liz Truss, one hopes for a rethink. But he's not proving to be a natural at this, is he?

Can someone gift the prime minister a designer spade? He wants to keep digging. If Keir Starmer were a celebrity, this week we'd be looking for the black hole in his publicist's brain. Alas, these are mildly testing times for anyone who bought into the always ridiculous idea of No Drama Starmer. The prime minister has officially graduated into his Some Drama Starmer era, and – like all prime ministers ever – is on the ineluctable journey towards his All Drama Starmer era. This journey is of variable speed, of course: sometimes it takes 11 years, and sometimes it takes 44 days.

The PM is never going to be Loves the Drama Starmer, though, judging by his amusingly defensive response that it is basically essential for him to be by far and away parliament's biggest receiver of hospitality and freebies, as well as being one half of the sort of couple on a combined salary of over two hundred grand who can't buy their own clothes, and also a guy who has a weakness for multiple pairs of designer glasses. Forgive me – 'luxury eyewear', with a value of £2,485.

I sympathise with his football security issue but can't quite keep a straight face over the hammy melodrama of the statement: '... never going to an Arsenal game again because I can't accept hospitality is pushing it a bit far'. We could be mere days away from an explanation that accepting £4,000-worth of Taylor Swift tickets off the Premier League is a basic human right. (I'm afraid my reaction to the phrase '£698 of Coldplay tickets' is: how many thousand Coldplay tickets is that?)

Nor did Starmer completely nail the tone when addressing the full-spectrum briefing war currently being waged between his chief of staff, who now gets paid more than him and is fine with that; internal enemies of his chief of staff, who get paid less than they were expecting and are not fine with it; his senior adviser and political strategist; lesser spads; and – I think? – the cabinet secretary.

I'm finding the angles on this quite hard to keep up with, but the general vibe of his No. 10 operation is the sort of snakepit you might have expected to find in the Kuntsevo Dacha 15 minutes after Stalin was discovered on the shagpile. I would even go so far as to say it could rival a breakfast television studio. I had to forcefully press my challenge buzzer when I heard Starmer explain to BBC South East that he was 'completely in control'. Oof. Once upon a time that was what Eamonn Holmes thought.

Moving on to the choice of donors, can we really judge a man by the man he lets smother him in high-end glasses? Let's hope not. Lord Alli was ennobled by Tony Blair – who, until he became one of them, was always pathetically impressed by very rich people – and is now the purchaser of the Starmers' wardrobes and arsenal of fancy specs. This latest piece of beneficence seems to have earned his lordship a temporary Downing Street security pass. As for the type of person we're dealing with . . . listen, I don't want to say Waheed Alli 'divides opinion', because you know what? This week I asked several people in the know about him to give their opinion, and they all said exactly the same thing. Unfortunately, it's a single word that we don't use in the *Guardian* unless it's in reported speech.

That all this should be taking place in the final weeks of a three-month scare buildup to the budget seems at best unfortunate, and surely something that one's chief of staff or political adviser or tailor should have spotted as a danger area. Even while he was droning on about his corporate hospitality, Starmer was declining to discuss next month's doom budget, on the basis that 'I don't want to risk putting the fear of God into people.'

Well, it's a bit late for that. Labour took office and immediately declared things to be so dire that they were going to have to do awful and painful things to combat them – but will have left it three months by the time they finally explain what those awful and painful things are. This, as the former chief economist to the Bank of England, Andy Haldane, and many others have pointed out, has created a sense of 'fear and foreboding and uncertainty among consumers, among businesses, and among investors'.

Truly the hat-trick. The current freebies row taking place during that particular information vacuum consequently feels even worse. It suggests that Starmer is a guy who talks to the public like an undertaker but in private likes the finer things in life. More than that, he feels entitled to them. That is no one's favourite combination.

Having said that, I don't think it's the within-the-rules odour of impropriety that is the biggest problem for Starmer, although it is definitely a problem. Taking essential things away from those with not very much at all, while giving the appearance of being perfectly happy to help yourself to luxuries, is not a great look. But the much bigger vulnerability, in my appraisal, is that thing that maps on to what a lot of people are always, always prone to thinking about Labour: that they're very free and easy when they're spending other people's money.

According to Ipsos polling in the *FT* today, half of British voters say they are disappointed in how Labour has governed so far, with Starmer's approval ratings worse than those of any of his predecessors, except Liz Truss. Considering that this comes more than a month before the doom budget outlines their plans for our money, Starmer may find the next set of ratings well worth misplacing his many pairs of spectacles for.

So ends the Keirbot's immigration week: literally everyone hates it. Possibly even him

16 May 2025

Several strongly worded X posts, a bungled Albanian scheme and the ghost of Enoch Powell. Once again, he's smashed it

On Friday morning, Keir Starmer was posting without compromise. 'If you're one of the smugglers putting people in small boats across the channel,' ran the prime minister's communiqué on X, 'we're coming after you.' Imagine the fear that would have struck into the hearts of all those people smugglers who follow his account.

Alternatively, you could consider the above as a performance for the benefit of people other than those to whom it appears to be addressed – which would certainly make it of a piece with Starmer's entire shtick for 'immigration week'. Because that really has been quite a performance, and one the critics are already calling unconvincing, excruciating and wooden. On several occasions the prime minister was outperformed by his lectern.

Monday was the big speech, which it is already clear will be remembered chiefly for Starmer's 'island of strangers' soundbite. Listening to any Starmer speech simulates the feeling of incarceration in a medium-security prison, and in this case it was like sharing a cell with a Chinese restaurant's Enoch Powell impersonator. Starmer plays this hardline stuff about as plausibly as Elijah Wood played a football hooligan in that terrible movie, which I would still have preferred to watch again over the spectacle of the prime minister droning on unconvincingly about the 'incalculable' damage immigration had done to his polling numbers. Sorry, to the country.

For the left, the problem was what he said; for the right, the problem was the absurdity of it being him saying it. These days, Starmer can't encounter two stools without falling between them, with the problem entirely of his own making. I once read a hideous story about a Kansas woman who had sat on a loo seat for so long she had become stuck to it, and I fear something similar might have happened here with a fence. Starmer has sat on one for so long, on so many different issues, that it has become fused to his form. We are now watching a live fence-ectomy, and it is painful.

Whatever the clinical bodyshock diagnosis, the vibes-based one is clear: the British public has never loved Starmer, and never will. On the rare occasions he reveals things about himself, they often in fact seem to be the absence of things. Starmer doesn't dream, we learned during his general election pitch last year, and couldn't name a favourite book. There is something of the slight to him, and he knows it – in fact, he knows it so powerfully that these days all his big speeches contain frequent, plaintive tells. Specifically, phrases like 'I believe in this' or 'I am doing this . . . because it is what I believe in.' If things were going convincingly, believing in the things you were saying and doing would surely be axiomatic.

But things aren't going convincingly, and so it is that we have a new gotcha question that Labour MPs – and, indeed, the prime minister himself – must most fear being asked. Namely, what is a Keir Starmer? The answer is – and I'm sorry to use a term that I know many people find offensive, but accuracy matters – a lawyer. A Keir Starmer is an adult human lawyer, as capable of advocating for this side as for that, or even both at once. And so it is that we have to listen to speeches like Monday's, in which the PM decries the 'incalculable' damage of immigration, at the same time as the Tories are posting videos from about 10 minutes ago in which Starmer is gurning, 'We need to make the positive case for immigration.' Again, what is a Keir Starmer? Can a Keir Starmer have both these views? Of course he can, and of course he does.

The counterpoint take is that the prime minister has a split personality, and both the personalities are somewhat insufferable. A legal manager in the sheets; a legal manager willing to talk tetchy in the streets. Strangely, the more Starmer tries to flesh out his immigration plan, the more the logic suggests that the only thing that could make coherent sense of it would be the UK leaving the European Convention on Human Rights. Yet at the same time, how could it, because the one thing the prime minister convincingly and consistently believes in is the primacy of lawyers.

Meanwhile, an incredibly wide spectrum of people find they can't really believe in what Starmer's saying. His speech contrived to unite Alf Dubs ('I don't think it's what he actually believes in') with Robert Jenrick ('It looked like a hostage situation where he was reading out words someone else had written for him'). The 'somebody else's opinions' stuff is becoming a recurring theme, recalling that BBC *Question Time* moment during the general election campaign last year when a member of the public put it to him that he came across like a 'political robot'.

By Thursday, he had travelled to Albania, and by most accounts, he was blindsided live on air by that country's prime minister ruling out the very idea of hosting processing hubs for asylum seekers. Perhaps it could be spun as a blessing in disguise for Mr Consistency. Arguably, the only thing worse than a defunct Rwanda scheme the taxpayer has paid hundreds of millions of pounds for is a notional Albania scheme that the taxpayer will get stung for, only for it to run into the same problems. But instead, No. 10 is trying to convince everyone that no Albanian hubs was the plan all along. Can you believe it? As with most things about Keir Starmer, 'no' would increasingly seem to be the answer.

Starmer's reno of the UK is going brilliantly. If you don't count the walls falling down

4 July 2025

Nothing says you've lifted the mood of the nation like having to haul your chancellor to a photocall at a 'wellbeing centre'

Well, British politics has served up another week of compellingly packaged action. Like *Drive to Survive*, but for clown cars. Leave it to No Drama Starmer to come up with the only thing weirder and more awful than watching the chancellor of the exchequer sob on the frontbench: wheeling her out a mere 22 and a half hours later for an unscheduled appearance at a wellbeing centre(!), where Rachel Reeves had to get her happy face on and pose for selfies.

The whole thing gave Keir Starmer the feel of one of those remorseless boyband managers who reacts to one of their young charges having a breakdown by getting them a special injection and shoving them straight back out on stage the next night. I think you can probably do it with a member of Take That or 5ive or whoever and only run the risk of them turning on you in a documentary decades later. But is it a vibe you want at the heart of the team in charge of the world's sixth-largest economy?

Yes, imply some allies of Reeves, who are now suggesting that because the (debunked) possibility that the chancellor was crying about losing her job clearly spooked bond traders, she has actually emerged in a stronger position from the whole business. Again: really? Having to physically hug your boss to calm the markets doesn't feel like a textbook power move, but look, like people kept saying last July, the grown-ups are back in charge.

Anyway, never mind last July. Watching the turbo fiasco of this week unfold, I kept thinking instead of a speech Starmer made in the Downing Street garden near the end of last August. I want to say it was the first reset of his government, but who's counting? This government has had more reboots than *Batman*. And, like that particular character's screen incarnations, it all just seems to be getting darker and grittier every time.

That August speech featured an extremely extended analogy between the country and a house that had some kind of rot but could be fixed by being completely made over, if you really had a go at overhauling the foundations. Rereading it in the wake of Labour's full-spectrum Commons chaos over the universal credit and personal independence payment bill reminded me of one of those movie scenes where an idealistic young newcomer is telling a guy in the town about the house they've just bought. It's a real fixer-upper, they're going to do it all themselves, it was quite the bargain, but it could be beautiful – and the guy just cuts them off as it dawns on him. 'Oh right,' he says. 'The murder house.'

No one is saying the House of Commons was built on an Indian burial ground, but this week's deranged farce certainly seemed to release the spirits of the Brexit years back into its cursed chamber. Much as Theresa May's 437 Brexit votes never actually achieved a Brexit, the universal credit and personal independence payment bill now has nothing about personal independence payments in it. If that doesn't take you back down memory lane, though, other throwbacks are available. Shortly after 9pm last night, the Coventry South MP, Zarah Sultana, announced she was going to 'co-lead the founding' (what?) of a new party with Jeremy Corbyn. And shortly after that, sources close to Corbyn let it be known he was furious and bewildered that this plan had been launched without consultation. According to what one ally told the *FT*, 'Zarah has really overplayed her hand,' which is believed to include the three of clubs, Mr Bun the Baker and an expired student railcard. Out loud, Corbyn said things like 'Zarah will help us' and 'discussions are ongoing'. Let's pray for peace – if not in the wider world, then certainly in this new and fractured party.

Then again, which part of our politics isn't fracturing before our very eyes? It is quite possible none of us will be able to escape the murder house's past. In some ways, the most bizarre thing about the welfare bill fallout was the cabinet ministers attempting to clean it up with the same strange, dead language that a growing number of people feel characterises most contemporary politicians bar Nigel Farage. No sooner had the horror show unfolded than cabinet office minister Pat McFadden was explaining that though there would be a cost, Labour would still stick to its manifesto promises on tax. Is this the gibberish about not raising taxes on 'working people'? It would seem so.

Yet even back at manifesto stage, this already felt like a deliberately obscure way of talking that just comes across as lying. Newsflash, Pat: you already have raised taxes on working people. People who run small businesses are working people. And the reason they haven't employed more working people, and in some cases have let go the working people they used to employ, is because you raised taxes on them. By chance I heard McFadden's interview right after one of my children told me he'd seen Reeves crying on loads of YouTube videos. He's 12, so I think that's what they call cut-through, and it underscores the feeling that you just can't control politics in the knackered old ways any more.

As for what we're feeling – all those wonderful working people out there in the dark – the answer is surely: like we've been here before, and that the dysfunction is more wearying for its familiarity. Starmer came to power promising his government would fix broken Britain. One year on, it would be a start if he could even fix his broken government.

It's Andy Burnham, the man who could be king. Will he, won't he – are we really still watching this movie?

23 January 2026

Many yearn and yearn for the Greater Manchester mayor to claim his Westminster crown. They should be careful what they wish for – as should he

Since Andy Burnham's will-he-won't-he return to Westminster is back in the news, permit me to advance a theory: Andy Burnham is Johnny Depp. Stay with me! We somehow have to make this more fun than immersing ourselves in the remorselessly petty mathematical dynamics of Labour's national executive committee (NEC).

So here goes: movie-wise, before *Pirates of the Caribbean*, Johnny Depp used to embody a desirable scarcity model. As a cultural asset he was high prestige, low supply, and every rudderless director thought that if only the mysterious Johnny was at the helm of their project, then everything would be rosy. He was different, he was cool, he was hyper-selective, he withheld himself, he didn't dress like the others, he wasn't your multiplex guy. And he was, crucially, *not available*. But *Pirates of the Caribbean* changed all that, and it changed Johnny Depp. After the unexpected mega-success of that film, the actor made himself available, and his aura evaporated. He made the conscious leap to middle-of-the-road A-listery and his cultural premium collapsed. Johnny Depp and his basic eye-liner were in everything, from franchises to mass-market fantasies to a couple of grim court cases with his ex-wife (obviously, Andy hasn't been involved in even the metaphorical version of the last one, though *Burnham* v. *Starmer* could be quite the rubbernecking spectacle). And honestly, most of it was highly indifferent. There was suddenly a lot less to him than had met the eye. Availability torched his cachet.

It's an old cycle. Scarcity gives you an aura, which gives you cultural leverage, but once the leverage has been deployed, you are no longer scarce and you lose the aura. These days, Johnny Depp has been cast out of the multiplex. Riyadh might be the only place he can open a movie, given he's been reduced to a lucrative bromance with Saudi crown prince Mohammed bin Salman. As *Vanity Fair* hilariously had it: 'Both men knew how it felt to suddenly go from golden boy to outcast.'

Sticking with this metaphor, mainly to avoid talking about Labour's endlessly excruciating internal politics for another paragraph, if Andy Burnham does contrive a return to Westminster to challenge Keir Starmer, he'll flop harder than Depp's outing in *The Lone Ranger*. And that thing really bombed. The whole point of Andy Burnham, the memoji-headed king over the water, is that he's over the water. Labour members want him, but they can't have him. He's like an illicit desire, a thing they yearn for because they can't possess it that's going to instantly seem less appealing the second they land him. Then, once again, the eyes will wander.

But will they land him? That's the other part of the drama currently gripping Labour, because there's nothing else to think about in this quiet and settled world. By way of a recap, the Gorton and Denton MP Andrew Gwynne is stepping down. When someone literally puts bits of his doctor's notes in his resignation letter, you know that there's going to be some other stuff you've forgotten about the story, so I thank Andrew for the inadvertent reminder that he was actually sacked as a minister and suspended after having been found to have sent various dodgy WhatsApp messages about constituents and other voters. Anyway, medically, he can't carry on . . . which might open up a seat for Burnham, who might ride south from Manchester to Westminster on a criminally overpriced train ticket and challenge Keir Starmer for Labour's leadership. It is ON!

But is it actually? It all depends on Labour's ruling body, the NEC. Over the years, many of you might have felt simply unable to face trying to understand how this impenetrable politburo works. So, to summarise: the NEC is a thing that any Labour leader who wants to do anything has to have 'sewn up', even though that leader will then be stopped from doing the things they want to do by the parliamentary Labour party, currently a 148-seat-majority brute force of myopic self-interest, even though most of them are going to lose their seats in the next election so might actually deign to think about the big-picture national interest and growth rather than themselves for two fricking minutes.

I hope that covers any gaps. The NEC is the entity that must give Burnham permission to resign as mayor of Greater Manchester and subsequently to stand as an MP, and current indications are that Keir Starmer has it so tightly sewn up that it'll block this one way or another. Even if it doesn't, alternative branches of future history are available. For instance, Burnham resigns as mayor of Greater Manchester, fights seat, loses to Reform. Or fights seat while the mayoralty is expensively lost to Reform. Or even fights seat but gets Boaty McBoatfaced by the Greens. Meanwhile, in most of the scenarios, the bond markets – which you'll remember Andy is not keen on us being 'in hock to' – have a little wobble every time his name is mentioned. In the circuitously reached event he wins the top job, they will have a mega-wobble.

Perennially frustrated by his name being linked with a leadership tilt, Burnham spent the hours after Gwynne's resignation defusing this latest blow-up . . . no, hang on. Yesterday he could be found in the *Guardian*, conveniently expanding on his political philosophy. It's no longer just a little bit of nationalisation and a little bit of wealth taxes. It's also something called 'Manchesterism', which – spoiler alert – is also not going to even touch the sides of the UK's deep problems.

As for how this plays out . . . For now, Burnham is able to bask in the happy worldview of every metro mayor: that everything good that happens is because of them, and that everything bad that happens is because of Westminster. Is this the moment for our self-styled indie star to go mainstream? Never underestimate the Labour party's ability to make a spectacular flop, of course, but I can't help feeling that Andy would be better off watching this movie rather than starring in it.

It's nothing short of TV gold: mix horror with wild comedy and call it Starmer's last stand

10 February 2026

The only reason we might not get our seventh prime minister in 10 years is that no one can find one

Keir Starmer is now the only person to have lost more comms chiefs than Meghan and Harry. After yet another day of drama, we kept hearing that the prime minister would be pressing the reset button. Not again! Starmer's reset button is like the 'OK' button on your TV remote – worn blank through overuse. He has pressed that thing more often than you've decided another 44 minutes of a crap thriller is somehow less of an effort than getting yourself to bed. Anyway, next episode in five, four, three . . .

Fine. One more.

The inciting incident for yesterday's deranged chapter was another comms chief leaving, followed by an objectively hilarious call for Starmer's resignation by the Scottish Labour leader, Anas Sarwar, that accidentally forced Labour's big guns to swing publicly behind Starmer. That said, you couldn't claim the cabinet came off as one big happy family, with a minister briefing darkly: 'We've all been made to tweet.' Buck up, Cruz. Think of Sarwar as the Labour family's Brooklyn Beckham, the latter having notably observed last month that 'Family "love" is decided by how much you post on social media.'

Anyway, having seen off Sarwar's desiccated power move, Starmer supposedly crushed it at Monday evening's gathering of the parliamentary Labour party. Entering the meeting room, the PM is reported to have got a standing ovation that lasted 37 seconds. But don't set too much store by a standing ovation. At the Cannes film festival, you can get double that even for a documentary claiming that every single Cannes film festival attender is a necrophiliac bestialist. A fired-up Starmer apparently told his parliamentary colleagues: 'I have won every fight I've ever been in.' The prime minister is now seeking a match-up with either Jake Paul or Tommy Fury.

He can butch it up all he likes, but the Peter Mandelson revelations have exposed Starmer as an alleged fallen nice guy and dubious ally to women. He's kind of the Justin Baldoni of Westminster. Who's the Blake Lively in all this? I desperately want to quit this analogy but find it impossible when Wes Streeting keeps claiming that he is being covertly briefed against by Starmer's team. If these dark arts start to impact unit sales of Wes's affordable haircare line, it may be time to go nuclear.

In fact, maybe that was what was already happening late yesterday afternoon, when Streeting went full drama, claiming Downing Street was briefing against him, then releasing his own messages with Mandelson. Do people now leak their own messages? It's so hard to keep up with the sheer naffness of our politics, particularly given Streeting's other sighting came during a media appearance, where he explained people needed to 'give Keir the chance [to turn it around]'.

Elsewhere, it emerged that Angela Rayner is doing all she can to get HMRC to hurry up and conclude its review of her tax affairs – so maddening when one has to spend more than five seconds in the political wilderness. We also learned that a partly constructed website that was apparently set to launch Rayner's leadership campaign, created by the same company that does her official parliamentary web page, briefly went live in January, before being instantly pulled. A Rayner ally described it as a 'false flag' operation. So, like Operation Himmler, but a website. Any other news? Oh yes, another cabinet secretary is on the way out – the third in eight years for a job that used to be all about stability.

When he took office, Starmer stood outside No. 10 promising 'to restore service and respect to politics, end the era of noisy performance, tread more lightly on your lives'. Yet his government has trodden on people like the Serengeti wildebeest migration, a million cock-ups and U-turns stampeding over a squashed Britain for 19 months, with absolutely no sign of any let-up. Even the attempts to defend his record sound like satire. Yesterday, allies sent round a rallying note explaining that the government was delivering 'on many areas of incremental change'. The trouble is, it delivers like Evri. Your incremental change has been left in a safe place. Not *your* safe place, obviously, but somewhere you may never find.

Arguably, the most intriguing line of defence yesterday came from two cabinet ministers, Shabana Mahmood and Bridget Phillipson. 'Labour governments don't come along often,' said Mahmood. After a day like yesterday, I can't imagine why. Phillipson went on to wibble: 'Change is hard. Government isn't easy.' Really? Many will be able to live without the pronouncements of the cabinet sounding like tactical self-care posts from an influencer who promoted a dodgy meme coin and is now on a sober-curious journey. No idea where we'll get to by the end of the week at this rate. The chancellor explaining that 'it's OK not to feel OK'? Anas Sarwar declaring, 'I've had to teach myself to hold myself in the moment'?

That said, it wasn't a massively edifying day for the news media, much of which could probably do with stepping away from the news as a wellness exercise. A mad world it may be, yet Chris Mason seemed somewhat overexcited by the idea that his audience wanted to see him as the White Rabbit. Next time you see the BBC's political editor on screen, imagine every report he presents being prefaced with the words: 'Oh my paws and whiskers!' It works better that way.

As for the many branches of what could happen next, Theresa May showed us that governing as a wounded meme was possible for at least two years, while some of the suggestions should a sudden replacement for Starmer be required are genuinely insane. Take the people suggesting that enough MPs could probably rally round John Healey as a unity candidate. Sorry, but what? And, indeed, who? In the most recent poll (Q4 2025), a mere 36% of the public said they recognised John Healey. I hate to break it to Labour's delulu-is-the-solulu power brokers, but after this rolling horror show, assuming the British people would be totally cool with some guy the vast majority of them have literally never heard of being anointed their prime minister may be a piss-take too far.

The fact is, the UK is on its sixth prime minister in 10 years, and at least teetering near breaking the glass on a seventh. We've had more CEOs in a decade than a failing 2000s telecoms firm. We're basically Yahoo. Or maybe it's worse. Maybe we're one of those countries that even the neocons refused to invade because there was no figure that a meaningful number of the local populace would coalesce around. It's all very last-days-of-the-frying-pan. As for Labour's next destination? Heard it's somewhere hot.

WHEN JEFF MET LAUREN

Having placed a personal ad in *Billionaire* magazine – 'top 3 Croesus seeks force of nature' – Amazon founder Jeff Bezos met Lauren Sánchez, and the rest is history. Their union enriches us all – if not via our countries' exchequers, then certainly in the gaiety-of-nations department. The couple worked hard, mostly struggling with the conundrum of how to give away money to those less fortunate than them. (Again, why not simply let an exchequer take care of it for you?) But they played hard, too, relieving some of that tension with mini-breaks, such as Lauren's all-female trip to the edge of space in one of Jeff's rockets. It's been said that in space, no one can hear you scream, but anyone who endured the simulcast of Lauren and her girlz hurtling towards the Kármán line heard little else than a hundred decibels of 'OMIGOD' for the entire 11-minute duration. Having conquered space, Jeff's betrothed headed somewhere famously even less hospitable – Paris – for her hen do. And the couple's love story reached its operatic climax in Venice, where they married in front of a crowd of friends they'd known if not for years, then certainly for months or weeks.

All hail Jeff Bezos the philanthropist! The rest of us will just keep paying our taxes

15 November 2022

The Amazon founder says giving money away 'is really hard'. Luckily, poor people do far more of it than he does

How bracing to wake up yesterday and read that Amazon founder Jeff Bezos had donated $100m to Dolly Parton's charitable endeavours at his own 'Courage and Civility' event. (Sarcastic air quotes: my own.) The many, many news reports about this act suggested it was a truly incredible sum from the second-richest man in the world, who, according to recent estimates, gets richer by about $205m a day.

Anyway, once I'd peeled myself off the ceiling, I got busy on the government's tax calculator. If you're on the median UK salary and you pay your taxes, your take-home pay is £72 a day. Looked at one way, then, Jeff's benevolence would be the equivalent of donating £34.56 to charity. Have YOU ever donated 34 quid to charity? Do you pay your taxes? If so, you're actually being *more generous than Jeff Bezos*, who, famously, avoids almost all of his. And yet, where's YOUR splashy write-up in all the fine news outlets of the world? Where's YOUR fawning TV interview? Why does no one refer to YOU as a 'philanthropist'?

We'll come to the obvious answers to those questions shortly, but for now, let's look at the stage-managed hoopla around these so-called Courage and Civility awards. And yes, that title does make it sound like Jeff just demanded a warehouse operative bring him two inoffensive abstract nouns that were out of copyright. In fact, Bezos announced the initiative last year, shortly after disembarking from his little space rocket, possibly sensing a planetary disdain being levelled at the kind of guy who could put himself in zero gravity for four minutes but couldn't figure out how to treat his workers properly.

Anyway, the Courage and Civility awards are now an actual thing. And alongside Sunday's self-effacing ceremony and his attempt to piggyback on the lifelong altruism and extraordinary charitable service of HRH Dolly Parton, Bezos granted an exclusive sit-down with CNN. First impressions? Jeff interviews like a chat tool and resembles your local area's most uncompromising and least-booked 58-year-old Vin Diesel lookalike. Having long refused to sign the Giving Pledge – a promise by many of the world's richest individuals to donate most of their wealth to charitable causes – Bezos announced that he intends to give 'the majority' of his money away during his lifetime, according to CNN. And yet, does he intend to do this? His answer – 'Yeah, I do' – feels somewhat vague and short on specifics.

But taking Jeff at his word, I mean it from the bottom of the heart when I say: BIG FRICKING DEAL. Most people give a significant amount of their money away during their lifetime, via a little something we call the taxation system. I know! Where's our red-carpet gala? I tell you what, next time our pay cheques arrive, why don't we all get our hair done and put on black tie or a big old dress and graciously twat our way down a red carpet, going 'You're MOST welcome!' for the cameras.

According to what Bezos told CNN, philanthropy 'is really hard'. It certainly seems to be for him. Do recall he was only dragged kicking and screaming to the giving-a-shit game, having spent years accruing billions before it was finally pointed out to him that not having some kind of philanthropic arm looked fairly abysmal. In 2017, Bezos asked Twitter users for ideas on how to help the world 'in the here and now', before embarking on a truly committed programme of ignoring every single one of those who suggested paying his workers properly and contributing a fair amount of tax.

A year later, he actually uttered the words: 'The only way that I can see to deploy this much financial resource is by converting my Amazon winnings into space travel.' That was the same year Amazon, by threatening to pull a huge building project, helped kill a Seattle tax on big firms that would help alleviate the homelessness crisis. The business and tech commentator Scott Galloway calls Bezos 'the mother of all welfare queens' for the vast benefits he's drawn from public money and the tax breaks he remorselessly chases and demands.

But, of course, Jeff is the kind of widely acclaimed visionary who simply lacks the vision to realise that the first way to help is by paying people a fair wage and forking out your taxes like an ordinary person – and not by turning up to dole out 'charity' after the event, like some bastard god of the purse strings. Unfortunately, he's part of that specific billionaire class that believes they should be allowed to hypothecate almost 100% of their own vast riches in whichever direction they wish, because the exchequers of the world are just junior personnel, and they know better than all of them how to spend it.

So, yes, for Bezos philanthropy 'is really hard'. What *he* does – fauxlanthropy – is much, much easier. Moving billions to non-profits you control, effectively awarding yourself tax breaks, buying media fawning with one of the lamest possible sleights-of-hand: these things, self-evidently, are a whole lot easier. What's hard to understand is why on earth we're still buying into this obvious bullshit from some of the most selfish people in the world. The poor give a far greater proportion of their money to charity than the rich. I don't mean to be uncivil, but what is courageous about letting Jeff Bezos pretend otherwise?

What does Jeff Bezos's new fiancée see in the world's third-richest man? Must be his enormous philanthropy

26 May 2023

Giving money away is hard, says Lauren Sánchez, who is currently touring Europe with Bezos on his 417ft yacht

One-click on a fascinator, readers, because there's a mega-wedding in the offing. Congratulations to Mr Jeff Bezos, Amazon kajillionaire, and Ms Lauren Sánchez, bralette-wearing philanthropist/immense force of nature. Although news of the couple's engagement seeped out this week after Lauren was spotted wearing a diamond ring in the south of France, Jeff has yet to release a formal announcement. So let's just draft one for him: 'Ladies and gents, she said Proceed to Checkout.'

Now look, you already know Jeff. World's third-richest man. Went to space. Looks like he should be appearing above a daytime TV caption reading: 'I make £40 a month as a Vin Diesel escort, and my fiancée loves it!' But are you fully across Lauren? I'll be honest: we haven't met. But from the outside looking in, my nose pressed against the glass of Google Images, I simply cannot get enough of this Nietzschean superwoman, the final form of the East German silicon-doping programme, who has missile-titted her way into my consciousness and now captivates me twice weekly with her insouciance, her outfits and her observations on just how difficult philanthropy is to do. Seriously, no one has ever thought harder about how to help poors while mooching round a Grand Prix enclosure with some kind of You Could Never Access All My Areas lanyard dangling from her belt loop. In some ways, I don't think I've felt this amused by a picaresque heroine since I saw a photo of Jennifer Arcuri biting the head off a fondant-icing Boris Johnson figurine from a Boris Johnson cake she'd had made. Yes, customers who liked Jennifer also liked Lauren. Not so much a gal-about-town as a gal-about-planet.

Anyway, the now-affianced Bezos and Sánchez are currently touring Europe on Jeff's new yacht, *Koru*, a 417ft three-master/three-peniser that is the largest such vessel ever built. To put things into perspective, this yacht is so big it has its own yacht: a 246ft 'support vessel' that lugs around boring little things like the helicopter pad and, reportedly, some kind of personal submarine. And this week, for the first time, we saw *Koru*'s figurehead. Ships' figureheads have traditionally come in various forms, of course: mermaids, Neptunes, angels – and now, Fox-News-anchor-in-transparent-singlet-with-erect-nipples. Suck on it, history! Our century is so the best. The Bezos yacht's figurehead is fingering a large pendant necklace and appears to be about to say something. 'Draw me like one of your French girls'? Either way, the vast boat it adorns only recently left the shipyard, hopefully while some urchin child on the dock cackled: 'Yeah, but you'll never be cool, will you, Bezos – YOU'LL NEVER BE COOL!'

But will the Amazon boss ever, really, even be a genuine philanthropist? We do seem to be at the stage of human intellectual decay where anyone who is a multibillionaire is also automatically described as a 'philanthropist', when in many cases 'misanthropist' would be better supported by the evidence. For instance, I'm forever seeing Dubai ruler Sheikh Mohammed described as a philanthropist. Is he the one who has at least two of his children missing/kidnapped at any given moment? Honestly, so what if he's built a sanitation programme too?

Back to Lauren, though, who last year declared: 'I'm immersing myself in philanthropy and strategic giving.' Which sounds a lot more fun than Amazon warehouse workers immersing themselves in strategic peeing-in-bottles. Yet it turns out this stuff is hard. 'You want to give money away,' claimed Lauren. 'You want to know that it's helping people and it's going to continue to help people, and that it's going to the right places. You *could* give it not-strategically. You can just give it away! But, we take it seriously.' Mmm. It feels like they've thought of everything except Amazon paying tax like normal businesses.

The question of just how much Bezos truly does want to give away is a thorny one, with his answers tending towards the vague. Or, as Lauren puts it: 'Jeff has always told me, since I've known him, that he's going to give the majority of his money away to philanthropy.' I hope you love the phoned-in generality of that 'to philanthropy'.

Even so, maybe 'I'm going to give the majority of my money away to philanthropy' is the kind of thing you say to get laid in the early stages of a relationship. I'm suddenly reminded of Anne Hathaway's former boyfriend, who told the movie star he was 'the chief financial officer of the Vatican'. 'My boyfriend is incredible,' Anne duly told the world. 'But when it comes to his charity . . . one of the most untouted aphrodisiacs in the world is charity work. Seriously, you want a girl to be impressed, vaccinate some kids, build a house.' Anne's boyfriend would go on to serve a four-and-a-half-year jail term for fraud, with probably my favourite detail in the FBI files being that he had fake Monsignor robes hanging in his and Anne's wardrobe at their $37,500-a-month Trump Tower penthouse.

But look, it's all a journey. And we're so, so lucky that Jeff's still in the pretending-to-give-a-toss stage of things with Lauren, taking a veeeeery long run-up to a minuscule percentage of 'strategic giving' on his half-a-billion-dollar boat. These fauxlanthropists may not give the world their taxes, but they do at least give us a few laughs. Strategically or otherwise.

What's more vacuous than an endless vacuum? It's Lauren Sánchez and Katy Perry's party in space

15 April 2025

The all-female Blue Origin flight on Monday broke boundaries and set records in the spouting of girlboss gibberish

Well, I watched every second of the buildup, flight and aftermath of the first Blue Origin all-female space trip. You've heard of one small step for man? This was one giant leap backwards for womankind. I'm kidding, I'm kidding! What could be more empowering or something than watching Lauren Sánchez make going to space sound like brunch with the girrrrrls. Sally Ride could never.

Anyway, if you missed this, Jeff Bezos's fiancée took an 11-minute trip to the edge of space on one of his Blue Origin craft on Monday, alongside some all-female passengers – sorry, 'crew' – who included CBS anchor Gayle King and pop star Katy Perry. So, yes, the 'Woman's World' video is no longer the most plastic feminist thing Katy's done.

Given the mixture of freebie rides and seats sold to the super-rich, the thing people always say about Blue Origin tickets is that prices range from zero to $28m. A bit like a seat on a Ryanair flight to Tallinn. But these spots were all personally gifted by Bezos and Sánchez because this was an Important Mission. Which also meant the whole thing was exclusively documented by Blue Origin's *Pravda*-like web channel. Here, the anchors and reporters kept explaining that – unlike when men went to space in the past – this mission was all about emotions. But look, it's great that we're valorising emotions above all things, because it gives me permission to say how very much I hated this entire, hilariously vacuous spectacle.

Lauren already bills herself as a children's author, helicopter pilot, journalist and philanthropist, and kept being told she was adding 'astronaut' to the world's longest multi-hyphenate. How did she find the trip? 'I don't really have the words for this, like . . .?' OK, but can you at least try? 'I can't put it into words, but I looked out the window and we got to see the moon.'

Back at the viewing platform in the West Texas desert, commentary was provided by, among others, Kris Jenner and a bottom-tier Kardashian (Khloé). Khloé glossed the moment of landing with the words 'it's literally so hard to explain right now'. Other insights? 'There's one woman whose grandfather is back there, and he is 92 and they didn't even have transportation back then.' I mean, the guy was literally pre-horse. Historic scenes.

Amid extremely stiff competition, the most hardcore gibberish emanated from Perry, who served up an entire word-salad bar involving the 'feminine divine' and being 'super-connected to love'. 'It's about making space for future woman,' she explained. 'It's about taking up space.' Imagine going to actual space and talking instead about therapy-speak 'space'. When Buzz Aldrin beheld the surface of the moon, he described it as 'magnificent desolation'. Honestly, if he wanted to feel desolation he could have just tuned into this corner of West Texas on Monday afternoon. When a STEM advocate came for her post-flight interview, we got to see the apparently lobotomised reporter shriek: 'How do you look perfect after just going to space?!'

In truth, how the women looked had been an overwhelming part of the buildup, by their own design. In an *Elle* magazine joint interview with the passengers, Lauren showed off the hot space suits she'd personally commissioned, inquiring rhetorically: 'Who would not get glam before the flight?' 'Space is going to finally be glam,' agreed Perry. 'Let me tell you something. If I could take glam up with me, I would do that. We are going to put the "ass" in astronaut.' A former Nasa rocket scientist said: 'I also wanted to test out my hair and make sure that it was OK. So I skydived in Dubai with similar hair to make sure I would be good – took it for a dry run.' Still want more? Because there was SO much of it. 'We're going to have lash extensions flying in the capsule!' explained Lauren. 'I think it's so important for people to see us like that,' explained a civil rights activist. 'This dichotomy of engineer and scientist, and then beauty and fashion. We contain multitudes. Women are multitudes. I'm going to be wearing lipstick.'

Ooof. I always thought space travel was futuristic, but this was the first time it came off as travelling back in time, in this case using their little capsule to take us back to the most ludicrous inanities of 2010s girlboss feminism.

Ultimately, it felt like a sign of the times that everything was about personal growth, rather than affording the wider world any new understanding of humanity. As King put it: 'I'm so proud of me right now.' Everyone, bar none, talked in whatever trite solipsisms language has been reduced to by a permanent diet of social media self-care. It all made me realise how much I miss humans who are not permanently crying on TV and who are able to find words that don't sound like they could be printed above a picture of a cross-roads sign on Instagram or maybe some sandy footprints on a beach.

Having oh-my-godded her way through some pure gibberish, Lauren eventually announced that she'd learned that 'We're all in this together. We're so connected.' Agreed. In which spirit, please please please could Amazon pay full and fair tax in all the territories in which it, one of the world's biggest companies, operates? Such an act of connection truly would be your and Jeff's gift to our planet – a planet you apparently got some kind of a perspective on while Katy Perry was floating around during the zero-gravity bit. Even if she did spend it pushing a butterfly printed with her next tour dates towards the camera. Why do I feel like the most meaningful thing to come out of this will be a three-minute song called 'Space Cowgirl'? Forget the right stuff. This was the wrong stuff.

Was this a hen do or a humanitarian mission to liberate Paris? Either way, give Lauren Sánchez an award

20 May 2025

The hemlines were high and the diamonds hefty as the world's richest fiancée and her entourage stormed the Seine. Formez vos bataillons!

To Cannes, in the country of France, where last night Jeff Bezos's fiancée, Lauren Sánchez, got what she deserves: a philanthropy award. Lauren was honoured at something called the Global Gift Gala, where she received the Women Empowerment Award for her commitment to climate justice, social justice and coming off at absolutely all times as a woman who refers to her breasts as 'my girls'. Regular readers will know I have a huge amount of time for her. She accepted her gong wearing a necklace with a diamond pendant that was slightly larger than an Amazon warehouse, once again redrawing the blueprint that other humanitarians will simply need to watch and learn from.

Meanwhile, if there were awards for hen nights – or bachelorette parties, in the American style – then Lauren would surely have taken one for her full-scale invasion of Paris last weekend, after French forces withdrew and declared the city open. Hand on heart, I initially assumed Lauren was the new US ambassador to France, but then remembered that State Department randos were probably seated in some windy overspill gazebo for Donald Trump's presidential inauguration, while Lauren had pride of place, ahead of the actual cabinet, as part of Oligarchs' Row. Plus, having just googled, I see the Senate yesterday confirmed Trump's pick for ambassador to France: his own son-in-law's former jailbird dad.

So, on Lauren's part, this was very much a private visit to Paris for premarital pleasure, a mood later reflected in her official Instagram communiqué to attendees and her 930,000 followers: 'To my girls . . . thank you for surprising me, lifting me up, and reminding me how much I needed this moment.' Remember, Lauren uses this same flattened palette of solipsistic language to dress everything: a spa day, a space trip, a humanitarian award, new swimwear.

Anyway, attendees at the hen weekend included fellow astronaut Katy Perry and the two most prestigious Kardashians – Kim and materfamilias Kris Jenner – as well as Eva Longoria, who travelled on to Cannes to present Lauren with last night's humanitarian award. If you're wondering which of the party goes back furthest with Lauren, I wouldn't waste your time. Typically, celebrities do not have old friends. They regard it as a moral failing and a sign that you don't really want the big time enough.

As for what was worn during the Parisian festivities, the dress code wasn't specifically themed as Marie Antoinette; necklines did plunge deep, in late-18th-century style, but hemlines had been guillotined somewhere near the Kármán line. One pharmaceutical billionaire's wife sported a vintage bronze-effect Issey Miyake breastplate recently purchased at auction for $54,000 (the girl-brunch equivalent of that time Nicolas Cage outbid everyone for a stolen T. rex skull).

Activities over the weekend included posting diligently to Instagram, the platform owned by fellow Oligarchs' Row occupant Mark Zuckerberg, while making sure to tag in their travelling makeup artists, hairstylists and lesser support-retinue members. There was also an ostentatious open-top boat ride down the Seine, where I think the ladies went to view the floating corpse of a trend once known as 'quiet luxury'.

In truth, it must be said that those curated and filtered Insta photos of the attendees looked startlingly different to the candid ones snapped by Parisian street photographers as they left the various venues. Had you shown some of the faces in the latter snaps to the average person 40 years ago, they would have assumed something awful must have happened to the women. Luckily, after decades of Botox, fillers and extreme 'work' going mainstream, our eyes have grown accustomed, so we don't notice the weirdness any more and read it instead as maximum hotness. Thank you, progress!

All in all, the entire special Parisian operation has served to heighten interest in the forthcoming Bezos and Sánchez nuptials, which are due to take place in Venice at the end of next month, after extensive lobbying by local Italian politicians for it to be chosen as the host city/organism. Venice's mayor informed *The Times* that 'we were in competition with other places but we won out'. As one Venetian official put it: 'It's going to be on par with a G7.' Truly, the fairytale. And if you happen to be visiting Venice as a tourist over the same dates, you should probably know that Lauren and Jeff have already 'booked every water taxi in the city'.

In terms of securing other things, Lauren has become quite the expert in acquiring trophies – and I'm not talking about Jeff. The Women Empowerment Award is far from her only humanitarian gong in the past year or so. She and Jeff also picked up Conservation International's Global Visionary Award, while madam alone somehow beat out the competition to win a humanity award from a charity called This Is About Humanity. Look, I don't pretend to understand the precise economics of throwing hugely glitzy charity galas to give climate awards to individuals who right at this moment are staying in Cannes aboard their megayacht, a vessel that emits more than 7,000 tonnes of CO_2 a year and is so large it requires its own support yacht to trail around after it. I don't think normies CAN understand these things. Our role is to simply admire them.

Even so, perhaps I'm not alone in feeling that it is becoming harder and harder work. In fact, the choice of Italy as host for the Bezos–Sánchez nuptials feels almost too on the nose. A few centuries ago, the super-rich of that country kicked off the Renaissance, commissioning a vast array of jewels of the visual arts. Our modern-day power players simply give us Instagram or red-carpet pictures. More of a Dark Ages dynamic, really, from which we might all fervently wish to be delivered.

Anna Wintour has spent decades dictating a certain look for the super-rich. Then along came Lauren

27 June 2025

The Bezos–Sánchez wedding is rewriting the fashion rules. And there's nothing the outgoing Vogue *editor can do about it*

How neat that Anna Wintour's resignation as editor-in-chief of American *Vogue* should occur bang in the middle of Lauren Sánchez and Jeff Bezos's wedding extravaganza in Venice. Top take-out? Anna's revolution is over. She lost. Not personally, of course – she accrued significant riches herself, and her name is literally hewn into stone over a chunk of the Metropolitan Museum of Art in New York. Just don't call her OzymAnnadias! But the things she represented are over, and nothing illustrates it in quite such withering fashion as the gathering on the Grand Canal of Instagram's apex predators.

Don't worry, this isn't going to be another article over-egging the fact that someone has unfurled some protest banner or something on a Venetian church. Very little needs refreshing quite as desperately as the eat-the-rich genre, which has started to feel even smugger than the super-rich themselves. I think we can all live without people who positively adored it when George and Amal Clooney took over Venice for their 2014 wedding now wetting their pants when the Bezos-Sánchezes do it. Besides, these days the super-rich behave more like revolutionaries than those supposedly committed to overthrowing them. Listen, I don't love the result, but you can't deny they've got on a lot better with ripping everything up than their opposition.

Anyway, the revolutionary style. British *Vogue* recently declared that 'chic is dead' – a comment that would probably have had to have been approved up the food chain in New York by the famously controlling Wintour. And certainly, someone as – how to put this? – *aesthetically sensitive* as Anna might have found it difficult this week to watch a series of Kardashians tramp down a series of Venetian jetties in a series of $10,000 bras. And yet, in her twilight professional years – and make no mistake, we have been living through them – Wintour ended up courting all these figures. Kim Kardashian was eventually admitted to Wintour's Met Gala in tacit recognition of her then unparalleled ability to create moments on the internet, a medium that has completely eaten magazines. Sánchez was 'helped' by Wintour with her outfit choice for her own Met debut, as well as given a *Vogue* photo spread.

All of that read like Wintour reluctantly having to attach herself to a type she'd spent such ferociously studious decades keeping out. This type was the way the wind was blowing, and it was better to be borne along by it than blown into irrelevance. But that in itself was the writing on the wall: Wintour was no longer making the weather. It is said she 'advised' Sánchez on her clothes for the current wedding celebrations. Maybe the only thing worse than helping Lauren with her outfits is not helping Lauren with her outfits.

And yet, if the second Mrs Bezos wants the clothes, she just buys them. Quick word on the Sánchez aesthetic: you might have heard of trends such as stealth wealth, quiet luxury, whatever. Forget about those. Lauren wants to look really rich and really sexy and like she's having a really good time, all of the time. In Venice, in space, at the presidential inauguration. And if you're even remotely tempted to comment that, actually, you don't find that type of look sexy, then you've missed the absolutely key thing about Lauren Sánchez, and what makes her hilariously, invigoratingly iconoclastic, in contrast with the billionaires' wives of yore. She literally *does not care* what anyone else thinks. Like, not at all. Sorry!

Her entire look says, 'I am wearing this and I don't care what you think,' whereas Wintour presided over a world where rich women's looks said, 'I am wearing this and I do care what you think.' Back in the day, someone passing from mere riches to mega-riches had a minefield to navigate, and knew it. The mines were mostly laid by women who'd got there about 10 minutes before them. Every single parvenue society queen felt this, and some even wrote it down. Barbara Amiel's memoir describes the milieu she moved into following her marriage to Conrad Black in excruciatingly absurd detail. Here she is, a billionaire's wife, yet gripped by constant social anxiety, forever agonising that she'd worn her best rocks to an event that actually called for 'patio jewellery' (necklaces $1m or under). She is constantly finding herself looking too much or too little. 'You don't wear white,' a caring society assassin tells her about the colour of her shoes. 'It's for sales girls.' As Amiel reflected: 'I was consumed by fear of not doing it right.'

In order for there to be people worried about getting it wrong, there had to be people decreeing what was right. And for a very long time indeed, the empress of those people was Wintour. She was a rarefied being who knew better than you, who had the power to help or hinder your passage even further up society's Mount Olympus, and who acted as a trusted and feared gatekeeper to a world in which you were, in some ways, still the rube you started out as. Even figures as recent in the timeline as Kim Kardashian kept the old ways and bent the knee to Wintour, but maybe Kim was the last.

Things go out of style – perhaps including style itself. Certainly, capital 'S' Style, as decreed by Wintour herself. If there's a *fin-de-siècle* vibe hanging over the Bezos wedding, it's Anna's *siècle* it's the *fin* of. The happy couple and their tribe have the distinct air of having only just got started.

DONALD TRUMP: TO ELECT HIM TWICE BEGINS TO LOOK LIKE CARELESSNESS

Donald Trump broke every law of politics – and was found to have broken a few laws of actual law too. But so what? In the looking-glass world we now live in, whether we want to or not, his convictions and court cases were widely judged to make his return to the White House more likely, not less. And so it seemed to prove, with Trump storming back to the Oval Office in November 2024. After that, he and his various henchmen used the White House to flog his sometime buddy's electric vehicles, sell out countries and self-isolate in when he really couldn't be bothered to pretend he was just another one of the guys at the G7. He would like you to know he was robbed of a peace prize, despite pulling off eleventy peace deals. You might ask, who or what comes after him? Then again, who says he's going anywhere?

So Trump moves closer to jail and nearer to the White House. This is our world in 2024

31 May 2024

This must be a day to reflect on the fact that in just one decade, it has become realistically possible for a multiple felon to lead the free world

No rest for political cartographers. It turns out that what lay beyond America's uncharted waters was some more uncharted waters. The unanimous verdict in Donald Trump's hush-money trial found the former president guilty, making him the first US president to be convicted of a crime. Forgive me: 34 crimes. A potential bar to security clearance, voting and owning a gun – but not, apparently, a bar to running for president. 'I am a political prisoner,' ran an instant campaign fundraising message from Trump, probably typed while on the same gold toilet he once pretty much ran the world off.

And might well again. Previous polls have indicated many Trump voters wouldn't switch sides even in the event of a guilty verdict, and the betting markets saw Trump's chances of re-election rise above 50% during the later stages of the trial. On the other hand, if criminal trial verdicts going the wrong way for you is such great news, how come Trump is trying so hard to stall the other three cases he's facing? By way of a reminder, those involve mishandling classified documents, trying to change the outcome of the 2020 election and fomenting the attack on the US Capitol on 6 January 2021. He was already found liable for sexual abuse and defamation in another trial last year and has been impeached twice. Take in his thousands of business-related court cases, and he's a one-man law degree.

That the import of Trump's conviction is even debated highlights the extraordinary loss of ideals we have lived through in a single decade. Even ten years ago, it would have been impossible to imagine a world in which a former president being convicted of 34 crimes would be regarded – including by many of his detractors – as quite possibly *beneficial* for his electoral prospects.

The ability to make people believe the opposite of things they see with their own eyes is not a new political trick, and even the version that defines this looking-glass era was perfected by Vladimir Putin long before Trump ever produced his own knock-off model. Perhaps Trump's most original achievement is to harness conspiracism, one of the great currents of the age, in his favour. I will never get over the vast irony of the fact that conspiracy theorists love this guy, when he embodies and proves so many of their worst fears. He ran, and may run again, a government that lied to them. He was head of a state that disappeared key documents, evidently into some of his own bathrooms. Every day he pulls a political false-flag attack of one kind or another. He was, and is, involved in any number of conspiracies. He really was out to get them. Yet their paranoia bell doesn't go off.

So free-speech nuts decline to see that this is a case in which Trump clearly sought to suppress free speech and, consequently, democracy. This is what authoritarians do. They decide what the 'truth' is going to be, and they manipulate events into making it so. Dissent is silenced. The people are judged too worthless and troublesome to be allowed to make up their own minds. Ideals that we might consider to be the cornerstone of a democracy – free speech, the rule of law – are regarded as things that need to be got around, subverted and ultimately crushed. Democracy, really, is the enemy. Control is the goal.

And if you're good enough at it, as Trump and Putin surely are, your former critics become your fawning court, to the point where no one can even imagine your successor, certainly not unless you anoint him (and it will be a him). To watch previous Republican scourges of Trump, such as JD Vance or Marco Rubio, fawning around him is to imagine a mirror of events that played out inside the Kremlin many years ago. And, indeed, during a succession of earlier Russian presidencies. Even Nikki Haley has recently folded and now says she'll vote for him, and she didn't even need to be tacitly threatened with nerve-agent poisoning to do it. A bunch of Wall Street big hitters have come around; maybe Trump will gift them some mining concessions or an oil company, like proper little oligarchs.

Right after the verdict, his ghastly strongman son Donald Jr popped up to declare, again, that America was turning 'into a third-world shithole'. To which the reaction of many overseas observers will have been: You said it, mate. Good of you to be so open, at least.

Naturally, I am not being entirely serious. But for many around the globe, the former US president has become like the country's gun laws – such a glaringly obvious negative that they honestly don't need some angry native to explain to them how actually it's all an aspirational local custom that they, an outsider, could never understand. Most people feel they understand it pretty well. No country is immune from making itself a joke – certainly, we Brits have had a few really determined goes at it down the years – and the US is currently the world's leading exporter of mirthless laughs.

Even those die in the throat when you consider that far from having always been there, full American democracy is less than 60 years old. And if its betting markets think that a former president being convicted of multiple crimes is a boost to his prospects for re-election, then the world must draw the conclusion that it is currently very sick, and quite possibly without health insurance. You can only wish it well.

There are 1,000 grotesque memes of JD Vance – and they're all more likable than the real thing

7 March 2025

Angry, rude and addicted to web troll-ery, the vice president has the Make America Awful Again portfolio. Seems a perfect fit

You may well be aware that *Backpfeifengesicht* is the German word for a face that is worthy of being slapped. Even so, how has this not been internationalised? Or at the very least Americanised, where its dictionary definition would presumably be adorned by a picture of the face of US vice president JD Vance, already faultlessly playing the role of worst American at your hotel? You can immediately picture him at breakfast, can't you? Every single other guest on the terrace with their shoulders up round their ears, just thinking: 'Where is he now? How unbearable is he being NOW?' Next, imagine breakfast lasting four years.

I say the *Backpfeifengesicht* definition would be accompanied by JD Vance's face . . . but then again, what is the face of JD Vance? The internet is awash with people suffering an acute case of not being able to remember it any more, having seen so many hideous comic distortions of Vance that those meme versions are not simply the only results on the first page of your own mental Google search, but stretch deep beyond the second and into the third. Somewhere on page four, where you might as well publish the nuclear codes or pictures of Taylor Swift giving cocaine to babies, is an unmodified snap of what JD Vance actually looks like. Or at least what he looks like with eyeliner.

Before you get there, your synaptic filing systems throw up every variety of Photoshopped Vancefake: swollen manboy, a face wearing a Minion suit, a bearded egg . . . I'm hoping that sooner or later an American news outlet will accidentally use a modified photo, because even the picture editor has forgotten what the vice president looks like, and then we can have one of those massively self-regarding legacy-media blow-ups, when the entire staff has to resign after a remorseless investigation by the executive editor reveals that Vance isn't actually a big purple grape. 'This is a stain on our newspaper's history. A big purple stain.'

Vance is more meme than man now, and it is, of course, something of a consolation that he is so extremely online that he can't help but to have noticed this. The VP is like a one-man government troll-feeding programme – please don't cut him, Elon! – which is probably why people have become so heroically committed to taking the piss. The probability of the vice president seeing you insulting him is basically one.

Just as previous holders of his office, such as Teddy Roosevelt and Richard Nixon, once did, Vance spent a notable portion of this week both denying he had suggested that Britain and France were random countries that hadn't fought a war in 40 years and replying to random X posters called things like 'Jeff Computers' to counter the suggestion that he wasn't loved and feted on his recent skiing holiday.

Over on this side of the Atlantic, it must be said that the latter vignette in particular serves as a helpful reminder of the cultural differences between our great nations – and, indeed, between our great anti-elitists. British politicians would rather admit they'd sexually harassed an intern than gone skiing. (You can, of course, do both, and many do.) If a British cabinet minister were to sally forth on to social media like Vance did and honk that, actually, he had a *great* time on the ski slopes, it would probably be the end of him. Let's face it, our rightwing politicians still make time twice a week to do a drive-by on 'latte drinkers', seemingly unaware that the only thing left on most high streets, and in quite a lot of people's lives, is a hot milky drink at a Costa. Yet in our country, would-be populists treat having the temerity to order a coffee as if it's Marie Antoinette skiing past a workhouse – which is a useful illustration of why we don't have growth, and why our many political failures speak to near-empty rooms at conservative conferences in the US.

Anyway, Vance. On or off skis – and I would prefer him to sod offski – the vice president can be judged successful in his deliberately adopted mission to become mesmerisingly awful. On British army talkboards this week, I spent some very enjoyable time watching veterans of the US's wars in Iraq and Afghanistan offer their thoughts on JD, who I believe was some kind of military journalist for about 15 minutes. Though that wasn't quite how they put it, naturally. Real soldiers can be hilariously creative with their insults, while Vance is drawn towards the artless, perhaps most neatly embodied in his decision to whine at Volodymyr Zelenskyy: 'Did you even say thank you?'

Then again, while I'm sure that the memes will keep us warm in the event of an unscheduled nuclear winter, it must be said that other forms of digital manipulation are, notably, passing without the comment they used to attract, even until very recently. So perhaps the moral slippage has not been entirely one-sided. I noticed this week that people who only a couple of years ago were hand-wringing about the horror AI deepfakes could wreak upon democracy were now cheerfully sharing synthetic scenes of Zelenskyy slapping Donald Trump in the Oval Office, or Trump crying like a baby, or some other eerie piece of fakery that felt qualitatively different from a still of a lollipop-wielding kiddie Vance. I think people used to believe this stuff was bad and corrosive and potentially politically dangerous? Maybe they still do – or maybe only when the other side do it.

Donald Trump, the president making anywhere but America great again

18 March 2025

The US stock market is spooked and his henchmogul's companies are floundering. Has the great dealmaker been building up . . . the wrong nation?

Naturally, I assumed the feeling would pass, but one whole week after the US president turned the lawn of the White House into a crappy car dealership, I keep finding myself feeling . . . optimistic. I know, I know. But if anything, I find myself feeling a little bit more optimistic every day – and sometimes a lot more. Not for America, which keeps electing him, but for the rest of the world. It really would take a heart of stone for governments, from Beijing to Delhi to Warsaw, to look at the clip of this old guy trying to sell his friend's electric cars and not think: 'Oooooooh, that is very, very bad vibes. Still, it's good for us!'

In China, they have ironically nicknamed Trump 'the nation builder', meaning he is doing an incredible, bigly impressive job of bolstering the Chinese nation. Not to be disrespectful to that ancient golf bore holding the little piece of paper listing his car-salesman talking points and gibbering, 'Everything's computer,' but can this guy even organise an oligarchy? He's certainly making his precious stock market run, stricken, in the direction of the nearest bathroom.

As for Trump's genius henchmogul Elon Musk, Tesla's share price has halved over the past three months, with the *FT* reporting today that hedge-fund short sellers have made $16.2bn betting against it. Last week, a J. P. Morgan note attempted to contextualise their grimly downgraded outlook for the firm: 'We struggle to think of anything analogous in the history of the automotive industry, in which a brand has lost so much value so quickly.' Listen, I'll take their expert word for it. But I feel like even I can think of something similar in the history of the social media industry. Last year, the entrepreneur and professor Scott Galloway observed of X since Musk's purchase of it: 'No company over $1bn in revenue has ever lost 60% of its revenues in a 12 month period in a non-war period. I don't think that's ever happened. Twitter is literally the worst-performing business in history since a change in ownership.'

Admittedly, as is now clear, X was a political project for Musk, so perhaps that was a strategic haemorrhaging of value. It certainly bought him a keyboard army, albeit one that doesn't appear to have a whole lot better to do all day than suck anonymously up to him. Indeed, for having the temerity to post this article on X, I expect a number of rape and death threats from Maga folk who are now, like some cowboy-booted modern take on the poor East Germans, being told to buy one type of car. Even worse, it's one of the electric type, which until very recently they were formally required to dismiss as soyboymobiles. So look, I understand: mandated ideological 180s are very upsetting. And in any case, I always threaten to rape and kill people when I'm winning an argument.

In the weeks after the Trump administration got under way, the pace at which it was smashing, cutting or walking away from things at first seemed discombobulating, frightening, even tragic. And it remains so for many Americans. But here, outside the US, the alternative view is that it has saved many years, potentially decades, of the various factions of the rest of the world dithering away while thinking, 'Maybe we should get it together? Then again, how would we get it together? We should probably get it together . . .' Thanks to the Nation Builder™, everyone is simply *having* to get it together, and fast. Defence is obviously the toughest issue, and suggesting otherwise is a level of facetiousness to which even this column couldn't aspire. But it's not undoable, mainly because it can't be. Meanwhile, stripping out the various moral dimensions, where is the money really going to flow? Towards countries like the one building factories where they make car batteries that can be charged in five minutes (sorry, Elon) and are so big you have to fly over them, or the one where the leader turned the seat of power into a garage forecourt?

Sometimes you don't need to be steeped in every economic and geopolitical detail to get a macrotrends gut feeling. Let's face it, all that the White House lawn spectacle lacked was one of those flailing inflatable tube men that entice/terrify potential customers. And I felt something similar again yesterday, watching the White House press secretary reveal herself as one of those countless modern idiots who have heard of only one war in history (the second world one), and who don't even understand that. Yesterday, Karoline Leavitt could be found declaring: 'It's only because of the United States of America that the French are not speaking German right now.' Bless! Taking a slightly longer look into history, I think America owed France a favour before it was the other way around. But getting lost in these stoopid yesteryear arguments is not really something winners do, is it? Anyone speaking at the superpower podium should at least give the impression of having bigger fish to fry.

On a local level, I've no idea whether the UK will be one of the nations Trump accidentally ends up building. On recent form, and with our proven propensity for taking dumb decisions and electing limited or actively awful leaders, you wouldn't put a whole load of money on it. But opportunities in a world that America has chosen to put in flux are openly presenting themselves. I can't help feeling that fortune will favour those who are blithely pushing on with it, not plaintively pushing cars literally in their own backyard.

Dear heads of state, Donald Trump won't love you back. He may be the worst boyfriend the world has ever seen

24 June 2025

The frantic attempts to decode his behaviour remind me of self-help relationship babble in the 1990s. Then, as now, it's not you, it's him

Until it finally opens, there remains much speculation over precisely which artefacts will occupy Donald Trump's eventual presidential library. My current view is that you could do a lot worse than fill it with all the volumes of text that have been written in the cause of 'understanding' him. These increasingly read like the most futile female-targeted self-help books of the 1990s. *You Have to Understand He Is Very Transactional. Take Him Seriously but Not Literally*. Guys, please – no more. We all urgently need rescuing from the Mind, Body & Statecraft section of the bookshop.

As I say, so many gazillions of words have been expended on this cause that Trump reminds me a lot of the men of the 1990s. Indeed, he was one. Back then, he had emerged from a decade of valiantly avoiding contracting STIs in 1980s Manhattan – a battle he would later describe as 'my personal Vietnam'. For much of the 1990s, the rest of mankind – certainly womankind – felt that personal victories of their own must be just around the corner. It definitely helped that the economy was booming and history had ended. But it was a time when people believed you could change everything through self-control/hard work/the right roadmap. In fact, speaking of roads, one of the biggest non-fiction titles of the 1990s in the US was M. Scott Peck's *The Road Less Travelled*, a hymn to personal growth that was treated by many as the key to all mythologies.

The vast, mostly female contingent of self-help-book buyers of this era seemed convinced that men were desperately trying to communicate with them, and that true harmony/a happy ending was possible if they simply learned how to decode the messages contained in totally inscrutable behaviour like not calling them back, not appearing to care about what they wanted or stating they were going to put tariffs on all non-US goods. One of those I might have misremembered. But the general gist was, what could it all mean? Once you had deciphered it, men would love you, and you could then set about managing them into their perfect final form. (This may also be what the rest of the G7 leaders thought once Trump got bored with the conference last week and left.)

Then along came an episode of *Sex and the City* – the absolute classic show about turn-of-the-millennium guys and the women who loved 'em – in which Miranda related to the girls (and one man) how her most recent date had gone. They'd had a nice evening, he'd told her he wasn't going to bomb Iran, but then he had. What could it all mean? No, hang on, I'm in a muddle – that was a different episode of something. Let's try it again. They'd had a nice evening, he'd kissed her, she'd asked him upstairs, but he said he had an early meeting, so he didn't come up. What could it all mean? Something really positive, think the girls. 'It means he likes you but he wants to take it slow,' is one of their verdicts. Men can be 'afraid of having their feelings hurt' or 'freaked out by their own feelings'. He could have been stressed out, on deadline, or have a migraine. When the only man at the table is asked for his opinion, he parts with it almost reluctantly. 'I'm not going to sugarcoat it for you,' he says. 'He's just not that into you.'

Well now. That last line of dialogue promptly became a real-life meme. Then the meme became a book when two of *Sex and the City*'s writers ended up writing an entire self-help tome, using the phrase as the title. And then the book became a movie, which continued to disseminate its essential message: stop wasting time parsing really obvious behaviour into whatever you want it – *need it* – to mean. Plus, by this point, among other things, it was the George W. Bush years, 9/11 had happened and people had learned that two of M. Scott Peck's children wouldn't talk to him and he'd cheated on his wife multiple times throughout their marriage. So, in many ways, everyone was waking up.

Watching the events of the past fortnight, in which any number of people have been blindsided, crushed, humiliated, whatevered by Trump, it felt like it was past time for a similar awakening for politicians and the analysts who love to comment on 'em. (Hi! I'm here twice a week, etc.) Instead, it feels like Keir Starmer could spend the Nato summit stuck drinking Cosmopolitans with his little gang of world leaders, going: 'I think I've worked out what Donald's trying to tell me – and it's incredibly positive! He's just COMPLEX, like all quality men! I don't think he wants to do any of these bad things; he's just left with no choice.' 'Yes,' the perfectly coiffed Emmanuel Macron might agree as he took another sip. 'He rang and told you his B-2s were on the way to bomb Iran a whole hour before other people found out – you have a really special relationship!'

Ladies, gentlemen, presidents, prime ministers, can I stop you? He Just Wants It to Be About Him. Everything being always about him is the position of maximum control and maximum attention. The end. Maybe someone could get a book out of it – God knows I've just got 900 words out of it – but honestly, save yourself time, money and emotion and wake up. He is not REMOTELY into you.

Compare Donald Trump with Kissinger and you'll be lost. But Taylor Swift? That's more like it

14 October 2025

As he conducts the symphony of applause for his Gaza peace deal, the key to understanding him is this: he's not a politician, not even close – he's a star

The old line that 'politics is showbiz for ugly people' is so good it should be true, but it isn't really. Politics has always been politics, and showbiz is something different. Not, however, in the unique case of Donald Trump. The current US president is best understood as a pomp-era megastar. Extraordinary, really, that Trump never even needed to get into cocaine. I think that when he dies, scientists will discover that his body naturally produced coke as a byproduct of digesting overcooked hamburgers.

Everything he says or does is redolent not of a politician, but of an ego-driven entertainment industry behemoth. Monday afternoon in Egypt, with all the awkward world leaders box-stepping behind him, was very much The Official Release Party of a Peace Process. Ego can, of course, be very creative, so it should be widely acknowledged that this hold-your-breath settlement simply couldn't have happened without our leading man.

In recent years, you may have read whole screeds on 'the Trump doctrine', often written by former foreign ministers or revered diplomats, and which singularly fail to capture the essence of the entity with which they are dealing. Maybe the reason they seem to have had so much trouble codifying things convincingly is that most of these people either regard showbiz as beneath them or know slightly less about it than they do about some obscure branch of theoretical chemistry. The muddle they get into is trying to compare and contrast Trump with Henry Kissinger or Benjamin Franklin or a pick-your-20th-century-Euro-dictator, when it should obviously be Elizabeth Taylor or Taylor Swift or turbo-monster-era Led Zeppelin.

The category mistake is even more perplexing because Trump makes his essential star-based ethos very clear. He speaks constantly about his ratings, releases the equivalent of political diss tracks twice a week, is pathologically allergic to anyone getting more attention than him, has a genius for staged events and subsumes team efforts wholly into himself. He is solipsistic, unpredictable and easily bored – all of those both innately and tactically. Showbiz monsters are both born and made. What we saw in Israel and Egypt yesterday was the modus operandi of a megaceleb in their most impossible-to-say-no-to era.

It's notable that in an age when the most consistently eulogised celebrity quality is 'authenticity', Trump is a politician about whom no one ever says: 'Yeah, but what does he actually believe?' It's all right up there on the screen. You're watching it. There aren't any methods really, or if there are, they are underpinned by the anti-philosophy that the first part of the word 'method' is 'me'. Everything he does, including the current ceasefire and peace plan, flows from the distinctly starry practice of having people bring him projects, which will get made only if his name becomes attached to them.

And people bring him all kinds of projects – international hotel developments, peace processes, fragrance lines. All of them become what Hollywood would call 'a Donald Trump vehicle'. There might well be merchandise associated with this ceasefire, if it holds and develops. Following the assassination attempt on him last year, Trump released a Fight, Fight, Fight fragrance, which is forever selling out on his website. Don't rule out some kind of Peace Through Strength aftershave hitting the online shelves soon.

Few megastars still do things solely for humanitarian or artistic reasons. Commerce becomes a way of keeping score and is the greater motivator. I somewhat suspect that Blake Lively declared legal war on Justin Baldoni when she was able to gauge how much an alleged covert smear campaign was affecting her commercial image via plummeting sales of her new haircare line. Taylor Swift went nuclear on Katy Perry when the latter tried to hire some of her backing dancers – or, as Taylor saw it, 'basically tried to sabotage an entire arena tour'. It's difficult to get past the sense that when Trump moved on this peace deal, he did so for selfish motives. Commerce is his special place, and you'd better not touch it without consent. In the case of Qatar, where the Trump family organisation had just done a $3bn deal to build a luxury golf resort, you'd certainly better not misfire some missiles in there. How dare you, Bibi?!

As I say, this kind of ego can produce some great material. The bit in Monday's Knesset speech where Trump 'went there' on Netanyahu's much-staved-off fraud and bribery trials was one of the most hilarious friendly drive-bys you will ever see in politics, and very difficult to greet with anything other than an involuntary laugh of disbelief. 'Give him a pardon, come on,' Trump digressed. 'Cigars and champagne, who the hell cares about that?' Amazing.

With that photocall in Egypt, we are now encouraged to think Trump has entered his peacemaker era. In fact, I know they're not each other's biggest fans, but the thing I've seen recently that it most reminded me of was Taylor Swift's album film, *The Official Release Party of a Showgirl*, whose centrepiece is the making of a video. In the film, Swift is shown constantly turning up and promptly offering the other creatives thoughts that they all treat like strokes of genius, despite them presumably having been on the process for weeks or months. Every one of these ideas conveniently ends up being adopted. Could they really all be credited to her? That is certainly the impression the director – a Ms Taylor Swift – gives us.

I imagine the White House works a lot like this. Actually, I don't need to imagine it. When he missed out on a certain Norwegian award last week, a White House spokesman pulled a full Kanye-interrupting-Taylor-at-the-Grammys move, declaring furiously: 'He has the heart of a humanitarian, and there will never be anyone like him who can move mountains with the sheer force of his will.' Well, there's always next year, by which time we could well be in new acronym territory. A whole 21 stars have an EGOT (Emmy, Grammy, Oscar, Tony), but only one is gunning for an EGONT.

Masked thugs, sneering elites and terrified citizens: a picture of the US today. We used to have a name for this

27 January 2026

Truly, I am the country's biggest fan. But in the spirit of free speech its leaders apparently love, here are a few things the rest of the world needs them to know

We in the rest of the world have had to hear a lot – *such* a lot – about what this US government and its hardcore fanbase think about us. So you know they'll be super-relaxed and free-speechy about hearing some thoughts about how they look from the outside. Let's use last Saturday as a single snapshot. In Minneapolis, they had the shooting by federal agents of a protesting nurse who posed no threat, an event promptly, provably and blatantly lied about at the highest level by Donald Trump's politburo. Then that evening in Washington, a lot of those same politburocrats turned out for the White House premiere of a ridiculous propaganda film about the president's wife, also attended fawningly by bloodless

Apple oligarch Tim Cook. And he's not even the oligarch who paid an insane amount for the film. Top line, guys: all this makes you look like what your president likes to call a 'shithole country'. Sorry! I assume it's fine to use officially licensed vocabulary?

Obviously, it's not a proper shithole country until the soft-skinned puppet masters in the presidential palace cut some grizzled local warlord off at the knees for following orders, so it's good to learn overnight that border patrol 'commander at large' Gregory Bovino has been pulled out of Minneapolis, possibly locked out of his social media accounts, and may soon 'retire', presumably a fall guy for the likes of stage-four homeland security tumour Stephen Miller. Bovino's the guy who has literally the same haircut and outfit as the Sean Penn character in *One Battle After Another*. But hey, at least he wears a uniform. Again, what are international outsiders to make of the spectacle of ICE's federal officers in masks and frequently dressed in civilian clothes, while images from protests across the States show resisting civilians increasingly drawn to military-style clothing? Can Trump's storm detachment not at least be issued with matching shirts? They don't have to be brown, but Maga chic desperately needs to make a first step towards getting itself together. In the entire history of the movement, only one follower – the QAnon shaman – has ever had true style.

With death threats being the sign of a deeply articulate and sophisticated political culture, I have cleared my inbox to make space for them. But I should say I have always truly loved America. I've visited 38 of its great states in my time, and have always dreamed of completing the set, but . . . not currently, let's be honest. I note that the US is currently experiencing a downturn in tourists from previously enthusiastic markets. Who among us can imagine why? Still, no doubt the numbers coming from Nato countries in Europe will rally if Trump (a five-time draft dodger) continues to piss on those nations' military graves. Reminder: Nato has activated its collective defence clause precisely once since its inception – at the request of the United States, in the wake of 9/11. Our troops fought and died in all their stoopid wars this century, but now, apparently, we have to listen to Trump's whiny little rants about how nobody really put themselves on the line.

Anyway, back to the events of Saturday and their fallout. Hard to pick the most mind-boggling reaction to the shooting of Alex Pretti, who never produced the gun he was carrying, for which he had a licence, before it was taken off him. But there's a strong argument for going for the statement from the National Rifle Association, which reacted to all the Maga zealots saying Pretti was always likely to have been shot for legally carrying a gun he had a licence for by thundering back that carrying a licensed gun is famously constitutionally allowed and calling for a full investigation into the killing. Maybe Trump's base is now more rightwing than the NRA? Or more leftwing? I can't tell. Are Maga now too woke on gun control for the NRA? Such are the sentences one can end up typing when we're this far through the looking-glass.

Speaking of the political upside-down, Saturday's other notable event was the *Melania* premiere at the White House, which, though flowing with champagne, was in some ways as grotesquely down and dirty as the scenes in Minneapolis. Consider the guests, who included the usual regime stalwarts, but also, intriguingly, Tim Cook. Days before, Cook had been posting on one of the other oligarchs' platforms about Martin Luther King's 'commitment to justice', only to watch videos of Pretti's execution proliferate across that same platform, but still popping on his bow tie and toddling off to clink glasses at the premiere. *Melania* is a 'documentary' about the president's wife, for which she serves as executive producer and has been paid an unspecified sum, while the entire thing has been bought by Jeff Bezos's Amazon for $40m (£30m) – a sum so staggeringly beyond what such a film should cost, by so many orders of magnitude, that it can only be read as a naked gift to the regime. A further $35m has been spent on marketing for its preposterous theatrical release.

But I guess that as the OGs in Russia have shown us, oligarchs have to take their turn to do expensive things, just so they can stay in the gang. At least they're getting something out of it. Much more tragic are the ordinary-folk foot soldiers dutifully coming out to defend the shootings by federal officers. I can barely think of anything more beaten than spending the day typing variations on the theme of 'it is good that law enforcement officers in my country shoot civilians who are no threat'. What a bunch of bootlickers. They might be too far gone to see it, but much of the rest of the world can.

How does Trump keep henchmen like Rubio in check? He literally makes them wear shoes that are far too big

13 March 2026

The art of the heel: if you want a shot at the US presidency, you better be ready to sartorially debase yourself on the world stage

The secretary of state of the United States of America is openly slopping around in a pair of too-big shoes that he has to wear because the president gave them to him. Why? Possibly as a piece of exquisite, complex satire about the size of his penis; possibly because Marco Rubio exaggerated his shoe size because he rightly assumed it would be linked to presidential speculation about the size of his penis.

According to the vice president, JD Vance, Donald Trump gives all his best boys a particular brand of shoe, after either guessing their size or making them disclose it. 'The president, he kind of leans back in his chair,' explained Vance a couple of months ago, 'and he says: "You know, you can tell a lot about a man by his shoe size."' Strong words, particularly from a president with such famously tiny hands. Incidentally, Vance casually dropped it into the anecdote that he wore a 13.

Anyway: Vance, Rubio, defence secretary Pete Hegseth – they all have a pair. Of shoes. I can't comment on the other, but let's just say they're about as likely to have the balls to stand up to Trump as they are to bin off the greasy pole of politics and risk it all in pursuit of excellence in competitive ice dancing. Certainly, they would like you to deny the evidence of your own eyes and agree that there is absolutely nothing obviously emasculating about your boss buying your shoes and you having to wear them, even though they don't fit and make you look stupid. As one White House official told the *Wall Street Journal*: 'It's hysterical because everybody's afraid not to wear them.' So everybody's a goody two-shoes.

All three guys are, of course, on barely covert manoeuvres for a future presidential run. And maybe there's a sense among these hopeful men that if the black leather slipper fits, they will be the one to gain the Maga movement's hand in marriage once the almost-80-year-old Trump has turned back into a pumpkin. Only instead of an ugly sister trying to jam her trotter into something far too small, we have a secretary of state trying to expand to fit a pair of far-too-big, reasonably priced black Oxfords. Impossible not to think back to previous occupants of Rubio's role – John Quincy Adams, George Marshall, George Shultz, James Baker – and not fall back on the obvious idiom: big shoes to fill. Rubio rightly resembles a small child playing dress-up with something he found in Daddy's wardrobe.

And regime-wise, it's aesthetically painful. So many of Trump's ideological forebears at least understood the importance of good gentlemen's outfitting. But it does all point to that peculiarly distinctive mix of vanity and indignity required in a Trump henchman.

You must take an excruciatingly obnoxious sort of pride in yourself, at the same time as submitting utterly to his regular humiliations.

Take Hegseth. Even that surname feels as though it might be a doubled-down-on slip of the tongue, like he's actually called Hesgeth but once said it wrong, refused to admit it and ever since then has just been butching it out. The defence secretary has certainly cultivated a similarly unapologetic yet absurd look: suits straining to cover his tattoos, and hair like one of the latex president masks the surfers in *Point Break* wear to rob banks. And, naturally, The Shoes. Alas, though, Pete's machismo is, in fact, incredibly vulnerable. This week, Hegseth became so incensed by 'unflattering' photos of him taken in the Pentagon briefing room that he has banned press photographers from taking pictures in that space. The only images available will now come from official Pentagon photographers, all of whom will presumably be ordered never to capture shots of his feet. Meanwhile, it is thanks to shoe-leather journalism, particularly by the *New York Times*, that we know the US has been found responsible for the Tomahawk missile strike on an elementary school in Iran on the first day of fighting. So what of shoe-leather defence-secretarying? In the Trump era, that demands lacking both the decency and the honour to admit to this devastatingly atrocious mistake.

Somehow, though, in this tale of three henchmen, the one on the least sure footing is Vance. All of us have had to grow accustomed to reading the Trump administration simply by vibes. And following his clearly lukewarm support for the war in Iran – as you might expect of someone who made 'no more stupid wars' his pitch – how would you define the current vibe around Vance? There is a distinct feeling, isn't there, that he is nothing but a spare part in this war, even frozen out of his role as chief shitposter, now that the White House social accounts are taking care of embarrassing war memes. Some speculate that Vance might well be headed sooner rather than later into what Anthony Scaramucci calls 'the woodchipper' – the inevitable destination of all Trump henchmen, in the end.

In fact, the war and his non-role in it have exposed both Vance's limits as an operator and the places his previous positions have boxed him into, when all he really has is form for bending himself to whoever he perceives to be the most valuable elite at any given time. Vance has always managed up and not down. He's not the little guy's guy; he's the big guy's guy. He is, ultimately, a creature of the boss who buys his footwear. So maybe he does wear size-13s – but all things considered, they're starting to look like dead men's shoes.

JEFFREY EPSTEIN AND HIS MANY FRIENDS

Who really was 'billionaire hedge-funder' Jeffrey Epstein, apart from a sex trafficker of women and underage girls? Manhattan financial institutions are littered with perplexed big hitters who say that none of their primary or secondary desks ever traded with the man, and who deem the source of his riches a mystery or a possible blackmail scheme. Even so, the deceased might go down as a figure more influential than he could ever have imagined in his wildest dreams. In the years since his death, Epstein has lurched like a zombie through the upper echelons of transatlantic politics, business and royalty, claiming the scalps of at least one financial chief executive and one ambassador, and the princely titles of one Andrew Mountbatten-Windsor. Is Jeffrey's trail of destruction fully wreaked? Some of the most powerful men on earth certainly hope so. But there may be life in the old corpse yet.

Is there a comeback more unwelcome and doomed than Prince Andrew's?

31 January 2023

If all the duke has is a bizarre mocked-up photo of two people in a bathtub, then he's in far worse trouble than he realises

In recent times, Prince Andrew has been the subject of both a televised comedy musical and a number of formal council petitions from Brits who no longer wish their street to be called Prince Andrew Drive or Prince Andrew Way. Yet, amazingly, the duke somehow still remains the most ridiculous thing about his own life. Barely a week goes by without some wince-inducing story about his comeback plans finding its well-sourced way into the news.

After many years of non-cooperation with any number of attempts to get to the bottom of her allegations against him, Andrew last year finally settled a civil claim with Virginia Giuffre, who was trafficked by the deceased paedophile financier Jeffrey Epstein. The settlement did not include any admission of guilt. Giuffre is now reported to be writing a book about her experiences with Epstein and beyond, and though her settlement with the duke would prevent her speaking out in detail about Prince Andrew, multiple articles suggest he is ready to launch a lawsuit, should she mention him. 'Andrew and his lawyers are ready to go on the attack,' a 'source familiar with the case' told the *Mail* at the weekend. 'Then her claims will be put under scrutiny for the first time in a court of law.' Finally! I don't know about you, but I always pay a reported £12m to settle a case out of court, when all I really want is for its claims to be heard in a court.

Then, last week, allies of the duke let it be known that 'details are about to be made public which will change people's perceptions of him'. Intriguing. Are those details . . . could they possibly be . . . a photograph subsequently published on the front page of the *Daily Telegraph* last Saturday? Unclear. But oh dear me, where to start on this picture, released by Ian Maxwell, the brother of Epstein's convicted accomplice, Ghislaine?

You will almost certainly have seen this truly cursed image by now. If you somehow swerved it, however, the details are as follows. Two (mercifully clothed) adults are sitting in the bath of Ghislaine's former Belgravia mews house, which, you will recall, is where Giuffre alleges she was first coerced into sexual activity with Prince Andrew. Around the faces of the two people in the photo – and I can barely believe I'm typing this, but here we are – there are elasticated, laminated A4 sheets of paper, worn as masks. Think of it as *Eyes Wide Shit*. One mask bears the face of 17-year-old Virginia Giuffre, from the notorious original photo of her with the duke's hand round her waist, taken in the house in question on the night in question. Odd choice – but not the oddest, let's face it. The other figure is wearing a contemporary photo of Prince Andrew, 62, which serves only to emphasise the bizarre grossness of what the reader is being asked to behold and consider. Unbelievably, actual lawyers had something to do with this nutso line of defence, which the *Telegraph* chose to headline 'The Photo That "Clears Duke" Over Bath Sex'.

We might begin by querying whether 'bath sex' is really the correct term for the alleged rape of a trafficked teenager. But wait, because there's more. The image is accompanied by quotes from Ian. I always feel I missed the point in time when the utterances of Ian Maxwell began to be treated with something other than quizzical contempt. When, precisely, did this switcheroo happen? Anyway, here is Maxwell on the photo, which he seems to have personally staged: 'I am releasing my photographs now because the truth needs to come out,' explains Ian, apparently dialling in from the Arkham Asylum of British public life. 'They show conclusively that the bath is too small for any kind of sex frolicking.' Two points: one, they don't show anything of the sort; and two, what? WHAAAAAAAAAAAT?!?!

'The family have even supplied the bath's dimensions,' gibbers the *Telegraph*, 'revealing that the base of the bathtub measures 1,359mm by 380mm.' I'm not sure any newspaper in the land can credibly take the high ground on the lunacies of other publications. There but for the grace, and all of that. But I don't imagine I was the only reader who saw this picture online and had to go to the source to check whether that really and truly was the actual front page. Yet it honestly was. Less of a marmalade-dropper, more of a stomach-vacater.

If that photo wasn't the gamechanging gambit at which Andrew's allies were hinting, perhaps it was last week's interview with Ghislaine herself. In this, Maxwell clutched one of the visiting-room telephones in the Florida prison where she is currently serving a 20-year-sentence for her crimes and explained through the glass that the original photo of the duke with his arm round Giuffre (in which Ghislaine herself is pictured smirking stage left) was a fake. If that was the de-smoked gun, then unfortunately all it took was for the news photographer who had originally snapped the image from a hard copy Giuffre handed him to produce his image of the back of that photo. This displays the standard developers' date stamp. It turns out to have been an ordinary printed snap, processed at a one-hour lab at Walgreens on 13 March 2001, three days after the date on which Giuffre alleged she was first forced into sexual activity with Andrew. The news photographer had gone back through his archives after being incensed by Ghislaine's interview last week. As he put it: 'I thought, "here we go again".'

And here we do seem to keep going again. For exactly how long the duke will fail to realise his comeback is doomed is unclear. News that he would no longer have offices at Buckingham Palace, which is undergoing a £369m refurbishment, was tempered by hints that he would probably be granted rooms at nearby St James's Palace. But for what, given he appears to have nothing to do other than mount a wildly ill-advised rearguard action against deeply unsavoury claims that he decided to settle?

Andrew no longer enjoys the range of confected positions that enabled him to be helicoptered between the world's finest golf courses. Does one really need a suite of damask-walled, lavishly gilded rooms with liveried attendants for his current activities? I can't help feeling that a lock-up with a single swinging lightbulb somewhere off the M25 might be more appropriate in the circumstances. That is the only staged photo any of us wishes to see. Failing that, a silent retirement for this lifelong self-saboteur would be in all interests, including his own.

Listen up, weaklings: there's no Epstein client list. Why are you so obsessed? Yours, Donald J. Trump

18 July 2025

It's the bonfire of the Maga hats. The real mystery is where their wearers got the idea of a paedophile conspiracy from in the first place

You have to feel for Donald Trump's Maga base. The one huge secret they didn't want disclosed was that he actually really hates them. He has that in common with most populists, obviously, but please, Mr President, respect the playbook! You're supposed to do it quietly. Regrettably, no one could accuse Trump of hiding his spite under a bushel after a week in which he described those of his supporters who want him to simply do what he repeatedly promised and release the so-called Epstein files as 'weaklings' and 'stupid people'. This is quite the (public) volte-face from the guy who originally swept to office declaring, 'I love the poorly educated.'

Most of you are unlikely to need a recap at this stage, but Jeffrey Epstein is the sex-trafficking financier and socialite who conveniently died in jail while awaiting trial, apparently by suicide. A woman, Ghislaine Maxwell, was convicted of conspiring with him to sexually abuse minors and is currently serving 20 years in a low-security Florida prison. But no big-hitting or even small-hitting male Epstein associate in the US has so much as been arrested for participating in what I believe the dead paedophile would have encouraged us to call his 'lifestyle'. This second Trump administration didn't just sweep to power while repeatedly screaming about the 'cover-up' of this story, but it spent a good portion of its early months assuring its ravenous base that Epstein's supposed 'client list' was on a desk waiting for release approval. Yet now, Trump and his associates say there is no list. Nope. Never even was a list. Where did these weakling idiots get that idea? To summarise his administration's position: 'We took a look at the deep state, and it turns out to be very shallow. Seriously, I'm standing in it right now, and it doesn't even come up to my knees.'

Understandably, a significant proportion of the Maga crowd are not taking this well at all. One of the key takeouts of Trump's rise has been that as long as you tell people that up is down or black is white in an engaging or sufficiently discombobulating fashion, truth is an extremely low-status commodity in contemporary politics. But, contrary to perceived trends, it seems that there do still exist some subjects on which you can push even your own people only so far. Maybe the ancient political adage still holds true: live by the paedo conspiracy, die by the paedo conspiracy.

Late on Thursday, as footage of people burning Maga hats spread online, a palpably frustrated Trump announced that he was instructing the attorney general, Pam Bondi, to seek the release of the Epstein grand jury testimony, 'based on the ridiculous amount of publicity given to Jeffrey Epstein'. Though you'll note the president failed to add the two key words: 'by me'. Still, it's good to hear Trump characterising what's currently happening as 'publicity', confirming that he sees even the desire to see justice served on a suspected paedophile sex trafficker and his associates as a form of limelight – which, like all limelight, should by rights be his.

It feels harder to sustain the idea that there is nothing to see here, especially when leading wingnuts such as the Georgia congresswoman Marjorie Taylor Greene, far-right activist Laura Loomer, Fox host Laura Ingraham, talk-show queen Megyn Kelly, Maga whisperer Steve Bannon and even the US House speaker, Mike Johnson, are out there pushing the base conviction that, actually, there might well be something to see here. 'It's definitely a full reversal on what was all said beforehand,' observed Marjorie, in a once-in-a-career alignment with fact, 'and people are just not willing to accept it.'

We have to take our laughs where we can, meanwhile, so do please consider the cavalcade of podcasters and Maga influencers who got jobs like 'director of the Federal Bureau of Investigation' and 'deputy director of the Federal Bureau of Investigation' and are now discovering that life comes at you fast. FBI chief Kash Patel spent the election campaign pushing Epstein conspiracies, and is now believed to be hiding under his big important desk wetting his pants. 'Listen,' his deputy, Dan Bongino, used to instruct his podcast listeners. 'That Jeffrey Epstein story is a big deal, please do not let that story go. Keep your eye on this.' Will do, Dan. Incidentally, a lot of people spent the weekend speculating feverishly that Bongino would sensationally quit his job, but in the end, he just came into work a bit late on Monday. What a tough guy. Make America Deep State Again!

Other developments? That are perhaps not unrelated? The *Wall Street Journal* reports that Trump had served as a contributor to some kind of cursed 50th-birthday scrapbook for Epstein, compiled by Maxwell, for which he'd sent a 'bawdy' letter. This missive was reportedly typed inside a drawing of a naked woman's silhouette, in which the famous Trump signature served as a kind of scribble of pubic hair. So far, so FDR. Unfortunately, particularly in the circumstances, the letter itself is said to conclude: 'Happy birthday – and may every day be another wonderful secret.'

Alas, the current president is not thrilled by this report, denying it completely, adding that he has never in his life 'wrote a picture'. (It goes without saying that all Donald Trump statements, always, are very much [*sic*].) Much more promisingly, Trump is furious with the *WSJ* owner, Rupert Murdoch, and threatening to 'sue his ass off'. Oh, please don't, Mr President! His ass is 94 years old and incredibly wrinkled. Also, half of Britain's political class still lives up it. Then again, perhaps Trump v. Murdoch is very much the desiccated-dick-waving contest the world . . . wants? Needs? Will have to endure? Unclear which of those applies at this stage, but let's hold out for the possibility that both men are wholly – and, indeed, literally – consumed by it.

Angles-wise, however, there are already signs that the *Wall Street Journal* might just be the common enemy the Magas need as an off-ramp for their civil war, allowing people who are obsessed with paedophiles to find common cause both with people who don't care about paedophiles and also with people who may actually have been close personal friends with paedophiles. There will probably be only one casualty, and it will probably be Pam Bondi. Women are great at taking these falls. Furthermore, the whole conflagration would once more pit a billionaire president against one of his billionaire buddies – exactly the kind of better world his supporters voted for, and a true testament to how truly, truly deeply he values them.

Just when Keir Starmer thought he'd got Jeffrey Epstein off his plate, look who's coming to dinner

16 September 2025

After a tough week for Labour, Donald Trump is touching down for a state visit. Let's hope the PM can stomach it

Quick update on Keir Starmer's government of 'national renewal': having just lost his deputy, and also housing secretary, over her failure to pay the required stamp duty, the prime minister has also lost his US ambassador over his known close association with a known child sex trafficker. Hang on – he's now also lost his director of political strategy for relating some dirty jokes about Diane Abbott.

Meanwhile, an increasing number of people think the solution to all this is Andy Burnham taking over, suggesting the current Greater Manchester mayor could run in a parliamentary seat that has only notionally become free because the previous Labour MP was suspended from the party after being found to have sent messages hoping a couple of constituents would soon be dead/'mown down', and is now apparently 'off sick'. On top of which, we're having the Americans round. US president Donald Trump touches down in the UK tonight, on the eve of the most hideously ill-starred dinner party since the vomiting scene in *Triangle of Sadness*. I don't think the nation could possibly feel any more renewed.

It's been a few days since Peter Mandelson's emails to Jeffrey Epstein were held up in front of the public using the hazmat tongs, and the more I've thought about them, the more I come back to one of the more obscure lines. Writing in apparent anguish on the eve of Epstein's incarceration in 2008, Mandelson opines to him: 'It just could not happen in Britain.' Maybe he was right, unwittingly or otherwise. Britain is very, very good at a sort of institutionalised looking away. Maybe Mandelson was, unwittingly or otherwise, characterising something grim about this country that pious old Keir Starmer would no doubt be hugely affronted to be caught up in. Except the prime minister *is* caught up in it – in fact, he's at the very centre of it. He is the one who looked away.

It's hard not to feel there is something necrotic and beaten about a government whose leader would appoint someone he knew had been very close to Epstein, who the entire world by that point knew was – and forgive me for repeating the words – a child sex trafficker. Association with him was already known to be such a horror show that the late Queen Elizabeth II had to sack her own son for it. And there is something worse about Starmer's horrifying lack of curiosity, even as the facts closed in, right till the bitter end, with No. 10 dithering for staggeringly long last week over a set of quite the most disqualifying emails, while Starmer fannied about defending Mandelson at the dispatch box.

This was, of course, the opposite dispatch box to the one at which Sir Keir plied his holier-than-thou trade in opposition. There's an old online rule that declares that if you tell someone off for their spelling or grammar, you will always end up making your own howler while you're doing it. Starmer spent his years in opposition telling off the Tories at every turn, instead of, for instance, coming up with a creative and coherent plan for growth. Inevitably, we now seem to be condemned to watching him and his administration warrant a daily telling-off as their offences and immoralities mount up. Why does this keep happening to him, etc.?

As for Epstein, we know that at the time Mandelson was writing to him, telling him to fight for early release, police in Palm Beach, Florida, had identified 36 girls whom the financier had sexually abused. Yet for all the many years of grim, grotesque revelations, it still feels as though we know remarkably little about him. Who was he, this mysterious paedo Gatsby, and where did all his money come from?

Shortly after his death, *New York* magazine ran a fascinating story in which real hedge-funders expressed pointed bemusement over how Epstein made his money, since none of them had really had any dealings with him. As one big hedge-fund president, Doug Kass, put it: 'I went to my institutional brokers, to their trading desks and asked if they ever traded with him. I did it a few times until the date when he was arrested. Not one institutional trading desk, primary or secondary, had ever traded with Epstein's firm.' Elsewhere, Kass confided to a different journalist: 'There's another guy who reminds me of Madoff that no one trades with.' Or as another hedgie remarked: 'It's hard to make a billion dollars quietly.' And yet Epstein had made no noise at all in the financial world. Its big hitters could barely find one investor. Their general theory was that the 'hedge fund' was simply a cover for a blackmail scheme.

Perhaps most amazing, really, is the fact that Epstein will be a ghost at the feast tomorrow night for more than one attender, as Trump continues to butch out his long and close association with precisely the type of evildoer his Maga followers are convinced runs the world. Epstein is a guy who really does fit the very template of their darkest conspiracy theories: rich and powerful, involved in the trafficking of minors, connected to a network of some of the most powerful people in the world. This is the sort of stuff they've been going on about for years – yet who should keep rearing his head in the story but their own beloved president.

Isn't it intriguing how many of them (currently) just can't bring themselves to believe it? Something to discuss over the starter tomorrow night at Windsor Castle, perhaps, as long as everyone can keep their food down.

Spare a thought for right-royal victim Duchess Fergie – it's been another truly hellacious week

23 September 2025

As more gushing emails emerge, Sarah Ferguson is once again rethinking her 'supreme' friendship with the super-rich sex trafficker Jeffrey Epstein

Last night, I found an incredible archive interview with Jeffrey Epstein, conducted by the *New York Times* on the eve of him beginning his 2008 prison sentence. 'He said he has taken steps to make sure the same thing never happens again,' the *NYT* relates. (Spoiler: it happened again.) 'For starters, Mr Epstein has hired a full-time male masseur (the man happens to be a former Ultimate Fighting champion). He has also organised what he calls a board of directors of friends to counsel him on his behaviour.'

Dearie me. Maybe that's what his friend Prince Andrew was doing in the famous photo of them walking in Central Park two years later, bundled up against the New York cold and an approaching tornado of sex-abuse allegations? Although, hang on, because that was the four-day house visit that Andrew said he'd made so he could break off contact for ever with Epstein. 'I took the decision that I had to show leadership,' he boasted to Emily Maitlis, 'and I had to go and tell him: that's it.' As most people wondered of the dim-witted old sleazebucket when that *Newsnight* interview came out: could you not have done it on the phone instead? But then of course he couldn't, because this was not actually the end of contact at all. An email from a few months later has already surfaced, sent from Epstein to what the UK Financial Conduct Authority redact as a 'member of the

British royal family', looking to set up a meeting between said royal and the since-disgraced former Barclays boss, Jes Staley. The response from the 'member of the British royal family' was: 'Keep in close touch and we'll play some more soon!!!' Look, maybe it was Princess Anne.

The trouble with being thick and telling this many lies is that you can never remember which one you've told. This is certainly the situation Andrew's former wife, Duchess Fergie, finds herself in this week, as some of her own emails to Epstein have surfaced, and have promptly detonated her 2011 statement to the *Evening Standard* that 'I abhor paedophilia and any sexual abuse of children and know that this was a gigantic error of judgment on my behalf. I am just so contrite I cannot say.' Fergie promised to 'have nothing ever to do with Jeffrey Epstein ever again'. We now discover it was just weeks before she was writing privately to Epstein, saying she never said all the things she definitely said.

Charities are dropping her left, right and centre, but what else can they do? 'I know you feel hellaciously let down by me from what you were either told or read and I must humbly apologise to you and your heart for that,' Fergie fawns in one email to Epstein. 'You have always been a steadfast, generous and supreme friend to me and my family. As you know, I did not, absolutely not, say the "P word" about you . . .' Absurd to find her too prim to even type the word 'paedophile', though not to be supreme friends with someone who had literally been to prison for soliciting minors.

Epstein had given her money, of course. She says fifteen grand. Then again, she says a lot of things. The duchess's debts were reported to be £5m at the time, because she has always spent money – other people's money – like water. Has she claimed this long-term trait was a mental illness yet? I wouldn't rule that out in the coming months. For now, her team are saying of these excruciating Epstein emails: 'Like many people, she was taken in by his lies' – a virtual cut-and-paste of Peter Mandelson's claim a couple of weeks ago that he regrets 'being taken in by [Epstein] as many other people do'.

The more I think about this fashionable line of defence, the more bizarre I find it. If I had a wildly rich and incredibly connected friend, and they still ended up going to prison for 18 months – even with the most shit-hot Rottweiler lawyers (Alan Dershowitz and Kenneth Starr!), even under the US's grotesque plea-bargaining system – then I would simply assume this friend had done the thing they were convicted of, and most probably much worse. It's called 'being realistic'. Do we truly believe that stretched local Florida police forces have the time or inclination to confect whole cases, spend years of asymmetric legal wrangling trying to push them over the line, get done over by a plea deal that bumps the case back down to state level and seals it, and do it all as part of some envious conspiracy? No. No way on earth. Any conspiracy ran the other way. 'This was not a "he said, she said" situation,' the police chief who led the probe said ruefully after the stitch-up. 'This was 50-something "shes" and one "he" – and the "shes" all basically told the same story.'

I'm not saying everyone in the world should have known this about Epstein back in 2008 – so many sex cases, so little time – and there was no reason most people would even have heard of him at that stage. But any close friend of his would have been following the reports. Any of them who didn't assume the grim reality just chose not to, out of moral cowardice, personal greed, staggeringly wilful blindness or sociopathic indifference. The end.

Epstein obviously cast things differently. In his nutty *NYT* interview, he 'likened himself to Gulliver shipwrecked among the diminutive denizens of Lilliput. "Gulliver's playfulness had unintended consequences," Mr Epstein said. "That is what happens with wealth. There are unexpected burdens as well as benefits."'

Do me a favour. And yet Fergie herself has played a version of this tiny violin for decades, and will again now that she has been found out, again. Her victim narrative has been surprisingly durable, even though she has helped burn through more fortunes than almost every other person on this planet will ever see: £20m chalets in Verbier; the £15m mucky mansion; houses she never even moved into; eternal luxury holidays; endless retinues of unnecessary staff... She has pulled in more than some of her charities ever will. How many of her financial empires have fallen, only for a new one to rise again when some Kazakh oligarch/sex Gulliver/other mysterious billionaire conveniently turns up in the nick of time to buy her out or bail her out? Rumour had it that even the King was still doing it until recently, probably dreading the deeper liability of her being outside the tent. It's unclear quite how long what we might call her personal 'charitable status' will be able to hold if further emails between Prince Andrew and Epstein emerge – as seems a distinct possibility.

Whatever happens, however, this is not victimhood. I'm sure one of Epstein's actual victims could explain the difference.

So the Epstein scandal is about politics? Silly me for thinking it's about the mass abuse of women and girls

6 February 2026

Obsessing over individual players and political chaos leaves less time to focus on the misogyny. And that's for the best, isn't it, guys?

Fair play to Bill Gates's ex-wife, Melinda French Gates, a woman who fronted up to appear on a podcast this week while so many of the men who feature in the latest Epstein files drop found that their diaries had them scheduled to stay hiding under their rocks. Melinda was asked about Jeffrey Epstein, obviously, and executed a very graceful drive-by. 'Whatever questions remain there of what I don't – can't – even begin to know all of it, those questions are for those people, and for even my ex-husband. They need to answer to those things, not me. And I am so happy to be away from all the muck that was there.' Oof. Yet she also said, more generally: 'I think we're having a reckoning as a society, right?'

Cards on the table, I don't think we're having one at all. Look at the headlines, or what's dominating all the news bulletins. We're talking about anything but the things that most need to be reckoned with. In the UK, we're talking round the clock about Peter Mandelson, the one guy in this we at least know wasn't making sexually abusive use of Epstein's trafficked women and girls. Even if he did offer Epstein image-rehab advice, which was a foray into the moral abyss. (Again.) But the frenzied, remorseless focus on the political fallout – and not the male-on-female debasement that is at the heart of this story, and always has been – is weird, isn't it? I had a mirthless laugh at the *New Statesman*'s cover this week, which characterised the Mandelson affair as 'the scandal of the century'. Guys, it's not even the biggest scandal of the scandal.

Let me be clear: I think our focus on all the tangential bits of the fallout is a mass displacement activity, driven subconsciously or consciously by men so we don't have to reckon with the fact that we now have searchable records of the way some of the most powerful guys in the world, who have huge sway over our lives, talk and think about women. And about girls.

In some ways, this is the dark switcheroo we should all have been prepared for. There really is no bad vibe/criminal abuse operation that a properly enterprising scumbag can't just buy up and take ownership of, and then flip into the appearance of do-gooding. There is an incredible clip of Epstein being interviewed in some wood-panelled, gentleman's-club-style room, shot in either late 2018 or early 2019. 'I made my living from old thinking,' Epstein reflects expansively in it. 'But the future is for the way women think.' We pan out to see that the interviewer is his buddy Steve Bannon. 'Is that a sop because of all the depravity you've done against young women?' asks Bannon. 'Your new sop is that women's thinking is the future?' 'No,' smirks Epstein. '. . . I'm a firm believer and supporter of Time's Up.' I wonder if he literally donated money to this #MeToo-era charity. I bet he did.

Anyway, all shapeshifters gotta shapeshift. A couple of years after Epstein's death, Bannon repackaged this footage into a documentary called *The Monsters* (producer: Stephen K. Bannon), and he now calls Epstein 'a globalist child molester'. Well, he would say that, wouldn't he? But oh, look – what do we have here? Also included in a recent file dump was some correspondence, in which Bannon spitballs a survival strategy for Epstein. 'What about establishing THE major center for human trafficking, teenage prostitution etc etc etc – global problem, needs to be solved.' You laugh – again, mirthlessly – but I firmly believe that only accelerating events, most pertinently the July 2019 arrest and incarceration of Epstein, deprived the world of The Jeffrey Epstein Underage Sex Trafficking Foundation. Sure, it sounds like an off-colour *Saturday Night Live* sketch idea that never made it to air, but sex abusers creating fake philanthropy ventures that bring them closer to vulnerable victims? Let's face it, we've seen it before, everywhere from the church to aid charities. And if these files show us anything, it's that there would have been so, so many mega-rich male donors. So many fathers of daughters who are quite happy to turn a blind eye to the use and abuse of other fathers' daughters.

Maybe the foundation's lavish fundraising brochure could have been shot by 'arthouse' bondage photographer Andrés Serrano. 'I was prepared to vote against Trump for all the right reasons,' Serrano moans to Epstein in one 2016 email. 'But I'm so disgusted by the outrage over "grab them by the pussy" that I may give him my sympathy vote.' Elsewhere, Epstein reckons the way to deal with any Senate hearing into his activities would be to ape Trump's successful supreme court nominee, Brett Kavanaugh, whose confirmation hearings notably featured him denying allegations of sexual assault. 'I guess I can mimic kavanaugh. "Yes senator I like pussy, pussy yes. Don't you senator."' Well, why not? For the benefit of the lawyers, I should clarify that those weren't Kavanaugh's words and he majored on how much he liked beer . . . But his approach famously worked, and Justice Kavanaugh will have huge influence over American women's lives for the rest of his. And even more famously, the pussy-grabber became president – twice.

So really, spare me the half-arsed elite pearl-clutching over Epstein's crimes and look at what is actually happening. What has anyone in power done, at all, to attack the structures and attitudes that allowed them to happen? We've known about Epstein's world for so long. As Julie K. Brown, the brilliant *Miami Herald* journalist whose watershed 2018 investigation into Epstein was built on the back of years of her meticulous reporting, stated baldly: 'Epstein got away with his crimes because nearly every element of society allowed him to get away with them.'

I agree. And years on from that investigation, we can see that the reaction to every file dump is born of the same look-the-wrong-way impulse that allowed it all to happen. From Noam Chomsky to Steve Bannon, from Bill Gates to the former Prince Andrew – this is nothing to do with left or right, or new money or old. There will always be something more important than grappling with the roots of misogyny – money, power, access, information, a political project, 'how the world works', whether you can use Mandelson to bring down Keir Starmer, 'philanthropy', realpolitik . . . A million other priorities. The abused women and girls are nothing but a plot device, just like they always were. It's the pussy-grabbers' world; we just live in it. The only difference is, you can now see it laid out in black and white.

So Epstein buddies Andrew and Mandelson have been arrested in the UK. And in the US? Zero, zip, *nada*

24 February 2026

At least the British gave us the perp-walk shots. But I fear that any Americans seeking real justice will have to wait, and wait, and wait

I can't believe the cops didn't max out the theatrics yesterday when taking Peter Mandelson to the police station to help with their enquiries. They didn't even do that thing where they put their hand on top of the suspect's head to ease him down into the back seat of the car. Absolutely *no* sense of occasion.

And you know, they really might as well have made the most of the moment. Misconduct in public office is such an archaic old law and so incredibly difficult to prove that you have most likely already seen the high-water mark of law-adjacent consequences for both Mandy and Andy. The perp walk is the punishment. No offence to the highly esteemed Metropolitan police and the various other forces who've found the rare grooming-gang scandal they can be arsed with, but it's hard to get past the deep-rooted suspicion that they are just looking busy. But look, we got one iconic royal photo out of it and a clip of Mandelson over which you could wonder absent-mindedly, 'Is this honestly the first time he's been arrested? I must be having a déjà vu, because it hasn't happened before, yet it feels so weirdly familiar. For whatever reason.' Anyway, allow me to reiterate that both of the men mentioned in this paragraph deny any wrongdoing.

So, in the UK, two guys have been arrested in connection with the Epstein scandal: a famously very clever one and a famously very thick one. What unites them? I have a theory about the many,

many friends of Jeffrey. And that is that the more desiccated and vulnerable the milieu they hail from, the greater the chance that they may feel the not-very-full force of the law. This may be why the only two arrests we have seen – bar Epstein himself and his accomplice, Ghislaine Maxwell – are from the British monarchy and the upper echelon of establishment British politics. Are either of these institutions in rude and red-toothed health? Erm, answer unnecessary. But if you are one of Jeffrey's big shots in big tech, or a high roller from high finance . . . well, as Holly Golightly once noted of the reassuring facade of Tiffany's, nothing very bad could happen to you there.

In fact, looking at what appears to have occurred, I'm not sure very much bad can happen to you in the US, as far as Epstein association is concerned. You hear a lot about the British establishment, but the American establishment has covered itself in even less glory. Come on, America – you've got to arrest *someone*. Haven't you? Even just one, for appearances' sake? Maybe pick up one of the little people, the ones who cleaned up after whatever took place with the girls, and book them for being an accessory. Again, just for appearances' sake.

If we accept even the most conservative estimates of what Jeffrey Epstein was up to for literally decades, then an awful lot of people would logically have to have been involved. Even those right at the top of the Trump administration say so. The billionaire commerce secretary, Howard Lutnick, recently assured the world that Epstein was 'the greatest blackmailer ever'. Yet apparently this all-time epic blackmail enterprise needed only one guy (deceased) to run it. Nobody else, at all, had anything to do with it or any knowledge of it. Even if we accept that preposterous premise, who does Howard reckon was being blackmailed by history's greatest blackmailer? Presumably quite a few people, presumably most of them sufficiently high-profile that they had enough to lose to pay up. It would be good if this supposedly fearless US administration, or the

FBI, or any of America's hundreds of thousands of law enforcement officers or 1.3 million active lawyers (!) could produce a single name and declare them an active person of interest – and even better if they formally decided to bring them in for questioning for so much as five minutes. And yet, nothing and no one has been brought anywhere near justice, except for Jeffrey and Ghislaine. For what we have long been assured was a huge criminal enterprise, Epstein Inc. seems to have been a real mom-and-pop business.

Not to the women and girls who were victims of it, of course. When the last batch of files was released earlier this month, almost a hundred survivors noted that their identities had been compromised in thousands of documents and photos, while they claimed that many of those who were their abusers remained protected. The Department of Justice later said that revealing victims' names and addresses and bank details and whatnot was due to 'technical or human error'. No doubt, no doubt. Why oh why does genuinely unbelievable ineptitude continue to dog this era-defining investigation?

So hard to say. Alas, I also have another theory on the Epstein scandal, held with infinite reluctance. And that is that no one else is going to be convicted for the sex stuff. No one at all. All those women, girls – children? – unavenged. No one, bar the dead man and the incarcerated woman, is ever going to get convicted, nor almost certainly get so much as charged, either here or in the US. It may be – indeed, is likely to be – that the biggest names from whom the public would really, really like to hear more are never even questioned. They will continue to be big shots, or under the radar, or people who simply don't fear a knock at the door because they understand perfectly well how the system works. And they always did.

ELON MUSK: SILICON CAESAR

What price being the main character on a social media platform? $44bn, for Elon Musk, who bought Twitter, turned it into X, and now boasts his own site's biggest follower count. Congrats, Richie Rich! Fortunately, American democracy is a lot cheaper, with Musk claiming his expertise – and daily $1m voter giveaways – were the difference between Donald Trump winning and losing the presidential election. Do we have to pay attention to anything he says? On the one hand, he's got a bunch of babymothers stashed in a purpose-built compound and is widely accused – including by Trump's chief of staff – of fuelling his mostly failed White House work with ketamine. On the other, his SpaceX scientists can catch a space rocket with some tweezers, and his ill-informed tweet-storms on the subject of grooming gangs in the UK undoubtedly sparked a chain of events that led to the establishment of a dedicated inquiry. Love him or hate him, let's just agree Mars would be a great place to keep him.

Is it wrong for Elon Musk to offer voters $1m a day to get Trump elected? That's a tough one

22 October 2024

The great and the good of US media and politics can't decide if the lavish giveaway is unethical or illegal. I'm no expert, but it seems off to me

For a guy who has spent his entire life making 'I am very rich' the keystone of his personal brand, there is something quite poignant about watching Donald Trump get financially cucked by Elon Musk on stage every night. Musk is much younger, much richer and has had a much more successful series of hair transplants. But needs must, it seems.

As you might be aware, Musk has recently decided to update the tired dystopian fiction trope in which impoverished citizens are forced to compete in deadly gameshows where the winner gets a life-changingly glittering prize and the losers are killed for sport. In Elon's rebooted version, the richest man in the world is giving struggling voters the chance to win $1m if they sign a 'petition' in favour of free speech and the right to bear arms.

You get $47 (£36) just for signing up – $100 in Pennsylvania, for *some* reason! – and only registered voters can apply. As long as they leave their names – and addresses, for *some* reason! – they're all good to enter the lottery pit. Also, it's not fictional but real, and it's happening in swing states every single day from now until the election in two weeks' time. On Saturday, Musk presented his first state-of-the-art cardboard cheque for $1m to a man at a rally in Harrisburg, Pennsylvania. On Sunday, it was the turn of a woman at a town hall in Pittsburgh. On Monday, his Pac (political action committee) launched a drive against election interference, because hey – above all, he's an ironist.

Like so many of the previous new lows of this campaign, once this tactic manifests itself you immediately find yourself thinking: *of course*. Of course, of course. Of course Musk, 53, would become a dark mirror version of MrBeast and use the YouTube giveaway playbook to go viral in the election endgame. It's at once completely shocking and also an October not-even-a-surprise. Perhaps the only mirthless smile it can raise is when you consider the utter yesteryearing it represents for Hollywood.

It felt quaint even at the time, but do recall George Clooney spouting off last year about how indispensable Hollywood could be to political campaigns. 'I always just say,' George just said, 'look, everybody keeps coming into Hollywood for cash, and they don't come to us for the one thing we do better than anybody, which is tell stories.' Mmm. And yet here we are, with the dark stars of the election bypassing the gold-standard magic of a movie industry everyone can see is in crisis and taking their inspo from YouTube, which isn't.

Anyway, in very familiar scenes, the old good-chap structures of political life are revealed as simply unable to cope with bad chaps who decline to play by the unwritten rules. In fact, even the written rules seem to be in doubt. Is Musk's stunt legal? Those scrambling to respond to this question are once again falling back on the old 'uncharted territory' descriptor. Alas, if you were hoping we could get a couple of cartographers out of bed for this one – like, yesterday? – then prepare for disappointment. What we have instead are leisurely headlines such as 'Elon Musk's Pledge for Daily $1 Million Giveaways Draw Legal Questions'.

The Pennsylvania governor, Josh Shapiro, opined on Monday of the giveaways that 'I think it's something that law enforcement could take a look at.' 'Could take a look at', questions being 'drawn' – I can't help feeling the vocabulary choices here indicate the sort of mid-tier to-do-list priority that no doubt the relevant cops/jurisprudence professors will get around to solving in a few weeks' time. No particular reason you'd want to rush this one. Is there?

In the meantime, seemingly nightly, we have the world's richest man on stage in service of Donald Trump. Or will it turn out to be the other way round? Only time will show, but given Musk is being touted for some kind of anti-regulation role at the same time as his businesses are involved in multiple anti-regulation lawsuits . . . let's just say this could go either way. In some ways, both parties could use a hand.

And yet, neither is an underdog. However many years we are through the looking glass now, I still boggle at the utter WTF-ery of Trump and Musk being able to present themselves as rank outsiders oppressed by the elites. 'One of the challenges we're having is, how do we get the public to know about this petition because the legacy media won't report on it,' whined Musk at the weekend, in comments promptly reported by the legacy media. Also: you own a media platform, shithead – please don't try to 'my struggle' this one. Other looking-glass lunacies include Musk's regular assertions that Kamala Harris will end democracy, which he makes while appearing to buy votes in support of a man who has already sparked one insurrection and has explicitly promised to be 'a dictator' on day one of his presidency.

They say democracy dies in darkness, but it currently appears to be suffering serious breathing issues under full stage lights. In fact, watching Musk go all out for Trump, it's hard not to get ominous circle-of-life vibes and feel like you're watching the simultaneous live birth of an American oligarchy. There have been vested interests as long as there has been US politics, of course. But, relatively, no robber baron of the Gilded Age was ever this rich or as artlessly open about what – and whom – a relatively tiny amount of money can buy.

How low will British politics go? Ask Elon, master of the Muskoverse – he'll decide

7 January 2025

The unedifying spectacle of would-be strongmen bickering over how to protect women and girls is just the beginning

Can it really be three weeks ago that Nigel Farage and Elon Musk were posing adoringly at Mar-a-Lago, in front of that hilariously naff painting of Donald Trump in the tennis sweater? I am as surprised as Nigel that his holiday romance has been built on sand. Or, to put it another way, that the African billionaire who promised to deposit *££££££££££* in his account has turned out to be not what he seemed. The Farage dumping seems to have occurred after the Reform UK leader failed to agree with Musk that he should ally with the imprisoned career criminal Tommy Robinson over the latter's stance on grooming gangs.

And so to grooming gangs – or rape gangs, as they are rightly and more accurately being called now. Maybe the first week of January has become the time when anger about things that have been going on for a long time reaches significant mass. Last year it was the Post Office, this year it is the rape gangs scandal. As for what it will be next year, the likeliest current forecast is: something that Elon decides. We all live in the Muskoverse now. It's a quirk of the age that the genius leading the race to the stars is also the idiot leading the race to the bottom.

Some facts are worth restating. There has already been a national inquiry into child sexual exploitation, faultlessly chaired by Professor Alexis Jay, who had previously chaired the specific Rotherham inquiry. The rape gangs scandal was one part of this second inquiry. It led to a searing report and a number of urgent recommendations. They should have been adopted in full by the government of the day (Conservative), but were not. They should be adopted in full by the new government of the day (Labour).

However, there is now a deep, if belated, conviction taking hold that the rape gangs scandal has not been sufficiently understood or reckoned with in this country. This is correct. It is frequently alleged that in at least several of the multiple areas where gangs operated – not just Rotherham – police and local politicians may have been complicit in cover-ups. My own belief is that further sunlight in the form of a new, swift and specific inquiry can be the only disinfectant for that institutional aspect of this horrific story. Gangs are still operating. Do they do so beneath a kind of wilful blindness that amounts to deep-rooted corruption or support? It feels long past time we tried to find out.

But if you want to talk hidden agendas, just look at the men muscling in now. Please remember that Musk has done absolutely nothing about this issue he suddenly cares about except post about it. Jess Phillips, the serially stalked and threatened safeguarding minister, had a career in helping victims of domestic abuse before she even entered politics, so what a surprise to find her literally being called a 'witch' by Musk. He'd like to put her in prison, as opposed to on a ducking stool or a stake. And that is the other grimness of the current spectacle: watching strongmen and would-be strongmen argue about how to protect women and girls. With all that entails – and all it may bode for the future.

Nigel Farage, Elon Musk, Robert Jenrick, Tommy Robinson – when have you ever heard these people give a shit about women's issues, let alone make a speech or put forward a policy dedicated to advancing them? Robinson very deliberately nearly collapsed a grooming trial, which would have put the victims back to square one and put them through the horror of having to testify twice. People threaten to rape and kill women pretty much every second on Musk's platform and nothing gets done about it; if I were him,

I'd be cleaning up my own streets. If he can't manage it, maybe he should immediately call for himself to be imprisoned?

In the meantime, women – and girls who will become women – should be in no doubt as to Elon's views on their ultimate role: handmaidening the world out of its problems. Musk is an aggressive pronatalist. 'Instead of teaching fear of pregnancy,' he wrote recently, 'we should teach fear of childlessness.' His father says even more out loud. Six weeks ago, Errol Musk told Sky News: 'One need only go to England and go to the Cheltenham area, the horse breeding area, and say, "Look, we're not going to breed the horses any more by any form of standard. I've got a few old horses I've found in Nigeria and we're going to just mix them with your race horses . . ."'

As for the political denizens of the knacker's yard, I boggled at the Tory shadow minister who was thrilled that Musk had shared a Badenoch post and who crowed to the *Mail* about Musk's dismissal of Farage by declaring: 'This is a big moment. Not just the Kemi retweet, but the split with Farage. It's like Hitler turning on Stalin and invading Russia.' Mmm. I want to say, 'Remind me how that went,' and yet a huge part of me simply cannot get past the phrase 'the Kemi retweet'. What can you say about the little tragedy of *The Kemi Retweet*, other than that it was not as good as *The Bourne Identity*? When leaders of once-serious parties and their allies are reduced to celebrating a retweet, they are completely beaten, even if they don't realise it yet.

And maybe most of them are. Please don't forget that Boris Johnson, a hero to a lot of those calling for a new national inquiry, described holding national inquiries into child sexual abuse as money 'spaffed up the wall'. A truly grotesque choice of words in the circumstances. Yet while all grotesquery might not be equal, it has definitely not been limited to one mainstream party. I find it difficult to forget now, and wrote about it at the time, but less than two years ago Keir Starmer approved and stood by an attack ad, disseminated on all the social media platforms, that used a picture of Rishi Sunak, next to the words 'Do you think adults convicted of sexually assaulting children should go to prison? Rishi Sunak doesn't.' Sunak's famous signature was added for good measure. Joining in the race to the bottom benefits no one, as the prime minister is now finding out. The sense that people like him have played politics rather than done politics is well entrenched.

Certainly, those starting the new year angry should not be lumped into one convenient mass of 'deplorables'. I have followed and admired for many years the campaigning work of Sammy Woodhouse, one of the Rotherham victims. Much as I might wish it were not the case, I can well see how she and others might feel they have been driven towards the hard right by what they have experienced as the failings of the mainstream political spectrum. Many of these people don't (currently) mind that the world's richest man, whom they will never be able to eject at the ballot box, is rapidly assuming the power to control their lives. Traditional politicians need to mount an urgent rearguard action to show them that there is a better way, and not simply keep telling them that there is.

It's Elon Musk's 'pronatalist' bonanza – so many families, so little time

25 February 2025

With the mothers of his kids begging for his attention on social media, he makes much of 'pronatalism'. Is that just a fancy word for bad parenting?

If only Elon Musk could impregnate humans at the same rate he's giving them the ick. Alas, polls show the efficiency tsar's US approval rating dwindling towards levels he has enjoyed for quite some time among the UK public. And as a country that lived through the Boris Johnson era, I think we have to warn the Americans that if a government figure can't or won't answer the basic question of 'How many kids do you have?', then he's probably going to turn out to be a disappointment. And the unspecified-number-of-kids thing might *even* have been a warning sign. If the WhatsApp group of his exes is bigger than Mumsnet, and 10 times as pissed off, then it's just possible you could be dealing with a guy you're going to end up feeling betrayed by.

Is Musk that guy? Who among us can say, certainly considering the sheer number and ferocity of the lawyers Mister Free Speech employs? I do know Elon is something called a 'pronatalist', but I increasingly wonder whether that's just a fancy new word for a very old form of shittiness. Consider the spectacle of his ex, Grimes, coming on to the social media platform Musk owns and outright begging him to get in touch with regard to a 'medical crisis' concerning one of their shared children. 'I'm not giving any details but he won't respond to texts call or emails and has skipped every meeting and our child will suffer lifelong impairment if he doesn't respond asap, so I need him to fucking respond and if I have to apply public pressure then I guess that's where we are at.' Her posts on this subject were either deleted or are now inaccessible, while one user suggested she had been 'shadowbanned'. Silly Grimes. If she had put a rape threat or some antisemitism in her APB, it would have stayed up.

Or as Ashley St Clair, mother of Elon's (maybe) most recent child, put it in an (also now deleted) X post last week: 'Elon, we have been trying to communicate for the past several days and you have not responded. When are you going to reply to us instead of publicly responding to smears from an individual who just posted photos of me in underwear at 15 years old?'

Aha. Think I'm starting to get a handle on 'pronatalism'. Gotta admit, I'd had my suspicions, ever since Elon portentously announced: 'Instead of teaching fear of pregnancy, we should teach fear of childlessness.' You'll notice that either way, for women, the situation involves fear. Fear of taking on the responsibility when you aren't ready. Fear of not populating the Earth. Fear that when you really need him to engage with the boring/terrifying realities of parenthood, he's going to be dicking around on a conservative political conference stage with a chainsaw. Literally shouting: 'CHAINSAW!'

Because that, regrettably, was where Elon could be found, wearing sunglasses indoors, at around the time Grimes's message was sent. The power tool had been handed to our power tool by the Argentinian president – the one who looks like some mid-2000s Kasabian manager who can't even get the girls that the band don't want and who once soiled himself at 6am in someone else's room at the Groucho.

Anyway, it's unclear which of Grimes's children with Musk has the alleged urgent medical issue. She reportedly has three, including X Æ A-Xii (X). You'll recognise X (which Grimes is far from thrilled about). He's the one Musk took to hang out with reporters and Donald Trump in the Oval Office, and I'd assumed he was the one currently being tried out for the successor role. Kind of a Musk Jong-un. Although in many ways, Kim Ju-ae, the North Korean leader's daughter and current apparent favourite, could be little X's closest thing to a peer. Their dads both root hard for Russia, and both kids have to watch a lot of rocket launches.

As for the wider impact of these increasingly icky glimpses into Musk's private world, it is beginning to feel like the Doge boss has flicked the public's 'weirdo' switch. None of us wishes to call this too soon, but it does seem as though the world likes Elon less the more they see of him. Given his lack of conventional charm, he is one of those who should have realised silence would be the most intriguing and awe-inspiring statement of all. Instead . . . CHAINSAW!

Meanwhile, St Clair is now pushing for sole custody of the baby alleged to be his. Motherhood can be quite crystallising, of course. Before it happens to you, you've got a load of free and easy ideas, you want to have a guy's 'rocket babies'. And then you do, and you send him a photo of you and your shared newborn in the delivery room, and he texts back a clipped 'All well?' Oof. Other messages she alleges are from Musk (and which are included in her court filings) explain that he can't visit her and the child because 'I'm #2 after Trump for assassination . . . This is not the time for sentiment at the expense of safety . . . Only the paranoid survive.' Mmm. Perhaps I must adopt this as my excuse to get out of any parenting I don't want to do this year. 'Guys, I'm so sorry, someone else is going to have to care about your jabs and your dentist and your, like, entire LIFE, because only the paranoid survive. I pay for it, don't I? Then what's the difference?'

There is a difference, though, isn't there? I would love to believe that this guy is going to be able to effect some era-defining revolution in governance that makes people have better lives. But a lot of stuff begins at home, and if Musk doesn't chainsaw America's way to playing happy families, we might just have to accept that there were one or two red flags on the home front.

So long, Elon: the cuts didn't go to plan, but you completely shredded your reputation

30 May 2025

Judging by Musk's approval ratings, Tesla investors won't be the only ones happy to see the dethroning of the king of Doge

I can't believe that Elon Musk is leaving Doge, the government department he named after a tired and basic meme that most of the internet had moved on from around a decade ago. 'As my scheduled time as a Special Government Employee comes to an end,' Musk wrote this week (capital letters: model's own), 'I would like to thank President @realDonaldTrump for the opportunity to reduce wasteful government spending.' Oh, man. 'Thank you for the opportunity'?! At some level, you have to salute Donald Trump's ability to turn even the world's richest man into an *Apprentice* candidate who leaves in week four after completely wiping out in the hotdog-stand task.

Musk arrived in government promising to slash spending by \$2tn. He leaves it a mere \$1.86tn short of that target, even by his own estimations. Meanwhile, the president's new tax bill is set to add \$2.3tn to the deficit. I imagine Musk thought his government finale would be a spectacular extravaganza – 'You're welcome, Washington!' – involving 2,000 chainsaw-wielding chorus girls. Instead, it's a tweet. And yes – we DO all still call them tweets.

Ironically, the thing that Musk has been most stunningly effective at slashing is his own reputation. Think about it. He arrived in Trump's orbit as a somewhat mysterious man, widely regarded as a tech genius and a titan of the age. He leaves it with vast numbers of people woken up to the fact that he's a weird, creepy breeding fetishist who desperately pretends to be good at video games and wasn't remotely as key to SpaceX's or Tesla's engineering prowess as they'd vaguely thought. Also, with a number of them apparently convinced he had a botched penile implant. Rightly or wrongly convinced – sure. I'm just asking questions.

But look, it's good news for Tesla investors, who have managed to end Musk's practice of WFWH (working from White House) and are now demanding he puts in a 40-hour week to save the company whose stock he has spent the past few months tanking. As the world order dramatically seeks to rearrange itself in the new era of US unreliability, no one should ever be able to unsee the president of the United States' decision to turn the White House lawn into a car sales lot for his sad friend. Did it work? It seems not. Musk spent a lot of this week airing his hurt feelings about his brrm-brrm cars. 'People were burning Teslas,' he whined to Jeff Bezos's *Washington Post*. 'Why would you do that? That's really uncool.'

Well, one thing we will no longer have to endure is this guy's decrees on what is or isn't cool. The time-worn thing about money and power is that they allow nerds to reinvent themselves as cool. You see it on Wall Street, where sea-beast financiers get manscaped by trophy wives who are no longer out of their league. You see it in Hollywood, where weird little guys become alpha movie producers. You see it in Bezos's transformation from puffy-chinos-wearing, dress-down-Friday dweeb to Bilderberg Vin Diesel impersonator. What you rarely see is the alchemy of that process in reverse, live and in real time. But we got that with Elon, and we have to take our laughs where we can. In some other businesses, Musk could have convinced himself it wasn't happening, but politics is a place where pollsters literally ask real people what they think of public figures every single week. Elon's approval ratings are underwater.

No doubt we're this close to him identifying the real problem: that we simply need new voters. Musk has long been convinced that people don't know how to handle his genius in all fields. Four years ago, he hosted *Saturday Night Live*, and sometime afterwards revealed on a podcast how the cast and writers had reacted to the uncontainably hilarious suggestions made by him and his team of bros. 'We come in just, like, guns blazing with ideas,' he honked, explaining he'd pitched a . . . bit, is it? . . . where he was 'going to take my cock out. So I'm going to reach down into my pants . . . and then I pull out a baby rooster. Like, "This is my tiny cock."' Oh, very good, sir. Absolute genius, sir. Presumably terrified that they would lose their jobs for ever to this superlative talent, the *SNL* team declined to 'yes-and' this genius sketch into the show's final running order, but Musk managed to get his own back – at least in his account of hosting an episode with a flattering 13% rating on

Rotten Tomatoes. 'There's a bunch of things that I said that were just not on the script. They have these cue cards for what you're supposed to say, and I just didn't say it. I just went off the rails.'

Mmm. Just like you have now. As for where Musk goes next, he's obviously building a Texan compound for the mothers of his many babies. But, psychologically, Mars would seem to be the answer. After a humiliation this big, only colonising another planet feels like the appropriately sized salve. It doesn't matter that Mars is an obvious shithole that looks like the least appealing disused quarry on Earth, a place so bleak and empty that if they found one single fossilised flower, it would be celebrated like the holy grail, even though the impossible majesty of the Amazon rainforest is right here. But, of course, the point of Mars is that it would be the place of Elon, Teslamandias, king of kings. And you know, I feel more confident than ever that we could all look upon his works and despair.

SO MANY COUNTRIES FOR OLD MEN

Good times for the global gerontocracy, as a slew of men in their late 70s, 80s and 90s continued to maintain that you're only as old as the entitlement you feel. Or, in the case of the Dalai Lama, the child you invite to suck your tongue. Retirement refusenik Rupert Murdoch tempered huge payouts over false Fox News claims of election fraud with getting engaged, breaking off the engagement, then getting engaged to someone else, all inside 12 months. Meanwhile, incumbent presidential candidate Joe Biden and his inner circle insisted his mind was like a steel trap. Or was it a teal strap? Either way, Sleepy Joe's belatedly relinquished insistence on running again was a gift to spring-chicken opponent Donald Trump, 78, who regained the White House – and immediately began nodding off in televised meetings.

Never mind the lies on Fox News, Rupert's getting married again. Just be happy for him

24 March 2023

I worry that the fuss about fraudulent election claims will overshadow the real story. It's love at fifth sight

'I was very nervous. I dreaded falling in love.' Ah, there goes newly affianced Rupert Murdoch, sounding for all the world like a widow who has previously lost her home and life savings in a romance scam to a guy falsely claiming to be an airline pilot. Dare she allow herself to open her heart again? Dare she, having been hurt before, permit herself one last surrender to the possibility of completeness? Dare she, 15 minutes after divorcing Jerry Hall by email, clap eyes on a former dental hygienist, model, singer-songwriter, Bay Area socialite and prison chaplain and declare simply: 'I want it'?

Reader, she dares. She *dreaded* falling in love, but she got back on the horse that bucked her and rode off. If not into the sunset, then certainly into the Delaware courtroom that is gearing up for a blockbuster libel trial in which Rupert's Fox News is accused of airing false and incendiary claims that the 2020 presidential election was fraudulently stolen from Donald Trump. Murdoch recently admitted he had known his hosts were endorsing lies, yet allowed them to continue.

But we're getting ahead of ourselves. Who wants to hear about stolen elections when there are stolen hearts to celebrate? Let's tell this week's happy stories first: at the age of 92, Rupert Murdoch is engaged to be married for a fifth time, on this outing to one Ann Lesley Smith, 66. We await the official engagement portrait. (Murdoch was, of course, first painted in 1533 by Holbein, stretched across the base of his celebrated work *The Ambassadors*).

Alas, this obviously hilarious news of the old boy's latest marital adventure has been met with the sort of strangled deference Murdoch tends to inspire in journalists. Though not, of course, to practise. The couple have marked the plighting of their . . . troth, is it? . . . by giving a short interview to Murdoch's *New York Post*, in which the proprietor declares: 'We're both looking forward to spending the second half of our lives together.' Or, as the bride-to-be puts it: 'I waited for the right time.'

Well, quite. If there were ever a right time to marry Rupert Murdoch, you'd have to say him being 92 was close to it. Though him being 110 would be better. As for what you get the couple who have everything as a wedding gift: anything other than a defibrillator.

If you're wondering what my favourite part of this entire fairytale is, I think I would have to alight on: everything. I want to hear much, much more about Ms Smith's prison chaplaincy, the standout occupation in a résumé that tends towards the eclectic. There is certainly plenty to enjoy in her characterisation of Murdoch as the humble beneficiary of largesse from the Almighty. 'For us both,' Ann claims to the *New York Post*, 'it's a gift from God.' Mmm. I can't help feeling that if madam's husband-to-be were truly to concede the existence of God, it would surely only be as a regional manager in his Churches division. The sort of guy you'd greet cordially on the annual facilities visit but certainly wouldn't invite to the corporate retreat.

Murdoch himself fails to cite divine intervention. He says he first clapped eyes on his new fiancée at one of his properties. 'Last year, when there was 200 people at my vineyard,' he explained, 'I met her and we talked a bit. Two weeks later I called her.' A post-providential encounter; indeed, it's nice to think that there is a level of wealth at which you can simply wander out into one of your gardens and the help will have laid on someone for you to marry.

For her part, Ms Smith last wed a very rich man when she was 48 and the gentleman caller in question was 75. He vexingly died a mere three years later, after heart trouble, plunging her into an unfortunate legal battle with his children, who claimed she had indulged in 'financial elder abuse'. The case was eventually dropped.

As for the timing of it all, it must be one of those mad instances of synchronicity that Murdoch broke the news of his love match just as his perilous court case was hotting up. In Delaware, his legal team this week argued that Rupert and other executives should not have to testify in Dominion Voting System's defamation case against Fox News, on the basis that it would constitute 'hardships' on said witnesses and would 'add nothing other than media interest'.

So if you thought this week's most preposterous spectacle was Boris Johnson arguing that a man of his character would never lie, here's a strong rival: lawyers for Rupert Murdoch's empire arguing disdainfully that media interest is not the same as public interest. We didn't hear much of that sentiment when – to pluck a completely random example from the air – the *New York Post* was carrying masses of detail about the sex life of Murdoch's fellow billionaire Sumner Redstone.

By the time Redstone himself was 92, this required the active assistance of a retinue of care workers. Rupert's paper slapped him with epithets such as 'horny feeble media honcho', gleefully repeating claims right down to the fact that the nurse would sometimes tell Sumner he had ejaculated 'when in fact he had not . . . Sumner appeared to believe him, not aware of the truth.'

Something to bear in mind, as the 92-year-old Murdoch looks likely to head to court next month for his money shot – and, indeed, down the aisle shortly after. Has Ms Smith's God-given fiancé always done as he would be done by? Juries literal and metaphorical will still be out.

Donald Trump, Rupert Murdoch, the Dalai Lama: living proof that no one is too big for retirement

11 April 2023

What do so many of the world's most powerful men have in common? In lesser jobs, they would have long been put out to pasture

'His holiness often teases people he meets in an innocent and playful way,' announces an apology from the office of the Dalai Lama, sounding for all the world like one of those statements issued in the first wave of #MeToo, as various older men made pained and absurd reference to 'unwanted hugs' (Pixar's John Lasseter) or a belief that they had been 'pursuing shared feelings' (talkshow host Charlie Rose). Students of these mea-not-really-culpas were left with the impression that the victims' misunderstanding was the real tragedy here, unless you counted the very belated losses of various glittering careers, which were obviously also desperately sad.

The specific 'people' to which this current Dalai Lama apology refers are, in fact, one person – more accurately, one young boy, who was invited to 'suck my tongue' by the spiritual leader of Tibetan Buddhism, on stage at a temple in India. The event took place in February but has belatedly gone viral, meaning an apology has only now been deemed necessary by his holiness, or rather by his holiness's office.

It is fair to say that the interaction with this distinctly unsettled child has not been taken by many people in the spirit in which the Dalai Lama's office retrospectively insists it was meant, despite that insistence being accompanied by the classic non-apology apology gesture towards any hurt 'his words may have caused'. In the interests of clarifying things for those pen-pushers/chime-tinklers in his holiness's office, it's not the words so much as the spectacle of an 87-year-old man sitting expectantly with his tongue out as a child squirms in front of him.

When is a seemly retirement age for a Dalai Lama, other than what we might broadly categorise as 'before this sort of thing starts happening in public'? The Dalai Lama retired as leader of Tibet's government in exile in 2011 – one year after he did the iPhone advert which promised that Apple's latest model was 'the most trusted phone ever' – but he retains his position as the foremost spiritual leader of the Gelug school of Tibetan Buddhism.

The process of identifying his successor has been inching forward for some time, though the Dalai Lama has mentioned dreams in which he sees himself living to 113. A few years ago, he twice stated that any female successor of his would have to be attractive or she would be 'not much use'. You don't see that particular quote of his bandied around as Instagram #inspo, though it did at least provide another occasion for his office to issue an apology.

The search for a successor continues, though an alternative Dalai Lama may also be chosen by the Chinese government. Speaking of which, the Dalai Lama's most committed foe, 69-year-old Chinese leader Xi Jinping, has rewritten the state rulebook to allow his own premiership to go on and on. It seems to be the fashion these days. Even Leonid Brezhnev was public-spirited enough to die at 76. Vladimir Putin is 70 but regards visibly dreadful health as absolutely no bar to office.

Over in that other superpower, the United States now appears fully committed to late-stage gerontocracy on both sides of the political divide. The next US presidential election may well be fought by a 76-year-old currently up on criminal charges and an 80-year-old president whose occasionally rambling public utterances have the effect of making one imagine his aides with their hearts in the mouths, somewhere just off stage, willing him to get to the end of them without further incident. Perhaps a lengthy and gruelling election campaign will flatter this presentational difficulty. More likely not.

Meanwhile, some of the most powerful companies in the world are run by men who in lesser occupations – such as mine and yours – might have been put out to pasture some time ago. It was Rupert Murdoch who once described the Dalai Lama as a 'very political old monk shuffling around in Gucci shoes'. Quite rude – the Dalai Lama is actually five years younger than the News Corp chairman, who is gearing up for a landmark lawsuit later this month over the 2020 'election fraud', a lie knowingly pushed by his outlets in a scandal in which he somehow felt powerless to intervene.

Murdoch's most recent engagement was celebrated in this column mere weeks ago. The distressing subsequent news that said engagement had been called off was buried on the day of the arraignment of Donald Trump, the aforementioned 76-year-old, a blockbuster event that also nudged headlines about the 74-year-old supreme court justice Clarence Thomas down the pecking order. Mr Thomas has accepted hundreds of thousands of dollars' worth of luxury hospitality from a major Republican donor, the 74-year-old Harlan Crow, whose hobbies reportedly include collecting communist dictator statuary and Nazi memorabilia. A thunderous leader column in Murdoch's *Wall Street Journal* obligingly referred to this as the 'smearing of Clarence Thomas'.

Mandatory retirement might be a thing at some places of work in the US and beyond, but for a certain stature of man, it is evidently not something that needs to be worried about. The idea of giving way to someone a few years younger, to say nothing of a few decades, does not appear to loom large in their minds, degenerated or otherwise. On they all go, really putting the 'ancient' into ancient wisdom. We can all celebrate a good innings, of course, but a remarkable number of today's biggest hitters do seem to have long passed the point at which a dignified walk back to the pavilion is in order.

Nixed nuptials, Fox in trouble and 'erratic' behaviour . . . Is Rupert Murdoch OK?

28 April 2023

In the grand tradition of his newspapers lasering in on public figures at their lowest moments, we really deserve to know

On page 3 of the *Sun*, I once saw the central 'i' of the word 'tit' asterisked out, not four inches away from a topless pair of the genuine article. So there's always been a ludicrous coyness to Rupert Murdoch and his many works. But surely we are not really to believe that the media mogul this week ditched his highest-rating news anchor, Tucker Carlson, for referring to a woman as a 'cunt' in an email? This is the take of the *Wall Street Journal* – proprietor: Mr R. Murdoch – which explains: 'Tucker Carlson's Vulgar, Offensive Messages About Colleagues Helped Seal His Fate at Fox News'.

Righto. It's fair to say the *Wall Street Journal* is not alone in the quest to make sense of Murdoch's recent behaviour. The week after he paid $787.5m to settle the lawsuit brought against Fox News by Dominion Voting Systems – Dominion's lawyers were going to force him to take the stand – Murdoch sacked Carlson via his son Lachlan. Media outlets have been scrambling to find logical explanations for actions that arguably, to deploy a euphemism, defy logic. After all, this is a 92-year-old who only weeks ago was delighting us with news of his impending fifth marriage – a whirlwind engagement to a former dental nurse turned prison chaplain, which was hastily called off a mere fortnight later. Apparently, Murdoch had become 'increasingly uncomfortable' with his fiancée's 'outspoken evangelical views'. Again: really?

The one thing we can say with certainty is that Murdoch would want us to pick over his actions and ask if he was still playing with a full deck of Happy Families cards. For decades, his newspapers have lasered in on public figures as they reach their twilight, premature or otherwise. Back in the day, a paparazzi picture of a painfully thin Freddie Mercury limping across the street was glossed with the *Sun*'s front-page inquiry 'ARE YOU OK FRED?' – one of those newspaper questions to which the answer is patently: no. No, he's not – what does it effing look like? So in the same solicitous spirit we must survey the recent actions of the mercurial mogul and ask, in the way he taught us: ARE YOU OK RUPE?

Put candidly . . . what does it effing look like? Last October, Murdoch announced plans to merge both his public companies, Fox Corp and News Corp, before being forced in January to abandon the scheme in the face of shareholder bafflement and dismay. March brought news of the bonkers betrothal and Murdoch's bizarre interview about how he 'dreaded falling in love'; April saw the engagement's abandonment. Murdoch was supposed to end the month testifying in the Dominion lawsuit; having settled that, he set about blindsiding even his allies by sacking Carlson. While legacy media oblige their own moguls by suggesting lucid cause-and-effect, some of the upstarts are finally breaking the glass on the word 'erratic'.

'Erratic' was certainly a word that came to mind when reading the epic recent *Vanity Fair* article on Murdoch, in which every line was a marmalade-dropper. Take the single paragraph that revealed that Murdoch had fallen and seriously injured himself while on a Caribbean superyacht trip with his now former wife Jerry Hall. Though it hastened to dock to get him to hospital, the boat was too big for the pier, resulting in Murdoch having to be precariously lowered down, after which he spent a night under a tent in a car park (the local hospital was closed). He was finally medevacked out, but, according to a family friend, 'kept almost dying'. LA medics discovered a broken back, noting from the X-rays that he had previously fractured vertebrae. The paragraph concludes: 'Murdoch explained it must have been from the time his ex-wife Deng pushed him into a piano during a fight.' (Ms Deng did not respond to the publication's requests for comment.)

It feels particularly piquant that all this is taking place against the backdrop of the final series of *Succession*. Murdoch is extremely, extremely relaxed about the show, to the point of having it written into his divorce settlement with Hall that she was banned from speaking to its writers. Jerry reportedly realised the Oxfordshire house she got in the settlement was rigged with cameras that were still beaming their footage back to Fox HQ, a discovery that prompted Mick Jagger's security guy to come and dismantle the apparatus for her.

Despite settling with Dominion, Murdoch's unfortunate courtroom dramas continue. This week, Prince Harry's phone-hacking case alleged Murdoch's News Group Newspapers reached a huge settlement with Prince William, but requested it be kept secret so as not to affect their ongoing legal battles with other claimants. Pleading favours off the establishment he has always regarded as his lawful prey – perhaps Murdoch is not so very different from other unhappy kings. Harry's statement suggested he had bonded with Rupert's boy James when they met at some Google event/creche for megarich estranged second sons. 'He made a real effort to try and come and talk to me,' recalled Harry of James Murdoch. 'I got the impression that, having broken away from the cult that is the Murdoch dynasty, he was starting to show signs that he wanted to do things differently . . . Given that he had broken away from his family's history, and I was about to do the same with mine, I felt that we were kindred spirits of sorts.' Real rebel hearts. As *Succession*'s Connor Roy once put it: 'The elites are scared.'

But are the shareholders a little on edge too? There is something increasingly preposterous in the spectacle of media outlets searching for rational explanations to explain Rupert Murdoch's recent antics. Surely at some point soon we might need to consider irrational ones instead?

Trump is too old and incited a coup. Biden is too old and mixes up names. America, how to choose?

9 February 2024

The special counsel has put the president's memory in the spotlight, but if we're talking about amnesia: 6 January, anyone?

To the US, where one likely candidate for the presidency delivers hour-long rambling speeches in which he explains that he's going to be a dictator, but all the chat is about whether the other candidate has lost his marbles. And yes, let me pre-emptively apologise, because I can already tell that we will be on only about the third paragraph of this column before I have exhausted the *Guardian*'s approved list of euphemisms for being a couple of world leaders' names short of a full set.

Anyway, our business today is with the president, Joe Biden, who called an impromptu press conference on Thursday night in which he hotly insisted that his memory was just fine. The occasion was the publication of a justice department report that cleared Biden of criminal charges over his handling of highly classified materials. This year-long investigation was carried out by special counsel Robert Hur, who happens to be a registered Republican, and whose report specifically mentions the president's 'significantly limited' memory. Mr Hur says that part of the reason he didn't bring charges was that 'at trial, Mr Biden would likely present himself to a jury, as he did during our interview of him, as a sympathetic, well-meaning, elderly man with a poor memory'. Oh dear. A real muffin-basket of an attack line gifted to Donald Trump there, and confirmation of my long-held conviction that fake sympathy is far deadlier a tone than open hostility.

Biden had almost left the stage last night when he returned to the podium to take a question on the Israel–Gaza conflict, in which he unfortunately referred to the Egyptian leader, Abdel Fattah el-Sisi, as 'the Mexican president'. On the one hand, this was always going to happen just at the moment he was insisting his memory was great, just as Theresa May's 2017 party conference speech to project strong leadership and control was fated to descend into a prolonged coughing fit, during which even the slogan on the backdrop began falling off the wall.

On the other hand . . . oh dear. According to polling, Biden's age and cognitive glitches are his biggest vulnerability with voters. As for his likely opponent, in my armchair diagnosis, the most terrifying thing about Donald Trump is that he is completely sane (unless you count advanced narcissism, which I suppose we have to these days). But Trump is a mere three years younger than Biden, often walks with a wobble, and himself recently confused Nikki Haley with Nancy Pelosi in a rant. So is it fair that the one should face infinitely more scrutiny on the lost-plot front than the other?

Alas, fairness isn't one of the base notes of political life. I'm afraid we could be dealing with Ye Olde Vibes Theory of Politics (est. 2022), which holds that the feels-based way in which a politician presents is more important than such trivialities as the facts or their record. Listen, I don't make the rules. But during the first 2022 Conservative leadership contest in the UK, remainer Liz Truss presented as more Brexity to the party's grassroots than leaver Rishi Sunak. Why? Vibes. Just . . . vibes.

The vibes on Biden's seniority are not great. Yes, he has led his country's exceptional and internationally envied economic recovery from the pandemic, so the large rational part of me judges that unfair. But another part of me, perhaps the irrational, can no longer watch any Biden speech or address without picturing his aides also watching backstage, mainlining cortisol, every fibre of their brace-positioned beings willing him to get over the line without making any unforced errors – and to then exit the stage without trying to use a flag as a door.

I'm sure this is complete fantasy and the only cortisol levels going through the roof are my own. Nevertheless: vibes. Can't fight 'em. I remember my heart feeling similarly in my mouth during the aforementioned Tory leadership contest, when runaway favourite Truss walked the wrong way off stage after her campaign launch. Did I think Liz Truss literally wasn't even up to finding her way off a stage? Of course not. Rationally, I knew it was just a silly mistake, of the sort that all of us make every day. At the same time, the irrational half of me felt the satisfying click of the right key turning in the lock. I knew that Liz Truss metaphorically wasn't even up to finding her way off a stage. There was some kind of ineffable psychological truth to it all that was far more powerful than the facts.

As someone who believes the likely Republican candidate is hideously, overwhelmingly worse, I fear that Joe Biden is gearing up for a gruelling election with precisely this vibes-based disadvantage. Both he and Trump are at the stage of life when sensible, ordinary people find the strength to turn to their families and ask: 'Be honest, should I still be driving?' Yet Trump's great power is defying rationality, like some dark lord of the vibes. He is possessed of a mesmerising ability to make every single thing feel like it is playing into his hands, which is why we now all watch news reports of various criminal charges being brought against him and go, 'Oh, this'll play well for him.' Will it? And if so, why should it? Who really knows, but the vibes say so.

After the last time I touched on the gerontocracy in these pages, the *Guardian* printed three letters from older male readers, under the headline 'What's Age Got to Do with It, Marina Hyde?' Ageism was mentioned, with one of the correspondents advancing details of how he spent his days, as an argument against what we might kindly have termed my own argument about when big hitters should leave the professional stage. Now no one welcomes a good bollocking on the letters page more than me, and all the three men were very nice about the rest of my output. Thank you!

However. At the risk of drawing further correspondence, I feel I still have to hold to the position that being president of the United States is not the same as 'writing, teaching, and volunteering in a residential home', and is a job for a man younger than Biden and Trump. Not a younger woman, of course – that would be genuinely insane, in the strictest clinical sense of the term. But younger than 86 at conclusion of office. So I end this column with a challenge: if any readers of the *Guardian* are able to get to the end of the lengthy forthcoming US election campaign and think it showcased a vibrant, healthy and sprightly democracy, then I urge them to write in on 6 November and suggest mandatory retirement for me.

Joe Biden now relies on instruction manuals, so here's a good tip: 'Walk to podium, smile, wave goodbye'

9 July 2024

He thinks he can run again; the signs say the opposite. Biden's best hope for beating Trump may be to let someone else do it

The Joe Biden re-election campaign is now a situation where you want to put your hands over your eyes, even when your hands are already over your eyes. Like mine, all your sets of hands may have been clamped tightly to your lids since Biden's franchise-killing performance in the first presidential debate 12 days ago, which his press secretary incredibly handwaved away by stating: 'He had a cold.' A cold what? A cold sweat? A cold day in hell? A cold dead hand he'd like you to prise the nomination out of?

In news that launched a million grimace emojis, the answer turns out to be: all of the above. Biden is on a fightback. Yesterday, he railed against 'elites' in the Democratic party, proudly deploying that great Donald Trump innovation whereby the actual president is somehow not an elite. In a strongly worded letter you strongly know was worded by someone else, Biden ordered the Democrats to stop worrying and love the bomb (I paraphrase slightly). A neurologist repeatedly came to the White House last year to treat other people who work there, the White House insists, while Biden last week told a meeting of governors that he was fine, reportedly adding: 'It's just my brain.' OK! Last Friday, he gave a sit-down interview, in which he was asked how he'd feel if he clung on in the race, then lost to Trump. 'As long as I gave it my all, and did as good of a job as I know I can do,' Biden judged, 'that's what this is about.'

Fact-check: I'm being told that is not at all what the forthcoming US presidential election is about. And listen, before we go on, please save your embossed-letterhead/well-meaning digital death threats. I already know who much the worst candidate is. Furthermore – and it's just a personal thing – I would very, very much like to see him beaten. Huge fan of American democracy here, which is to say, huge fan of the country of America having democracy. In fact, speaking of colds, you've probably heard the expression 'When America sneezes, the world catches a cold.' Most of us in the droplet radius have zero clinical interest in discovering what the world catches when America does . . . whatever *this* is.

Which makes it somewhat painful that I am currently looking at White House-issued instruction pictures taken from the wings of various stages, about 10 footsteps from where you'd expect any occupier of those stages to make a speech – pictures with the heading 'Walk to podium'. These are the leaked official templates for those guiding Biden through forthcoming events. There will doubtless be plenty on hand to claim that this is standard procedure when event-planning at this level, to which the only reasonable response is: please, please tell that to the countless millions with access to televisions and the internet who have already seen Biden struggle with any number of stage entrances and exits! Please tell that to the optics! Please tell that to the vibes! In the meantime, please tell it to my subconscious, because every time I look at one of these pictures, it immediately rearranges itself into the image of a yawning hellchasm, beneath the heading 'Walk to the abyss'.

This is all more than beginning to feel like the path leading over the edge, which the Democratic establishment has thoughtfully plotted out by its truly time-worn tactic of hoping for the best and in no way preparing for the worst. 'What's the worst that can happen?' ask people who already saw the worst happen once before. Fool me once, shame on you. Fool me twice . . . autocracy? As far as Biden's cognitive state is concerned, if only there had been different signs to all the signs there were.

Then again, only last year did the Democratic leadership in the House – which had a combined age of 973 or something – finally begin giving way to some non-thinned blood, having clung on in varying stages of decline out of . . . what? Selflessness? A fundamental/fundamentalist belief that they were the good guys? Forget the audacity of hope – this is the obnoxiousness of hope. The arc of history is now bending in the direction of the hellchasm. Why should it be a toss-up between Trump and a guy who in all conscience no one should say is operating without impairment? How dare this be the choice? This, alas, is the other reflection sparked by those 'Walk to podium' instruction manuals. Oh, NOW you're planning every last detail! Well, it's like they say: micromanage all the tiny little things now and it absolutely won't matter that you macro-fucked-up the big thing back when finessing a change wouldn't have been a last-minute scramble.

Possibly the only minuscule bright spot currently is the amusing scenes in Hollywood, where starry donors are reportedly turning on Jeffrey Katzenberg, the DreamWorks co-founder-turned-Biden campaign co-chair, for supposedly concealing the president's true state of mental fitness from them and making them part with infinitesimal percentages of their money. As the Endeavor mogul Ari Emanuel remarked mildly last week: 'We are in Fuck City.' (On the plus side for Katzenberg, the worst thing he's ever done is no longer Quibi.)

None of this is how healthy democracies operate. Non-democracies? Oh yes. Petrostate princes are kept alive in western hospitals long after natural causes have kicked in, with their vast entourages of dependants somehow unwilling to switch off the life support machine, what with it being connected directly to the cash tap. The Russians used to joke about Leonid Brezhnev that his daily routine ran as follows: reanimation, makeup, banquet, awards ceremony, clinical death. The people couldn't do a whole lot about it, but they knew. Everyone knew. *Spitting Image* portrayed his successor-but-one, Konstantin Chernenko, as something kept in the freezer and reanimated only when occasion demanded. There are currently flashes of this vein of satire in every opening monologue on the US late-night TV shows.

As far as ways forward go, there are not exactly a whole load of tried and tested walks-to-podium. But the Democrats have surely exhausted the limits of irrational hope as a victory strategy. The gruelling presidential campaign has not even got fully under way. In the absence of a candidate who appears consistently rational, rational solutions must be found. In the meantime, we might prepare some simple briefing notes of our own for Biden's strategists. You're not going to defeat the world's biggest 'anti-elite' conman by railing against 'elites' in the Democratic party. You're not going to defeat the world's biggest liar by being economical with your own *actualité*. And you're not going to defeat the world's biggest gaslighter by gaslighting people in your own way. There's more than one way to be a hero. Sometimes the greatest legacy is knowing when to walk from the podium.

BIG TECH IS NOT GOING TO SAVE YOU

Even as their products were found to have atomised, narcotised and traumatised the world, Silicon Valley's finest continued to explain that they just wanted to make it a better place. Sure, there were a few broken eggs, but to regulate their firms in any way was to be anti-omelette. Meta's Mark Zuckerberg was repeatedly summoned to Washington to be told something must be done, by the very lawmakers who could do something, but somehow didn't. At a certain point, he stopped saying sorry, except to declare that he was sorry he had ever even said sorry. Meanwhile, the tightly fought competition to be the worst tech lord gained an audacious new entrant in the form of OpenAI boss Sam Altman, who in 2016 was likening Donald Trump's rise to Hitler's in 1930s Germany, and in 2025 was attending Trump's second inauguration and dining at the White House.

When Mark Zuckerberg can face US senators and claim the moral high ground, we're through the looking glass

2 February 2024

Tech CEOs who have ruined people's lives, or politicians who back misery and mayhem? That's a low bar and a tough choice

Did you catch a clip of the tech CEOs in Washington this week? The Senate judiciary committee had summoned five of them to a hearing titled 'Big Tech and the Online Child Sexual Exploitation Crisis'. There was Meta's Mark Zuckerberg, TikTok's Shou Zi Chew, Snapchat's Evan Spiegel, Discord's Jason Citron and X's Linda Yaccarino – and a predictable vibe of 'Senator, I'm a parent myself . . .' Listen, these moguls simply want to provide the tools to help families and friends connect with each other. Why must human misery and untold, tax-avoidant billions attend them at every turn?

If you did see footage from the hearing, it was probably one of two moments deliberately staged as clippable news content. The first was when ranking committee member Lindsey Graham addressed Zuckerberg with the words: 'I know you don't mean it to be so, but you have blood on your hands.' Well, ditto, Senator. 'You have a product that is killing people,' continued Graham, who, strangely, has yet to make the same point to the makers of whichever brand of AR-15 he proudly owns, or indeed to the makers of the assault rifles responsible for another record high in US school shootings last year. Firearms fatalities are the number-one cause of death among US children and teenagers, a fact the tech CEOs at this hearing politely declined to mention, because no one likes a whatabouterist. And after all, the point of these things is to just get through the posturing of politicians infinitely less powerful than you, then scoot back to behaving precisely as you were before. Zuckerberg was out of there in time to report bumper results and announce Meta's first-ever dividend on Thursday. At the time of writing, its shares were soaring.

Anyhow, if it wasn't that clip, maybe it was the one of Zuckerberg being goaded by sedition fist-pumper Josh Hawley into apologising to those in the committee-room audience who had lost children to suicide following their exploitation on his platform. Thanks to some stagey prodding by Senator Hawley, who famously encouraged the mob on 6 January 2021 (before later being filmed running away from them after they stormed the Capitol), Zuckerberg turned round, stood up and faced his audience of the bereaved. 'I'm sorry for everything you've all gone through,' he began. Helpfully, a transcribed version of this off-the-cuff moment found its way into a Meta press release minutes after the event.

So I guess that was the hearing. 'Tense', 'heated', 'stunning' – listen, if adjectival clichés were legislation, this exercise would have been something more than pointless. And yet, they're not, and it wasn't. There really ought to be a genre name for this kind of performative busywork – the theatre of failure, perhaps.

Other outcomes were available once. Back in 1994, the CEOs of seven big tobacco firms took their oaths before a Senate committee, then spouted the communal line that nicotine wasn't addictive. Within two years, all seven had quit the tobacco industry – a development not unrelated to the fact that all seven were under investigation by the justice department for perjury. Those were different times, and not just because we probably wouldn't slap them with the 'seven dwarfs' moniker now. These days, you can't escape the sense that some old guys were shouting in vain at Zuckerberg at a hearing six years ago, while he offered 2018's variation on his favourite blandishment: 'We know we have more work to do.' And you suspect they'll be shouting in vain at him again in five years' time, when he will still know they have more work to do. 'If you're waiting on these guys to solve the problem,' sniffed Graham of the tech CEOs, 'we're gonna die waiting.' Again, the senator speaks of what he knows. There is always talk of legislation, but there is never really much legislation.

There's a line near the start of the movie version of *Ready Player One*, the cult dystopian book about a VR world that weirdly feels like the lodestar for Zuckerberg's pivot towards the metaverse: 'I was born in 2027,' explains the teenage protagonist, 'after the corn syrup droughts, after the bandwidth riots . . . after people stopped trying to fix problems, and just tried to outlive them.' It was hard to watch any amount of Wednesday's hearing – it's hard to watch a lot of news about the intersection of politics and mega-business these days, in fact – and not feel we are in a very similar place. Few of the politicians giving it the hero act could be said to have left the world in a better place than the one in which they found it when they took office. A necrotic form of politics has gripped the Republican party in particular, and while they were busy with it, they have been downgraded by corporations they don't even understand, let alone have the will, foresight or political skill to control.

'Companies over countries,' as Mark Zuckerberg said a long time ago. This once-unformed thought becomes more realised all the time, with the Meta boss last year explaining that 'Increasingly, the real world is a combination of the physical world we inhabit and the digital world we are building.' The added irony is that the more the Lindsey Grahams fail the real world, the more people retreat further into the unregulated embrace of the worlds that the Mark Zuckerbergs run. It's going to take so much more than the theatre of failure to solve it, but bad actors currently dominate the bill.

Hail, Zuckus Maximus! The master of the metaverse is finally sorry . . . for being sorry

27 September 2024

Mark Zuckerberg is embracing both AI and full-on imperial monomania. As for petty gripes about elections and teen mental health, so what?

The good news is that Mark Zuckerberg has become bored of looking like an answer to the AI prompt 'efit of a teen villain'. The bad? While the Meta overlord has grown out the Caesar hairstyle that has sustained him since 2016, he is now leaning in to open imperial monomania. This week's Meta Connect conference saw Mark take the stage in a T-shirt reading 'Aut Zuck Aut Nihil'. Either Zuck or Nothing. The original was 'Aut Caesar Aut Nihil' and was enthusiastically adopted as a motto by one of the worst Borgias (tough field) . . . but look, I'm sure it's ironic. Mark's such a gifted ironist.

We'll get to the magic glasses and AI feedspam he was pushing at this week's event in a minute, but before we do, let's recap. Easily the most significant thing Zuckerberg has said this year was that he isn't sorry any more – in fact, that he wished he'd never said sorry for most of what he'd ever said sorry for. I paraphrase only slightly. A couple of weeks ago, Zuckerberg appeared on stage for a podcast and called Facebook's willingness to offer stakes-free apologies for things he wasn't to blame for – like election manipulation or the effect of social media on teen mental health – 'a 20-year mistake'.

'And I think it's going to take another 10 years or so for us to fully work through that cycle,' he reflected, 'before our brand is back to the place that it maybe could have been if I hadn't messed that up in the first place.' Please, imagine the force Meta could have been if only it hadn't been held back by extremely intermittent synthetic contrition.

The upshot is that we might never again hear Mark drone all those Facebook phrases for 'sorry' – 'We will learn from this'; 'We know we have more work to do.' That said, the counterpoint to his soz-regret is that they've played quite well for him. Sure, every now and then he's had to pitch up at Congress for hearings that are always described as 'aggressive', 'pointed', 'intense' and even 'sharply critical'. But these have repeatedly proved themselves to be nothing more than the theatre of futility. Not one federal law has ever been passed to regulate Meta or the other big tech firms. So if the occasional few hours in Washington for a besuited 'my bad' has been the price you pay for being the world's most powerful oligarch, selling the lives of three billion monthly users via a platform that has incentivised hate, then . . . can you not just pay it? Apparently, not any more.

Of course, you may be one of those who feel trepidation at the idea of living in a world where Mark Zuckerberg is no longer minded to take responsibility for things. In which case, he has another world to sell you: the metaverse. Like so many of the tech titans, Mark really does offer an end-to-end service: they make the world worse, then they claim to be leading the escape. Elon Musk with his Mars aspiration, Jeff Bezos with his space programme, Zuckerberg with his virtual knock-off of the real world, whose landmark upgrade is that he controls it absolutely.

That would certainly appear to be its sole advantage. For a man seemingly without a cultural hinterland, perhaps it's no surprise that the fantasy world Zuckerberg's firm has come up with is a place of such utter conceptual dreariness. We are forever being told that the metaverse is a place where you can shop, have meetings, do real-estate deals, attend conferences . . . I mean, honestly. Just add 'answer infinite email' and you really have simulated paradise.

We aren't quite there yet, Mark admitted this week – honestly, it's just round the next corner – but in the meantime, he'd love to show you some augmented reality glasses and a cheaper VR headset than the one he asked you to buy last time. Also, now people don't post so much on Facebook and Instagram any more, he is going to start gradually pumping their feeds with personalised AI images that have been created by Meta AI. Mmm. Ideally, we will eventually eliminate the need for any human posters at all. Or, as the Meta founder prefers it: 'We are trying to build a future that is more open, more accessible, more natural, and more about human connection.' Go on. 'Feeling truly present with another person is the ultimate dream of social technology.' Historically, of course, there has always been another way to feel truly present with another person, which is to be truly present with another person. But this is not what the emperor would wish for his citizens. He prefers the world atomised, mediated via his machines. One of the most lunatic moments at his event saw Zuckerberg call an affiliated creator on to the stage, but then proceed to have a conversation with an AI chatbot version of the creator on a giant screen, while the genuine article stood on stage like a lemon, just watching.

Watching this eerie spectacle, I was reminded of what Mark once said to a Facebook employee whose job eventually became serving as his ghostwriter. Kind of a flesh-and-bones AI (very 1.0). She had asked him what he meant by the three-word essay prompt he'd given her – 'companies not countries'. 'I think we are moving to a world in which we all become cells in a single organism,' Zuckerberg replied, 'where we can communicate automatically and can all work together seamlessly.' Oof. Well, there you go. Who could fail to be happy that a guy who thinks *this* is now only sorry that he was ever sorry?

Oh, I'm sorry, tech bros – did DeepSeek copy your work? I can hardly imagine your distress

31 January 2025

If China has done to Sam Altman what his OpenAI has been accused of doing to creatives, it would take a heart of stone not to laugh

I once saw an episode of *America's Dumbest Criminals* in which a man called the cops to report his car stolen, only for it to turn out he'd stolen it from someone else in the first place. I couldn't help thinking of him this week while watching OpenAI's Sam Altman wet his pants about the fact that a Chinese hedge fund might have made unauthorised use of his own chatbot models, including ChatGPT, to train its new little side project. This is the cheaper, more open, extremely share-price-slashing DeepSeek.

As news of DeepSeek played havoc with the tech stock market, OpenAI pressed its hanky to its nose and released a statement: 'We are aware of and reviewing indications that DeepSeek may have inappropriately distilled our models, and will share information as we know more,' this ran. 'We take aggressive, proactive countermeasures to protect our technology.' Oooooooooh! I want to say, 'Welcome to America's Dumbest Tech Barons,' except I can't, because I think we all know that no law enforcement is coming to get Sam for the stuff *he's* alleged to have made unauthorised use of first. That was the good type of alleged theft, whatever the claims of all the lawsuits belatedly trying to claw something back for the alleged copyright victims of his firm's own inappropriate methods.

So, to put it another way . . . wait, Sam – you're not telling us that the Chinese hedge fund crawled all over your IP without asking and took it for themselves? Oh my God, IMAGINE?! You must feel used and abused. Financially violated. Like all your years of creativity were just grist to some other bastard's mill. Like a host organism. Like a schmuck. Like Earth's most screamingly preposterous hypocrite.

Anyway, are you particularly familiar with Sam Altman? I think he's becoming almost my worst of all the tech bros. Elon Musk remains the edgelord overlord to beat, of course, but honestly, it's getting extremely difficult to avoid appreciating just how much of a super-irritant the OpenAI boss has become. Physically, he resembles the kind of actor who shows up to an audition thinking he's a perfect leading man, but who gets cast as the puppy-eyed loner who just happens to take a trophy from each one of his victims. Which, in a funny kind of way, I guess he is. Sam's got every living creative down there in his basement well. 'It feeds my machine its script, or it gets the hose . . .' I think I have to say here that he and OpenAI deny all this. The unauthorised scraping of human creativity, I mean – I'm not sure if anyone's asked him about the basement well, so do consider that one unsolved.

But where were we? Ah yes: the Altman journey. In 2016, he was declaring Trump's statements akin to Hitler's during his rise in the 1930s. But now? Well, purely going on Sam's own rather crass analogy, he seems to have turned into one of those German industrialists who gladly popped into the Chancellery for a slice of cake. And, indeed, for a slice of *the* cake.

But as I say, that's Sam's analogy; anyone who's ever skimmed over his recommended books list knows he's never met a bland popular history book he didn't love, and consequently he shouldn't be relied upon to produce a single comparison that isn't with either the Third Reich or ancient Rome. If you want to feature on his recommended books list next year, just get the freebie version of ChatGPT to fart you out something called 'Rome: The First Reich'. He will find it 'fascinating', 'unexpected' and 'really thought-provoking'.

Needless to say, Sam was there at the inauguration of the current American Caesar. As far as I could see, he didn't make the cut of those tech titans placed in front of Trump's supposed actual cabinet. I did, however, note that he was filmed having some bulging-eyed chat with Jake and Logan Paul – YouTubers, podcasters, energy drink dealers and 'boxers'. I suppose one of the comic pleasures of these times is watching the nerds making common cause with the guys who would 100% have given them a wedgie in school, purely because they are now all rich. Money's one weird side effect is to unite some of the worst wedgers and wedgees.

Alas, like the rest of the Silicon Valley horror-moguls, Sam is now a fact of all our lives, and – along with the Trump administration he is thoroughly cosied up to – is telling everyone how to think about DeepSeek. This is really a key dynamic of the next few years: being told we should be very worried about what the authoritarian Chinese are doing by Silicon Valley authoritarians whom we should also be extremely worried about. For us little people, the choice seems to be between being data-jacked and screwed over by the undemocratic Chinese, or being data-jacked and screwed over by the post-democratic tech bros. Once again, it's the old syphilis or Ebola menu choice.

The only thing worse than being this impotent and option-free is having to listen to the Silicon Valley gazillionaires whining about it all and demanding more public money to defend themselves. But why wouldn't they? Their whining always works. Every time they say we should get rid of all government subsidies, while keeping their own, or threaten to abandon building projects if required to pay normal taxes like everyone else, they get what they want. Already Trump's AI tsar is gibbering obligingly that it's 'possible' that theft of OpenAI's IP has occurred.

As the entrepreneur and investor Scott Galloway has pointed out on numerous occasions, the big tech firms are the biggest welfare queens that have ever stalked the Earth. They've all drawn vast benefits from public money, chased countless tax breaks and demanded even more. Far from being some heroic form of risk-taking done without a single handout, theirs is the capitalism of the school bake sale: someone else buys all the ingredients and does most of the cooking, and the kids then claim they have turned a profit for the good of humanity.

Meanwhile, it's left to sidelined Cassandras to flash the warning lights. This week, Yoshua Bengio, the Canadian computer scientist and a so-called godfather of AI, warned of the shock arrival of DeepSeek that 'It's going to mean a closer race, which usually is not a good thing from the point of view of AI safety.' You'll note that barely a day goes by without someone described as a 'godfather of AI' coming out to caution against its increasingly malign potential and capabilities. AI seems to have more godparents than even Sleeping Beauty. And, regrettably, more than one significant prick.

Amazing: of all the books in all the world Mr Free Speech Zuckerberg wants to ban, it's the one about him

14 March 2025

Whether the Meta boss and his ex-lieutenant Sheryl Sandberg are truly beyond awful is neither here nor there, but I thought he was done with fact-checking?

I am as shocked as I am confused that Mark Zuckerberg is going all out to block a memoir by Facebook's former director of global public policy, Sarah Wynn-Williams. I thought information wanted to be free? I definitely heard that speech should be. We know Meta's revolting oligarch doesn't write his self-serving public pronouncements, but he should at least make time in his busy Magafication schedule to read them.

Anyway, even if you think the stories in *Careless People* are untrue – and I don't, not for a single nanosecond – I thought the Meta boss said disinformation wasn't a thing any more? He recently binned off all his fact-checkers to 'dramatically reduce the amount of censorship'. Yet here we are, reading stories of how Meta this week launched an emergency action in the US to ban Wynn-Williams from promoting or further distributing copies of her book. It argued – successfully, for now – that it would face 'immediate loss . . . in the absence of immediate relief'.

Honestly, Mark: TOUGHEN UP! It was only about 10 minutes ago that you were telling Joe Rogan that corporations needed more 'masculine energy'. If something's wrong or dangerous or really seriously harmful, just let everyone keep seeing it – because freedom – but pop a 'community note' on it. As for how you put a community note on a book, my advice to you would be to go and stand outside Pan Macmillan, which bravely published Wynn-Williams, with a little sign saying 'Context'. Listen, if it's a good enough bulwark against the risk of genocide in some boring old developing-world backwater, then it should be good enough for you.

The grounds for Meta calling in emergency lawyers to block Wynn-Williams's book seem to be that she has gone against the terms of her severance. Luckily, none of us has a 'non-disparagement clause' against Zuckerberg, who on this evidence and so much more should be disparaged every minute of every day in the countries where he operates, and even in the ones where he doesn't. There's a lovely bit in the book where his company is said to be 'dangling the possibility that it'll give the Chinese regime special access to users' data'.

In conversation, I overuse the phrase 'the worst people in the world', but the Facebook/Meta top brass really are up there. Wynn-Williams's book is that simultaneously satisfying yet horrifying thing – an insider account that shows you that absolutely every single one of the awful things you already suspected apparently really did go on behind closed doors. As did a few you didn't suspect. I knew Sheryl Sandberg's brand of 'lean-in' feminism was bullshit, but I didn't think it involved female employees being encouraged to lean into her lap/bed on private planes.

Shortly after turning this offer down, Wynn-Williams nearly dies in childbirth. Once she's back at work, her male boss tells her she was insufficiently 'responsive' during her absence. 'In my defence,' says Wynn-Williams, 'I was in a coma for some of it.' For light relief, we meet a shadowy Zuckerberg aide who supposedly games his boss's own algorithm so his posts have mega-engagement. Mark's senior staff all let him win at Catan.

And that's just the office politics stuff. The hardcore business – what we might call the politics politics stuff – is so much worse. Meta is currently insisting that Wynn-Williams was ultimately fired for 'poor performance and toxic behaviour'. But it's amazing to think anyone at Meta could get fired for 'toxic behaviour'. I'm sure whatever they've done didn't actively stoke a genocide, like the Rohingya claim that the firm's negligence did so in Myanmar. I'm sure it couldn't be as bad as betraying vulnerable citizens in exchange for market penetration.

Quite early on in Wynn-Williams's 2011–17 stint at Facebook, a US Treasury official tells the Facebook execs that tech firms like theirs are two years away from being hated as much as the investment banks. Well, that turned out to be adorably optimistic. I think we all *love* the cuddly old banks compared to companies such as Mark's or Elon's. But, of course, the tech firms are way, way too powerful to care.

Meanwhile, the world's children have simply been allowed to become hideously and destructively addicted to their products by politicians who either implicitly or, as is often claimed by Wynn-Williams, explicitly thank the companies for assisting in their electoral success. We non-American outsiders bang on about the US gun laws and how unspeakable it seems to us to raise children in a world of active shooter drills and school massacres. But *all* western countries and plenty beyond have failed to protect children from the known iniquities and poison of social media. Australia alone has just banned it for under-16s. I've no idea where Zuckerberg's children (the first born of whom he apparently asked Xi Jinping to name) go to school. But, like metaphorical crack dealers, many Silicon Valley bosses have sent their kids to a specific local Steiner school, where it's all crocheted textbooks and chalkboards and no one is stupid enough to let the little scions near the narcotising horrors of the product.

So on Meta sails. There are words and phrases for these supranational organised enterprises that harm societies and seemingly do whatever they like, and none of them is the nerdily bland 'tech firm'. What was it that the Indians used to call the period of chaos and social instability instigated by the East India Company, that rampaging entity/'honourable company' that I increasingly feel Meta is most redolent of? Ah yes: the anarchy. We live in a modern form of it now, thanks to Zuckerberg and others, and it's way past time we did more than simply scroll defeatedly on.

It's Sam Altman, the man who stole the rights from copyright. If he's the future, can we go backwards?

10 October 2025

His AI video generator Sora 2 has been reviled for pinching the work of others. One giant leap for Sam; for everyone else, not so much

Take a look at Sam Altman. I mean, actually do it. Go to Google Images, where you can find countless photos of the OpenAI boss smiling in a kind of wan genius way, the humble lost puppy of Silicon Valley. But I urge you to simply cover the bottom half of his face in any of these pictures, and you will immediately clock that Sam has the sad-psycho eyes of the lost woman's boyfriend whom the police have asked to front the missing person appeal. Please come home, Sheila – we're all worried sick and we just want you back.

If that joke seems off-colour or crass or some kind of manipulative stretch, please, don't worry. I'm using the OpenAI gold standard of giving-a-toss, where the unwilling subjects of any generated content have to formally, time-consumingly and bureaucratically opt *out* of being used/abused/exploited any way anyone likes. I haven't heard from Sam, so my assumption is that he's fine with me saying that he knows exactly where Sheila is, because he put her there. He is, after all, fast emerging as precisely the type to appear alongside the phrase 'in plain sight'.

For Sam, the past fortnight has involved the release of AI video generator Sora 2 – a staggering upgrade on the Sora of barely 10 months ago – and its instant descent into a sludge of stolen copyrighted goods. We also saw the announcement of another web of circular bargains between OpenAI and chip firms like Nvidia and AMD that brings OpenAI's frenzied-deal tally to over $1tn this year alone. That absolutely does not mean that in addition to enabling you to watch videos of meticulously created characters get pixel-puppeted by aggressively bigoted and talentless losers, OpenAI will also enable you to lose your home in a financial crash if the bubble bursts badly.

And look, no offence to Sora's 'creators'. I often walk through art galleries and realise the stuff on the walls would be so much better if I simply stole it and drew hilarious penises or whatever on it, and that they wouldn't have made it publicly viewable if they didn't want that. Furthermore, no tech titans have a cultural life, so they can't possibly imagine what could be so creatively valuable that you wouldn't want a robot to desecrate it for cash. If you've seen Sam's frequent reading recommendations, you'll know they're literally the Business Philosophy section of a second-tier airport bookshop. This week, he mainly wanted us to know Sora 2 was all cool and fun. 'It is way less strange to watch a feed full of memes of yourself than I thought it would be,' Sam posted reassuringly. So everything's fine! Although I guess it helps if you're one of the most powerful people in the world and making untold billions off this stuff, not just getting revenge-porned in a Byzantium simulation because somehow historical prompts seem to confuse the 'guardrails'.

I've seen it said that OpenAI's motto should be 'Better to beg forgiveness than ask permission,' but that euphemises it preposterously. Its actual motto seems to be: 'We'll do what we want, and you'll let us, bitch.' Consider Altman's recent political journey from Cassandra warning of Trump's Hitlerian tendencies to regular guest of the man himself. 'Thank you for being such a pro-business, pro-innovation president,' Sam simpered to Trump at a recent White House dinner for tech titans. 'It's a very refreshing change.' Inevitably, the Trump administration has refused to bring forward any AI regulation at all.

Meanwhile, please remember something Sam and his ironicidal maniacs said earlier this year, when it was suggested that the Chinese AI chatbot DeepSeek might have been trained on some of OpenAI's work. 'We are aware of and reviewing indications that DeepSeek may have inappropriately distilled our models, and will share information as we know more,' his firm's anguished statement ran. 'We take aggressive, proactive countermeasures to protect our technology.' Hilariously, it seemed that the last entity on earth with the power to fight AI theft was OpenAI.

It was left to Hollywood talent agencies this week to extract some kind of momentary pause from Altman, who posted some flannel about trying to direct, if not hard cash, then certainly some 'new kind of engagement' at those he openly called 'rightsholders'. Many of us remember a time – about 15 minutes ago – when rightsholders meant *the people who hold the rights*. I mean, the clue's right there in the word. But Sam is post-rights. The question is: if he's post-creative rights, can we honestly believe he isn't effectively post-other kinds of rights?

OpenAI wants what all loving platforms ultimately want: its users never to have to leave its confines. It's clearly positioning towards being seen as the new default homepage of the web, as Meta once did. Can a heartwarming coming-of-age privacy horror show/election distortion scandal/child harms crisis be far behind?

Because, incredibly, we've already gone through this life cycle. But we're going to do it again, aren't we? Or, more accurately, given the unprecedented speed Sam's firm is moving at, we already *have* done it again. We've initially lauded some mysterious tech Pied Piper as a brilliant, unconventional altruist, then belatedly realised he is not as he seemed and that his technology is more dangerous than imagined, then still failed to regulate, and are now being victimised by it. In more ways than one, this is just the terrible AI version of a movie we've already seen. If Altman's models can learn, why can't we?

WINDSOR KNOTS

It was unclear how the British people would react to the death of Queen Elizabeth II, after her seven decades on the throne. In contrast with the aftermath of the death of Princess Diana, it turned out to be the retail brands and not the people who went mad. (If there was any bubbling public anger, it was a gusher that officialdom managed to cap – at least until four days after her late majesty's funeral, when it surged up beneath the personage of new prime minister Liz Truss and her mini-budget and washed them clean away.) Enter King Charles III, whose coronation was written up as a time of immense joy, even though all with eyes could see he looked old, exhausted and sad. The new king's cancer diagnosis was treated with less demented prurience than that of the Princess of Wales, who was pursued and trolled by crazed royalists, conspiracy theorists and the provisional wing of the 'be kind' brigade. No conspiracy theorising was required, of course, for the piss artist formerly known as Prince Andrew, whose behaviour was so bad that it contrived to get him fired from an institution whose entire point is that it has precisely nothing to do with meritocracy. An achievement of sorts, after a lifetime of avoiding them.

Britain has become One Nation Under Brands, detained in our Center Parcs lodgings

16 September 2022

When the revolution against corporate twee comes, I'll be down the front with a plastic putter and a bow and safety-arrow

For all the horror and tragedy of death, the aftermaths of many bereavements produce unexpected moments of light relief. As long as the deceased is an adult who has lived to a ripe old age, you can pretty much guarantee that there will be some sudden instant – usually when you're shoulder-deep in making the arrangements – that reduces you and perhaps a sibling or two to truly helpless giggles. We all need a pressure valve, and few things can be taken entirely seriously for 10 whole days.

Of course, you can never predict quite what is going to set you off. It might be as random as the undertaker leaning towards you, steepling his fingers and asking in hushed tones bordering on reverence: 'And did she have a favourite wood?' Nope, sorry. I've gone. I've absolutely gone.

In the wake of the Queen's death, these moments of hopelessly unintentional, tenuously sane hilarity have surely been produced by the behaviour of any number of our commercial brands. Them and Nicholas Witchell, anyway. It's been like a competition to see which retailer can act the most preposterously, the most self-regardingly, and with the most complete commitment to the twee.

Could it be Morrisons, announcing that it had turned down the volume of its till beeps 'out of respect'? Could it be pawnshop chain Cash Converters formally announcing its self-seclusion from social media? Or could it be – and this one's the correct answer – Center Parcs decreeing that holidaymakers must be thrown out of its villages for the day of the Queen's funeral 'as a mark of respect', before backtracking and permitting customers to remain on site, while ordering them to 'remain in their lodges'?

Yup, I've gone. Completely gone. If you've felt slightly 'managed' by aspects of the relentlessly choreographed elements of the past week, then this really was your Triumph of the Corporate Will. It was, all of a sudden, simply impossible not to picture oneself in one's wood-effect, lodge-effect detention hut, cowering by the forest-mural feature wall as village guards toured the site with loud-hailers while screaming: 'REMAIN IN YOUR LODGES!'

Thank heavens for a glimpse of the indomitable spirit of piss-take, as various online posters offered a masterclass in why brands really should avoid running their firms via the Pooterising diktats of social media. 'Good luck removing guests from the parks,' ran one Twitter response to Center Parcs (heroically refusing to submit to the 'parcs' affectation). 'You've trained them in archery, shooting, swimming, canoeing and swinging through the trees like apes. You've basically got five village-loads of ninjas to clear out.'

Majestic. Yet still the brands came. No doubt the Queen's death has taught us many things, but one of mine has been that I absolutely don't need to be contacted about it in yet another non-Spandex-related email by a luxury UK yoga-wear brand. I didn't need to hear from them after the death of George Floyd, and I sure as heck don't need to hear from them again now. Honestly, get over yourself. You're in retail! Just sell me your crap and be on your way.

The commercial landscape is awash with this nonsense. I know our society is measured by how it treats its most wantonly evil members, but my finger does hover over the 'deploy whole-life-tariff' button when I read about Innocent Fruit Smoothies not tweeting for a few days 'out of respect' for Her Majesty's death. But of course – of *course* – Innocent would take this immensely self-righteous stand. Its products are just a few among an ever-growing mountain that are plastered with terrible, pious catechisms all over their packaging, where the words 'the good stuff' are supposed to signify something moral as well as nutritional. Sorry, but no. Stop managing me. Just sell me your crap and be on your way.

What have these companies been doing all week since the Queen died, other than getting it amusingly wrong and reminding us that, for all their tactical social positioning in the course of flogging more units of this or that, they actually have precisely zero idea how to behave in a situation that, amazingly, doesn't require any input from them at all? The ludicrous attempts at managing their customers have sparked hugely funny and invigorating backlashes. Arguably much in need of a pressure valve, sections of the public have been given a fantastic opportunity to let out a cackle and shout the simple, inescapable truth at whatever screen on which they're viewing the brand announcement. Namely: 'No one cares! Literally NO ONE CARES what you do or don't do!'

I'm not suggesting everyone has woken up from some late-capitalist slumber with a howl of realisation that actually some bunch of plonkers at British Cycling are not in fact the boss of them. If they want to go for a bike ride on the day of the funeral, they don't need permission. Alas, this is still a country where the annual release of the John Lewis advert is obediently greeted as though it's one of the formal parts of Christmas. But what a great showing-of-the-arses the past week has been for so many firms and organisations, and a reminder that we really shouldn't submit to our brand overlords, because they know very little and matter even less. The important things in life are nothing at all, ever, to do with retailers and brands. Any of them suggesting otherwise deserves total ridicule – or perhaps some chaotically boring little American academic to accuse them of 'centering themselves during a national tragedy'. Which is obviously a fate worse than total ridicule.

Quite how we've got to this ridiculous place where irrelevant retailers feel moved to act like the Archbishop of Canterbury is unclear, but the past week has certainly underscored the necessity of getting out of it before we submit fully to becoming One Nation Under Brands. Every one of these botched attempts at gravitas now turns me full *Braveheart* – and I very much hope you are with me.

Are we going to be confined to our metaphorical lodges by the preposterous posturing of retailers? Are we going to allow death – any death – to be part of their ridiculous 'brand positioning'? Are we going to be told how to act by a flipping pawnbroker? No. No, my friends, we are not. Instead, let us rise up in defiance of the tyranny of corporate twee. Let us take up our bows and our safety-arrows, our plastic putters and our laser rifles. Let us defy the orders of our corporate oppressors and roam the village of human piss-take and possibility, and beyond. They can take our cash, but we can NEVER take them seriously.

A day for Charles, our mournful monarch: in his pomp but out of his time

5 May 2023

It's everything he had hoped for, just the wrong era. Still, one makes the best of these things

Are you all set for the coronation? Whether you plan to pay the 'people's homage' – swearing aloud the newly proposed oath of allegiance to the King while watching it at home – is, of course, a private matter between you and your television set. This morning, Charles's friend Jonathan Dimbleby suggested that this faintly controversial innovation was some ghastly evangelical idea of the Archbishop of Canterbury's (I paraphrase), and that Charles himself would find it 'abhorrent'. Which feels fairly definitive.

Even if the Archbish hasn't made a bish, it must be said that the full-spectrum reverence of the run-up to the coronation can leave one always on the point of collapsing into giggles. I hugely enjoyed a *Spectator* article this week about the spoon used to anoint the sovereign with holy oil, which was described as a 'very special one' (agreed), 'one of the most beautiful examples of that humble genus' (OK) and 'doubtless the world's most important spoon' (sorry, I've gone).

Royalty remains, with a few notable resignations, a family firm, and Prince William and his wife, Kate, have spent the big-game buildup engaged in tasks typical for the royals of our era. They go to a gym, where they must gigglingly ride exercise bikes; they go to a pub, where they must gigglingly pull pints. The giggling is key: the royals must show themselves to be keen to laugh at their relative ineptitude at these tasks, gamely participating in photographs whose message always seems to be: 'We are not skilled enough to be ordinary people such as your good selves – thank you for bearing with us!' This maladroitness is very bad when politicians do it (see Rishi Sunak at the petrol station), but very good when the royals do it. It is the form of duty on which we have settled in the modern age.

The quality of that age is not unalloyed. Talking to Elizabeth II's biographer, Ben Pimlott, Princess Margaret recalled the 1953 coronation as a 'phoenix time', when everything was being raised from the ashes of the immediate postwar years. This current moment is very clearly a different one, when to many the coronation does not feel part of a general sense of renewal and optimism, with the new sovereign merely the most gilded boat being lifted by a rising tide. Instead, it is a time of contraction, with state pageantry frequently described as the last thing we do peerlessly. By 2024, the average UK household will enjoy a lower standard of living than the average household in Slovenia. By 2030, we will have fallen behind Poland. But will they have such world-beating royal spectacles? No, they will not. A win is a win, even if it is in a game few other countries seem very interested in playing any more.

There is absolutely no question that we do these things rather amazingly. Indeed, we have done them rather amazingly rather a lot recently, what with the platinum jubilee, the state mourning and funeral of the late Queen Elizabeth II, and now the coronation. Some of the golden hardware is starting to look very familiar from recent seasons of the show. The Duke of Norfolk's organisational skills increasingly seem like the administrative apogee – perhaps he could be persuaded to take over a government department or three in the post-coronation lull? At this point, there is virtually no question of him doing any worse.

The contrast between the state of the country and the state of royal occasions was best illustrated for me by the formation of two queues this week. The first was the expected one of those citizens and tourists staking out the best spots along the procession trail. And the second was one of hundreds of people, which started building well before dawn on Tuesday in King's Lynn, Norfolk (population 48,000), after the sole dental practice in the town that treats people on the NHS announced it would be accepting new patients.

Twenty-four hours before the 1953 coronation, hundreds of thousands of people were already camping out in London to see the procession. Some of those doing so this time around have said some fairly odd things to the microphones pointed their way, but you can't mention this or it's elitist. If you're keeping a taxonomy of things that are and aren't elitist, raising an eyebrow at someone fuming about Prince Harry's 'porn book' is elitist, but riding past him in a gold coach with the demeanour of Leeds players largely ignoring young fans at the team hotel is not.

As for the man at the centre of it all, Charles remains oddly – perhaps ominously – unknown. His belatedly saluted prescience on environmental matters has left the depth of his creed unexamined. A totally fascinating article in the *New Statesman* this week saw its author, Will Lloyd, travel to Transylvania, the rural region of Romania with which Charles is under-the-radar obsessed. He owns two properties there and has visited every year since 1993, holding it up as an idyllic rebuke to modernity. 'It's the timelessness which is so important,' our king is quoted as saying on a tourist website. 'The landscape is almost out of some of those stories you used to read as a child.' To this pre-modern simplicity Charles is in wild thrall, which is in some ways understandable, given that Transylvanians do things like gratefully show him their breads, and – to my knowledge – have never put a private call in which he expressed a wish to be his now-wife's tampon on a premium-rate phone line to titillate local peasants.

But Lloyd visits the typical Transylvanian village of Buneşti, where people have no shoes and their animals grub in the dirt. His taxi driver points out the sole anachronism in this otherwise ancient peasant scene: satellite dishes bolted to every shack. He tells him that our world is beamed into their houses, and that these people want it. But evidently Charles does not want them to have it. He apparently prefers them to exist in this 'simplicity', which to other eyes looks merely like grinding poverty. Can a man of many palaces – who famously lamented the departure of the servant who squeezed his toothpaste on to the brush for him better than anyone else – truly reconcile these aspects of his character with the back-breaking existence he so romanticises in others? Maybe it all makes sense in the sort of mystic feudalism that seems to amount to his philosophy.

Yet so many of Charles III's chosen works echo with melancholy, a sense that he has arrived past the point in history at which he would have liked to have lived. Perhaps the new king feels like that other uneasy head of a family, Tony Soprano. 'It's good to be in something from the ground floor,' reflects the mobster soon after we first meet him. 'I came too late for that – I know. But lately, I'm getting the feeling that I came in at the end. The best is over.'

The royals bring on their B team, captained by Prince Andrew. No wonder some fans think it's all over

1 March 2024

With details scant about the Princess of Wales's health, diehard royalists are losing their minds. Into the vacuum steps Andy

Say what you will about King Charles's previously fanfared vision for a 'slimmed-down monarchy', its injury woes suggest it could do with buying another striker. If that isn't how it works, then it's clear that despite thinking they are the greatest fans in the world, many diehard royalists are simply not happy with what they're seeing out there on the pitch and are voicing their increasingly hysterical discontent. The King's cancer treatment and the Princess of Wales's convalescence from abdominal surgery have come at the same time, and social media posts are awash with the type of bizarre and brutal conspiracy theories in which so many of the #BeKind contingent specialise. Traditional media are trying to lose their mind with dignity, and – as so often before – tragically failing.

The royal family itself is playing its second team, the implications of that perhaps most eye-catchingly laid bare at this week's memorial service for the former king of Greece. As Constantine's godson, Prince William had been scheduled to do a reading, but pulled out at the very last minute due to a 'personal matter'. So, bring on the under-70s Bs.

And who's this barrelling along at the very front of the family party, grinning and leading the way next to his unestranged ex-wife, Fergie? Could it be Prince Andrew, a man who has spent two years formally in the wilderness (the 30-room Royal Lodge in Windsor Great Park, which comes complete with several staff cottages)?

Could it be a man who regards that most luxuriously cruel and unusual punishment as more than enough for paying multiple millions in an out-of-court settlement to a trafficked woman he didn't have sex with when she was 17? Yup, I think it could. Not to suggest that Andrew indecently relished the chance to step up, but the photographs outside the church give the impression he was pretty much doing the Lambeth Walk on the approach. The moving footage is slightly more forgiving, but the vibe was the actor playing Hamlet going off sick and being replaced, not with the understudy, but with a particularly dim competition winner. Hopefully Andy was more suitably restrained during the actual service for the man the media kept referring to as King Constantine of Greece, even though Greece doesn't have a king and hasn't for 50 years. Still, what do the newspapers know?

Not nearly enough, seems to be their general consensus. Barely six weeks after Kate was admitted to hospital for planned surgery, much of the media here and around the world has wholly exhausted its fabled supply of patience and is demanding detailed updates on the health of a woman who clearly, clearly doesn't want to give them. Kate's feelings do not remotely seem to matter, despite the fact that Kensington Palace indicated from the start that she'd be 'unlikely to return to public duties till after Easter'. Almost a full month out from that date, some are already veering in the direction of the weirdness that broke out after the death of Princess Diana. Specifically, the unreal part when the late Queen was somewhat bullied back from Balmoral – where she was engaged in the rather more real business of comforting her bereaved grandsons – to comfort the nation. 'SHOW US YOU CARE', demanded a typical headline (in that case from the *Daily Express*), somehow lacking the imagination to grasp that children who have lost their mother are rather more important than grown-ups who didn't even know Diana and not two weeks before were lapping up every obviously intrusive paparazzi shot of her. I always love the historian Ben

Pimlott's line on the madness: 'A private crisis had become a public one, even though nobody knew what it was about.'

These days, nobody really knows what anything is about, with one *Mail* columnist declaring that Kate's current absence from public life 'feels almost like a bereavement'. (No, it doesn't.) 'The King has been open about his cancer diagnosis,' ran another impassioned cry. 'Why can't Kate be open about her surgery?' Mm-hmm. I think it's because she doesn't want to be? The general tenor of these rapidly snowballing articles is that of your worst nosy neighbour coming round shortly after you've had some surgery you don't want to go into, even though you've expressly said no visitors, and screaming through the letterbox: 'How are you feeling "down there"? I am a well-meaning friend!' Then posting the whole exchange online.

In terms of what 'well-meaning' royalists do want from the unwell people they claim to adore, some sort of worldwide privacy tour would seem to be the answer, ironically. Naturally, they can't own up to this position, preferring instead to couch it in terms of what they, as the King's subjects, 'need'. But isn't this simply bollocks? The people don't really 'need' anything at all, they would just quite like it, which isn't the same thing.

Yet we live in an age where the royal family's chief challenge is itself. All its crises come from within – deaths, divorces, diseases, decampings to America. The trouble for the royals, ultimately, is that you need those diehard fans to be on your side. The base must be rallied. As Queen Elizabeth II famously put it: 'I have to be seen to be believed.' Perhaps the monarchy will end up considering the wisdom of slimming itself down to the point where it might almost provoke one of those other classic headline templates of intrusive fake concern: 'Fears for Painfully Thin Royal Family – Pals Say Its Health Drive Has Gone Too Far'. In the meantime, could someone please urgently substitute Prince Andrew or sell him to the Saudis in the transfer window?

I feel deep sympathy for Kate and I'm glad she's better. But this dance with the media devil won't work

10 September 2024

A woman emerging from chemotherapy feels obliged to be filmed in a wheat field to appease the public. What does that say about the monarchy – and us?

I wonder if we will come to look back on that supposed great virtue of our age – controlling the narrative – and see it for the cornered form of submission it so often is. I felt nothing but immense pity for the cancer-stricken Princess of Wales before the release of her intimate family video yesterday, and the sheer weirdness of the resulting enterprise has only magnified the pathos of her situation. Watching the three-minute film, shot by some ad man, I wondered who could possibly feel it was anything but sad that a recovering post-chemo mother should feel that this is her best option for keeping 'well-wishers' at bay a little longer.

A lot of people could, it seems from the feverish coverage since it dropped – meaning that convention demands I couch the notion that the existence of the video is in any way weird as 'my unpopular opinion'. In which case, allow me to chuck in another unpopular opinion: this sort of thing appeals precisely to the grown-ups who, when Diana died, regarded their own supposed emotional state as in more urgent need of attention than that of her grieving 12- and 15-year-old grandsons. On this pretext was the late Queen – their grandmother – media-stormed back to London. The selfishness and self-importance of a certain stripe of loyal subject is at best demandingly prurient and at worst grotesque. We hear a lot about the male gaze. The royalist's gaze could do with more unpicking.

Hilary Mantel understood this voraciousness where royalty was concerned – recognised it even in herself. 'Royal Bodies', her epic 2013 essay for the *London Review of Books*, began with a passage on Kate – itself disingenuously and enthusiastically misconstrued by the tabloids. Later on in the piece, the *Wolf Hall* author described coming up close to the late Queen at a palace reception. Mantel confessed: 'I am ashamed now to say it but I passed my eyes over her as a cannibal views his dinner, my gaze sharp enough to pick the meat off her bones.'

And so to Kate's video, shot by a man who has also shot campaigns for Uber Eats, and who made Tesco's 'Food Love Stories' commercials. Something else is being served up here, which for some reason he has decided to make look like a Center Parcs ad. Despite artfully included clips of Prince George asking of a camera, 'Is this filming?', the video was captured not by a GoPro on a picnic rug, but by a crew and a significant post-production operation, who made studied use of filters and slow motion, switching from sweeping shots to grainy scenes designed to ape cine film. Unlike the private home movies in the opening titles of *Succession*, the footage shows a happy family, but for my money, the sense of menace is still there. But whereas the Roys are menaced from within, the menace to the Waleses comes from the outside, and it is the endless and thankless task of appeasing it that dictates that this video must exist at all.

Various media have added to the threats that always beset the throne, and with its scenes of picnics and secluded country days, this video explicitly echoes Queen Elizabeth II's famous decision to allow the cameras into her private family life in 1969 for the famous/infamous *Royal Family* documentary. That was an attempt by the crown and its courtiers to meet the medium of television on its own terms. Decades later, opinion is still divided as to whether it was a PR masterstroke or the moment the rot set in. 'It was difficult,' concluded the historian Ben Pimlott in his biography of the late Queen, 'once the genie of this kind of publicity had been let out of the bottle, to put it back in again.'

Fifty-five years on, the Princess of Wales's video feels like an attempt to meet social media on its own terms. Social media is, of course, the arena in which hunting Kate became a jolly global blood sport earlier this year, when – despite having been explicitly told that she would not appear in public before Easter owing to significant illness – the #BeKind brigade grew bored within weeks and whipped up a vicious feeding frenzy of conspiracy theories regarding her absence and the reasons for it. Despite condemning the ghouls of social media, sections of the traditional media merely put quote marks round their vileness, running coded versions of precisely the same hounding. Kate tried silencing it with a Mother's Day photo; minor editing glitches immediately became a 'scandal', for which she absurdly felt obliged to formally apologise. Next, multiple royal experts and headline writers explained that the true problem was that the palace had 'lost control of the narrative'. Eventually, a video in which a poised yet fragile Kate revealed her cancer diagnosis was judged the only way to regain it.

Inevitably, meanwhile, the same critics who detest Harry and Meghan's barefoot California content decline to look at the style of the Waleses' video and consider that the Meghanisation of the royal family continues apace. Things that are bad when the Beckhams do them are axiomatically good when royals do them, selling the crown being an activity from which the news media arguably profit most of all. This accounts for much of their magnanimity towards Kate's latest video.

But service is not the same as people feeling forced to serve themselves up. It was often said, back in the mid-1990s, that Diana learned to control the narrative. Did she really, though? As David Beckham stagily remarked in infinitely lighter circumstances in a recent candid film of his own: 'Be honest.'

Now Andrew has been fired from the Firm, a nation wonders: who'll be next?

31 October 2025

The King is reduced to a blustering CEO, Prince William to his head of HR. This de-princing could leave the entire House of Windsor facing redundancy

Incredible news for residents of the likes of Prince Andrew Drive and Prince Andrew Way, who in recent years have sought name changes from their local councils to remove the unfortunate association with You Know Who. Thanks to last night's historically dramatic action by the King, the dignity of those aforementioned small stretches of Britain has been restored. (If anyone happens to live in Andrew Mountbatten Windsor Close, my commiserations.) But has the dignity of the British monarchy – current custodians: the House of Windsor – been restored? No, I reckon. In fact, this has made it worse.

By way of background, the royal family's crises have not been external for some time. It is not beset by marauding forces, or rival claimants to its throne, or parliamentarian revolt. All its greatest crises over the past few decades have come from within. These have been marital, financial, even clinical – and have just avoided being criminal. The royal family has proved to be its own worst enemy. The things that have happened have not happened *to* it, but *because* of it. The call's coming from inside the castle.

I've covered this particular Andrew story for well over a decade, and it hopefully goes without saying that the ex-prince is an utterly grim, utterly dim disgrace. But for my money, this latest Windsor crisis is the most dangerous variety yet for the crown: philosophical. Far from securing the monarchy's future, the de-princing of Mr Mountbatten Windsor has hastened its end, in the great scheme of things. Don't ask me to put a number of years on 'the great scheme of things'; all I can tell you is that it's a real rush writing a column that will be proved right or wrong only long after I'm dead. Tony Blair must feel like this every time he says history will judge him kindly for the Iraq war.

But look, here's the take: when there isn't a royal family any more, analysts will look back and see the unprecedented, enforced commoner-ing of Andrew as a key moment. Not *the* key moment – that was the abdication. Forgive me getting all *Stranger Things* on this story, but 1936 was the moment the Windsors opened the gate. Once they started suggesting that people could be fired from Earth's most committed non-meritocracy – unroyalled, as it were – then they played around fatally with the idea of royalty itself. Now you might well think that the idea of royalty itself is stupid, but it is what it is. They're not just another random rich family. They're supposed to be special and ethereal and not subject to personnel issues. There's no way in the world they should want to be stepping out of their realm – which is, quite literally, 'the realm' – and into the plebeian waters of appraisals and feedback and mandatory discrimination training and whatnot. Though all that would, as always, make a fun three-minute comedy sketch.

The most almighty number of shitbag relatives have been harboured by the British royal family down the centuries. Obviously, it was easier when you could just poison your errant brother or whatever, but for those who couldn't (most of them after the 17th century), you lived with it via exile and so on, because total de-royalling torpedoed the entire idea of what it was you were born into. The British dukes who had their titles removed for fighting for Germany in the first world war were distant foreign randos. Andrew remains eighth in line to the throne.

So, yes, the abdication was when the Windsors opened the gate. After that it was – and will be – whack-a-mole. Every crisis will draw out significant numbers of people who will ask why you couldn't cut off whoever was displeasing them in that moment. And why not? You got rid of one: the precedent is set. My theory is that the late Queen Elizabeth realised this, and consequently knew that to avoid making matters worse, she would have to work as queen till literally her dying day. Don't forget that for quite some time, people seriously suggested that the crown should skip the then unsatisfactory Charles and be passed straight to William. Don't forget that later on, people kept suggesting that Elizabeth abdicate in favour of Charles, having put in decades of exemplary service and being deserving of retirement, as though monarchy really were this ludicrous 'firm' they keep telling us it is.

But it isn't. It isn't a firm, or a small-to-medium enterprise, or a place where you pick and choose which family member gets the big jobs. They're not the flipping Murdochs. As far as the long-termist stewardship of the thing they are above all charged with protecting goes, I think that, philosophically speaking, you have to play the cards you're dealt. Now public opinion has managed to get the King to issue a P45 so close to home, it will be that much easier to call for the next personnel change. The King won't have too many more years in the managing director role. But William, that supposedly iron-fisted current HR director, is a very indifferently gifted individual who will probably prove to be overpromoted in the role of king. I wonder who or what he'll cancel under his strange, self-styled guise as protector of the mental health of the nation. I guess we'll find out.

For what infinitely negligible amount it's worth, I'm in favour of having a royal family, mainly because they're insanely good copy and arguably better than having Peter Mandelson or whoever as head of state. (I'm kidding: I understand third ways are available.) Given the sheer amount of merriment/discourse they generate, they add to the gaiety of the nation – certainly to the compulsive prurience. People love to love them or love to hate them. It seems to be a complete misery machine for those involved, and certainly not one that any of us ordinaries would in our right mind want our children to marry into. (I will never get over the Middleton parents' reported keenness for Kate to take a gap year so she could switch her university application to St Andrews, once it was confirmed Prince William would be attending – and all this after the cautionary story of Princess Diana had come to its awful end.)

Speaking of tragic stories, the law has decided Andrew can't be investigated further over the late Virginia Giuffre's allegations, with the FBI dropping its probe into him earlier this year. The King's statement on the de-princing appeared to hint that he doesn't entirely believe his brother's denials, so perhaps Charles's actions are a sort of synthesised justice, designed in part to show that no one is above the law. And yet, the royal family is above many laws – and this will only hasten the goodbye to all that.

Some PR advice for the Andrew-stricken royals: try something that looks less like a £12m cover-up

13 February 2026

A loan to keep the case out of court doesn't quite add up to 'thoughts and prayers to Epstein's victims'. Working with the police might be a start

'I could have worse tags than "Air Miles Andy",' the then Prince Andrew once reflected. 'Although I don't know what they are!' I think it's safe to say he does now.

Almost all senior members of the royal family are biologically capable of sweating, and what really brought them out in a cold one four years ago was the thought of this honking liability testifying in a

New York courtroom. So they paid millions upon millions to make sure it didn't happen. The late Virginia Giuffre's civil case alleging that the former prince abused her on three occasions in London, New York and the US Virgin Islands was never heard, because the late Queen seems to have decided that it shouldn't be, at almost any cost. (Andrew denied all claims of wrongdoing.) And yet, as many of us predicted at the time, this would never be the end of it, and the royal family are now playing a failing game of catch-up with the institution's own actions. Andrew's de-princing – an attempt to keep it all in-house – already hasn't worked.

The Windsors are incredibly tight with their own money and have spent generations indulging in arguments and internecine sulks about how it is spread around. Before the Duke and Duchess of Sussex stepped away from their roles, money rows were a big part of Harry's, but also William's, friction with their father. The idea that this bunch would reportedly fork out over £12m, plus seven figures' worth of Andrew's legal costs, without some fairly frank family discussions is just bollocks. Yet they clung to their public silence. They shielded Andrew from what lesser mortals would know as the consequences of their alleged actions. This is proving to be extremely consequential for them.

Whose were the millions? As of yesterday, the King is letting it be known via courtiers that he didn't chip in, with the money coming mostly from the late Queen and the estate of the Duke of Edinburgh. It is often assumed the late Queen paid from her secretive private funds, but others suggest it came from the Duchy of Lancaster, the earnings of which are public money. It would be good to know. In fact, it's one of many Andrew-related questions that senior royals would surely have got the answer to behind closed doors many, many years ago. It would be good to know, for instance, how come in 2007 a Kazakh oligarch paid our former trade envoy £3m more than the asking price for a mansion the late Queen had given Andrew as a wedding present – and an estimated

£7m more than the market value – and then was happy to let it go to ruin. Please don't tell me they never asked the question.

This week, the Windsors' approach to the gathering peril has shifted. Now, say Charles, William and Kate in statements issued on their behalf, the King and Queen 'stand ready to support [Thames Valley police] as you would expect', while the Waleses 'remain focused on the victims'.

And yet, some victims are very specifically asking the royal family to focus on how they could help in more active ways than thoughts and prayers. It would, for instance, be a lot more helpful if they focused on security logs at Buckingham Palace and Balmoral, as well as internal household emails, and all the other documentation that could be dredged up. A leaked email last year suggested that in 2011, Andrew had asked one of his taxpayer-funded royal protection officers to dig up dirt on Giuffre. The officer in question reportedly couldn't remember the events in question, and the Met closed its investigation into the matter. Have police ever even so much as spoken to Andrew about any aspect of this case? We don't know. We should.

The general approach of the monarchy and the establishment or whatever you want to call it has always been to imply that no one knows whether Andrew, who had 24-hour top-level protection, was where he said he was at any given time. But every now and then, someone refuses to play ball. Take the late Thomas Harris, former British consul general in New York, with whom Andrew claimed to have been staying in 2001, meaning he couldn't have had 'activity' with Giuffre at Epstein's Manhattan house. 'It doesn't sound like he stayed with me,' Harris stated in 2019, saying he had no recollection of the visit and it hadn't featured in the Court Circular, which would have been standard. What a puzzle. One for Buckingham Palace's remorselessly dogged internal affairs department, perhaps.

Andrew himself spent years playing a two-faced game, suggesting to Emily Maitlis that he'd certainly help US investigators with their Epstein inquiries, if asked. Yet soon after, the then US attorney for the southern district of New York stated for the record that Andrew had offered 'zero' cooperation up till that point. A few months later, the situation remained unchanged. 'If Prince Andrew is, in fact, serious about cooperating with the ongoing federal investigation,' the attorney declared, 'our doors remain open, and we await word of when we should expect him.'

The trouble comes when that two-faced game is perceived by the public to have spread to those at the top of the institution, who certainly have no part in the alleged crimes, but have not dispelled the increasingly noxious impression of the institution having been adjacent to a cover-up.

Statements this week indicate that senior royals are still playing this dangerous game of publicly really, really wanting to help, while not revealing anything useful of substance. No doubt they think this is the only game they can play. They are not brilliant strategists, but then the royal family is, somewhat famously, not a meritocracy that can promote the best and the brightest. They eventually worked out that doing nothing was not an option. I wonder how soon they'll clock that doing a bit less than nothing isn't either?

WAR AND PEACE IN 280 CHARACTERS

You hear a lot about 'the changing nature of warfare', but nothing brings it home quite so powerfully as Elon Musk tweeting out a Ukraine peace plan and turning off his Starlink system in the middle of a Ukrainian counteroffensive so that their drones fell out of the sky. No, wait: nothing brings it home like the United States' national security adviser accidentally adding a journalist to a *Real Housewives*-style group chat that also included the defence secretary and the vice president, in which live operational details of a US forces mission were shared, alongside punching-fist emojis and metaphorical drink tosses at the Europeans. Sorry, wait again: nothing brings it home like the US president using his private social media platform to share an AI-generated video of a swimming-trunked him and Benjamin Netanyahu sipping cocktails on sun loungers in a lavishly redeveloped 'Gaza riviera'. Actually, final answer: nothing brings it home like the US piggybacking on Israel's plan to bomb Iran, declaring the war had been 'won' on the first day – but also 'not won enough'. Despite all this, and very regrettably, the reality is that your tweets don't end wars, these guys do. Or, unfortunately, don't.

And then Elon Musk said there'll be no more war – not via his satellite. Aren't we lucky to have the world in his hands?

8 September 2023

The tech deity reportedly shut down his Starlink system to foil a Ukrainian attack. Is he the guiding force we need right now?

When Elon Musk posted a personally crafted 280-character 'peace plan' for the war in Ukraine last October, a Ukrainian diplomat offered a carefully considered review. It ran to a full two words: 'Fuck off.' This week's allegations that Musk shut down his Starlink system (on which the comms-shattered Ukraine relies to defend itself against Russia) right in the middle of a counteroffensive last year – apparently, deliberately to neuter it – forces a new question: when he does finally make it there in his big space rocket, will even Mars be far enough away for Musk to fuck off to?

For now, it's time to take another turn around the block with Phoney Stark, as Musk's biographer Walter Isaacson reveals that the edgelord magnate (and edgelord magnet) ordered his engineers to switch off the Starlink satellite communications network during a surprise attack on the Russian fleet in Crimea last year. Or to 'disrupt' the attack, as CNN puts it, still clinging embarrassingly to the preferred Silicon Valley argot that surely ought to have been discredited once its boy kings started becoming more powerful than many of the world's actual countries. I can't help feeling that the benefit-of-the-doubt era with these guys ought to have officially ended back when Y2K fashion was just fashion. Yet until very recently, Musk was still being breathlessly judged as a net good to humanity, what with his electric cars and his hyperloops and the fact that he once smoked a joint on a podcast. So! Very! Cool!

Elon was endlessly covered by the media as a kind of fascinating, eccentric inventor, as opposed to someone with a vast amount of power who should be held to account accordingly. Just as it was with Mark Zuckerberg before him, by the time people realised a lot of what was happening, it was rather too late.

Anyway, back to this strategic Starlink blackout, which was apparently prefaced by Elon wailing to his biographer: 'How am I in this war?' The question appears to have been rhetorical, but demands an alternative answer to the one towards which Musk was apparently gesturing. (He followed up by explaining that Starlink was 'so people can watch Netflix and chill and get online for school and do good peaceful things, not drone strikes'.) You're in this war because you're literally a defence contractor, just as you're in the news this week for demonising the Jewish Anti-Defamation League (ADL) because you're literally a media mogul. Man up.

Instead of accepting the complexities of the consequences of his own actions, Musk seems to have simply buzzed in on the answer to that age-old question: how can a just tech god permit suffering? The Ukrainian drones were thus stopped in their tracks, while the Russian fleet remained unharmed and able to launch future attacks itself. Musk himself returned to other based-deity pursuits, such as enabling the dissemination of Moscow's propaganda and Twitter-polling on what should happen to Ukraine. This last gambit fell squarely in the tradition of the Treaty of Versailles, of course, which famously asked Allied users whether Germany should be punished extra-hard and offered three options: 'Hell yeah,' 'Hell no' and 'I don't care – just show me the numbers.'

It's not that Musk doesn't have a consistent worldview so much as he doesn't even have consistency. Barely a week goes by without him making threats and failing to follow through. By now it should be clear that Musk isn't going to have a cage fight with Zuckerberg. He isn't going to sue the ADL. He probably wasn't even really going to buy X (formerly Twitter), and only ended up going through with it because the courts forced him to. He just says any old stuff for attention or a laugh or because he can. The key question is whether someone who just says any old stuff for attention or a laugh or because he can should have quite this much supra-democratic power.

Alas, this is not a question being asked by Elon's fanboys, that whole heaving army of betas out there defending him minute by minute on his own platform, in the hope that he sees their posts and perhaps . . . what? 'Likes' them? Oh, man. It's too poignant. Yet the second this latest story about the Starlink shutdown broke, you couldn't move on X for Muskovites suggesting that if Ukraine doesn't like the deal it signed up to, it can terminate its contract and sign up to another service. Please, let's put much, much more of our future security in the hands of people who treat war and the fallout from an unsolicited invasion like a broadband contract.

Ultimately, it remains one of the more pathetic tragedies of our age that Musk is seen as a superhero analogue – but perhaps also an inevitable one, given that superheroes connote institutional failure. After all, if society and its institutions were working as they should be, we wouldn't need them. This is certainly the mood that Musk likes to play into, forever fanning the sense that the world and its problems are too hard to manage for everyone, from ordinary people to police chiefs to politicians and supranational bodies. Only recently, he was speaking tellingly of himself as Earth's 'other option' to Mark Zuckerberg. Yes, have no fear, because Elon's here. Until – as the Ukrainians seem to have discovered at something of a crucial moment – he suddenly isn't.

Ah, here's Trump's peace plan for Ukraine – or rather, a plan to leave it in pieces

14 February 2025

And despite having ample time to prepare for this moment, why do Europe's and Britain's leaders seem so surprised?

In the wake of Donald Trump's decision to instigate his Ukraine 'peace plan', it's great to hear from US defence secretary Pete Hegseth that 'everything is on the table'. Also, would President Putin like to keep the table? I get the feeling that Hegseth would be very willing to throw in the table, which is likely to be hewn by Saudi craftsmen. That's not a bone-saw euphemism: Trump says the putative peace talks could be hosted by Crown Prince Mohammed bin Salman. For now, though, the world had to settle for Hegseth popping into a Nato defence ministers meeting in Brussels to announce: 'Make no mistake, President Trump will not allow anyone to turn Uncle Sam into Uncle Sucker.' So this week offered an opportunity to watch Eisenhower quotes get Disneyfied by a defence secretary with a Crusades tattoo. Good times!

Anyway: the peace plan. I expect this lesson is contained in Trump's seminal business text, *The Art of the Deal*, but one fairly reliable principle of negotiation is that if you say a number first, you end up negotiating down from it. If you get the other side to say a number first, you can negotiate up from that. For whatever reason, and supposedly before formal negotiations have even begun, Hegseth has already effectively surrendered most or all of the land taken by Russia since 2014, the possibility of Ukraine joining Nato and the threat of any future European security being guaranteed by the US. I image Vladimir Putin will simply accept the terms by pointing at him and saying, 'You're hired!'

This wasn't the exact way Hegseth billed it in his scene-stealing turn on the eve of the Munich security summit, going instead with the assertion that Trump will be 'the perfect dealmaker at the table'. As mentioned, the president's going to lose the table, but so what? Like he cares. Ever since he got much of a country to kayfabe that he won an election which he definitely lost, he must have known it would be a piece of piss to get them to agree that he had pulled off the most elegant peace treaty of all time. That, really, is the art of his deal. Also, he has bone spurs.

Other interested parties should be engaged in far deeper self-laceration. I kept reading and hearing yesterday about how European leaders were left 'in shock', 'reeling' and 'blindsided' by the US gambit, but . . . how? What did they think was going to happen? The signs have been spelled out for more than a year by Trump, who said he was going to end the Ukraine war on day one of his presidency, so if anything, he has been slow in pulling the rip cord. Furthermore, I wouldn't say Hegseth was hard to read. In fact, as indicated, you can quite literally read him. He has a US flag enmeshed with an assault rifle on his biceps, and a number of handy clues to his strategic thinking emblazoned, in writing, down both his forearms.

As far as mealy-mouthed statements you'd struggle to fit on a forearm go, hats off to the German foreign minister for responding to Trump's move on Thursday by declaring: 'It is now crucial for us Europeans to make it clear what is important for our own peace.' Now? Hate to be the bazillionth person to point it out, but 'now' feels a bit late for Europe to finally get its multiple-cheeked backside in gear on this front. Europe has spent years – diplomatic technicalese ahoy – dicking around and not acting to prepare for the possibility of the US withdrawing support.

Shortly after Putin invaded Ukraine three years ago, EU leaders met at Versailles. You would think that this particular location would be sufficient to crystallise the minds of those present in a spirit of 'Let's not cock this one up'. And yet. No one could have accused what emerged from Versailles *that* time round of going too far. Despite the French president, Emmanuel Macron, announcing that while Versailles 1919 divided Europe, Versailles 2022 was bringing it together, that couldn't meaningfully have been said to be the case. Instead, and unsurprisingly, the declaration that emerged from that meeting found Europe retreating into its happy place of fine words and forever consultations.

And here we all are. Nobody but the US administration and Putin is in their happy place, with Ukraine in the unhappiest place of all. Asked whether it was equal partners with Russia in these high-handed negotiations over its own future, Trump replied: 'Hmm, that's an interesting question.' Which I guess is your answer. Not only is Ukraine not in the driving seat, as various people keep mildly observing, but it may well not even be in the car, condemned at best to run along after it, and at worst to be run over by it.

In terms of where the UK stands in all of this, the answer increasingly feels like 'nowhere particularly'. This morning, Keir Starmer was assuring Ukraine's president by phone that his country was on 'an irreversible path' to Nato membership. Hmm. Meanwhile, Hegseth was on the ground in big-spending Poland, saluting it as 'the model ally'. The UK's ego has long been writing cheques its body can't cash – and certainly that its chancellor refuses to cash. Starmer looks about as likely to make the cut of a modern-day Yalta photo with Trump and Putin as he is to be revealed as Dressed Crab on *The Masked Singer*. As for Trump, he's never going to get a tattoo. But if he did, it should read: 'APRÈS MOI, LE DÉLUGE'.

It's war and peace with Donald and Pete – and the worst group chat the world has ever seen

25 March 2025

We absolutely won't tolerate leaks, they said, before looping in a journalist to top secret war plans. Feel safe? Me neither

Once again, we find ourselves having an anguished debate about mobile phones and online safety, in this case asking: should we ban the devices for US national security advisers under the age of 60? Do you know what your national security adviser is doing on his device? Is he using it to stay in touch with other guys in the big-man-osphere to talk about bombing Hooters? Or did he maybe add the editor-in-chief of a leading general interest magazine to a Signal group in the crucial period running up to a highly sensitive US military operation in Yemen, seemingly committing so many alleged crimes that he should have a full-body orange jumpsuit tattooed on him for ever?

By now, you will have caught up with the tale of one of the most idiotic breaches of security imaginable, seemingly executed, regrettably, by the actual US national security adviser. Mike Waltz seems to have been aided and abetted in his full-spectrum fatuity by other ultra-senior figures, including the vice president, JD Vance, and the defence secretary, Pete Hegseth, who shared detailed operational and strategic information in a chat to which *Atlantic* editor Jeffrey Goldberg had been accidentally invited. Is Hegseth OK? Has he returned to being – how to put this delicately? – someone you probably don't want to give important tasks to 'after lunch'?

On another tangent, meanwhile, was there some extremely senior military or government official with either the first name

Jeffrey or the second name Goldberg whom Waltz actually meant to add? And did that intended Jeffrey or Goldberg wake up the next day, see the Yemen news and feel a deeply wounded sense of Fomo? 'Wait, you guys bombed Yemen without me? I hate you ALL. I demand you put me in the group chat NOW, just so I can immediately flounce off and leave the group chat.'

The breach exposes so many things that it is difficult to know where to start. It certainly highlights the almost immeasurably rich lexicon of emojis. You realise that a certain type of guy deploys the same three emojis for taking out a Houthi target as they would if Bryson DeChambeau nailed a slightly tricky putt on the 14th at the West Palm Beach Pro-Am. Punching fist, USA flag, flames emoji. Let's GO, Bryson!

That said, the emojis are obviously the best of it. Less easy to scroll past is the bit where Vance, or his proxy, says: 'I just hate bailing out Europe again.' Then Hegseth replies: 'I fully share your loathing of European freeloading. It's PATHETIC.' Mmm. Three weeks ago, we had Vance offering a blanket disparagement of European forces as 'some random country that hasn't fought a war in 30 or 40 years'. Now we have this Signal chat – yet another sweet memorial to all the European service personnel who gave their lives in the US Republican party's endlessly stupid 9/11 wars. We never asked to be reimbursed for that military assistance – very BAD! very Wrong! – and are now repeatedly hearing that it meant nothing to Marine-adjacent shutterbug Vance, who remains the most unbearably loud and rude American at the luxury hotel breakfast. They really should make a darkly satirical TV show about these absurd, degenerate, unpleasant people. Call it *The White Potus*.

Needless to say, the first instinct of the Trump administration has been to insult the journalist, when in less responsible hands than Goldberg's this could have been catastrophically endangering information for the US service personnel and intelligence operatives involved. At the time of writing, Hegseth's sole comment on the bed he and the guys just shat involved attacking the man to whom they personally served this scoop, calling Goldberg 'a deceitful and highly discredited so-called journalist'. Is he, though? Come on, Pete! Given the same information in real time, your boy Joe Rogan would have livestreamed it, and you know it. At least Donald Trump would have been up to speed with it that way. 'I don't know anything about it,' was the president's sleepy verdict yesterday, a day he spent wetting his pants about some oil painting of him hanging somewhere in the Colorado state legislature.

As for consequences, do please remember that we are dealing with the biggest hypocrites on the planet. Consider their own thunderous statements on infosec. Here is the chief Pentagon spokesman, Sean Parnell, just last week: 'If you have a private that loses a sensitive item, that loses night vision goggles, that loses a weapon, you can bet that that private is going to be held accountable. The same and equal standards must apply to senior military leaders.' Also last week, here is Trump's director of national intelligence, Tulsi Gabbard: 'Any unauthorised release of classified information is a violation of the law and will be treated as such.' Was Tulsi on the Signal chat? Course she was! If you still want more, here's Hegseth mining the seemingly endless potential of Hillary Clinton's careless use of a private server for classified information back when he was a Fox News host: 'If it was anyone other than Hillary Clinton, they would be in jail right now.' 'When I'm president of the United States, neither she nor any of these other people are going to be above the law,' was the previous verdict of one Marco Rubio, last seen on the Houthi chat appearing in the role of secretary of state of the United States.

We'll have to wait and see if these clowns will hold themselves to their own very high standards. In the meantime, please enjoy European diplomats declaring that as far as the relationship between the continent and the US goes, this is 'the writing on the wall'. If only it HAD been written on a wall – that would actually have been more secure and secretive. Come to that, it would genuinely have been more secure and secretive to hire a skywriting plane. Great job, guys! Punching fist, USA flag, flames emoji, etc.

Hurry, hurry, hurry! It's Trump's great Ukraine giveaway. Bargains galore, if your name is Vladimir Putin

12 August 2025

The Art of the Deal, The Art of War*: I doubt the US president has read or understood either. If Zelenskyy is a worried man, who can blame him?*

Good to have it confirmed that Donald Trump and Vladimir Putin will be talking about Ukraine behind its back on Friday in Alaska, as the US president rambled through a press conference on Monday in which he explained that Putin 'wasn't going to mess with me' and that Ukraine was going to have to accept new borders. And listen, you'll agree that territorial pronouncements mean so much more coming from a guy whose staff once shamelessly redrew a hurricane impact map to stop him looking stoopid. It's a true honour for the Ukrainians to see their country effectively carved up by someone who would prefer to post-rationalise any old crap with a Sharpie than admit he doesn't have the first clue about it and cares even less.

Leave it to the tasteful visionary behind the Gaza Riviera to categorise what he's doing as trying to get back some of Ukraine's 'oceanfront property'. 'In real estate we call it oceanfront property,' Trump said on Monday, demystifying this term of high art for non-developers who haven't contrived to bankrupt several

Atlantic City casinos. 'That's always the most valuable property.' Thanks, Mister Mogul! It is assumed that the stretch of high-end primo coastline Trump was referring to included Mariupol, the utterly ruined port in which many thousands of civilians perished during the Russian siege. In international law we call it a possible war crime; in real estate we call it . . . what? Strategic pre-construction? Spa-chitecture?

Certainly, how we put things is a matter of concern to this supremely sensitive president, who can find words very hurty, particularly when allied to optional concepts such as truth or the law. 'I was a little bothered by the fact Zelenskyy was saying, "I have to get constitutional approval,"' he whined on Monday of the Ukrainian leader's desire to put any peace deal to the Ukrainian people via a referendum. 'He's got approval to go into war and kill everybody?' Again, whether Ukraine 'go[ing] into war' is a fair categorisation of its being invaded by Russia is not something that bothers the Sharpie king of the White House.

As for the precise nature of the forthcoming cartography, Trump spent quite a lot of time talking suspiciously nebulously about 'land swapping'. Can you swap things on behalf of someone who doesn't want to swap them, and without them being present at the table? If so, I would like someone to swap me one of Trump's second-tier golf courses, and would expect him to be very relaxed about it. He'll just have to take my word that it's in the wider interests of everybody.

In terms of what he deems to be the interests of interested parties, there has been a strong suggestion in recent days that the Trump administration thinks it would be a win for Ukraine to abandon the bits of the Donetsk and Luhansk regions that are not even occupied by Russia, with only a ceasefire and the promise of some future better deal to show for it. Which would certainly be the absolute wrongest reading of a land deal since the *New York Tribune* called the Alaska purchase a folly and a waste of money.

In fact, it would explain Putin's willingness to travel to that very territory to hold Friday's peace talks instead of doing it on neutral turf: you can probably afford to concede on the meeting's location if everything else is likely to be such a complete gift to you. The Russian president might even bring along another hideously flattering portrait of Trump as an ice-breaking present, having already commissioned one as a personal gift earlier this year, which was passed on to Trump via his special envoy, Steve Witkoff. Witkoff said it was a 'beautiful portrait' and that the president was 'clearly touched by it'.

And so to the buildup to Friday. We'll have to see how excited Trump gets about the chance to join some sort of German-organised conference call with European leaders on Wednesday. For the US president, the negotiating table is a place that seats only two people, one of which should always be him. For Putin, many fear through bitter experience, the negotiating table is a place where you simply obfuscate and buy time to regroup before renewing your aggression. Rather like Holly Golightly at the window of Tiffany's, nothing very bad can happen to Putin in Alaska. Merely turning up avoids the threatened sanctions. If, as seems likely, Trump decides he should be appeased with some land, any Ukrainian refusal to rubber-stamp this would leave the US president frustrated with, and lashing out at, Zelenskyy, not Putin. (Give the orange guy his peace deal and then his peace prize, dammit! He's getting bored out here.) And if a ceasefire is somehow agreed, it would surely, on the form book, be regarded by Putin merely as a strategic buying of time. The Russian leader is obsessed with Ukraine in a way the Trump administration seems incapable of, or indifferent to, grasping.

Look, maybe geopolitics really will turn out to be just a simpler version of commercial real estate. Maybe someone who has lost almost as many fortunes as he has gained in that particular trade really will turn out to be a maverick master who refreshes the parts traditional diplomacy can't reach. Maybe! But the sheer lack of jeopardy for Putin in Alaska feels far more significant than the mood music. The best-case scenario is that Europe and Ukraine prepare themselves for the artlessness of the deal. The worst-case scenario is a darker pathway altogether – and one we seem increasingly likely to stumble on to.

Boycott the banquet, send a tweet. But ending the horror in Gaza still relies on the worst people in the world

29 August 2025

This humanitarian catastrophe is barely of passing interest to Donald Trump. The curse of our times is how little we can do about it

Day 222 of Donald Trump's presidency, and Russia's war in Ukraine, which he promised to end on day one, shows no sign of having got the memo. This was not a single-use Trump promise; he made it at least 53 times. Yet the US president has failed to keep it, either literally or in his favourite manner, figuratively. Can you figuratively end a war? Not even, apparently.

What his most recent round of failure means, however, is that Trump is pivoting back to another war, the grotesquely horrifying and unlawful humanitarian catastrophe unfolding in Gaza. Not the way he'd phrase it, possibly. This week he swerved commenting on either Israel's invasion of Gaza City or the mounting declarations that famine and starvation are clearly under way in the territory, and instead announced: 'I think within the next two, three weeks, you're going to have a pretty good, conclusive ending.' Righto. Trump's recipe for an ending to the horror has hitherto seemed to resemble the famous business plan of the *South*

Park gnomes. Phase 1: Collect underpants. Phase 2: ? Phase 3: Profit.

In the US president's version, this runs along the following lines: Phase 1: Grotesquely horrifying and unlawful humanitarian catastrophe. Phase 2: ? Phase 3: Beach resort. Strange to look at the Yalta conference photo of Churchill, Stalin and Roosevelt and think how much more quickly the three Allied wartime leaders could have wrapped things up, had they shunned various complexities and understood the world as a simple selection of waterfront real-estate opportunities. And yet, perhaps even stranger to imagine that while we don't have a group selfie of Donald Trump, Vladimir Putin and Benjamin Netanyahu, the curse of our times is that the fate of so many appallingly desperate and persecuted people in the world hinges on three men who might well be imagined to be in jail were they not in office.

But these are the realities. The path to peace in Gaza runs through Trump, not social media posts, or window flags, or creatives 'using their platform', or any of the other gestures that, while the wishful might cast them as speaking truth to power, in fact only throw our era's increasingly pervasive sense of powerlessness into even sharper relief.

Nor, in any non-gnome sense, does it run anywhere near Ed Davey's announcement this week that after much thought and prayer, he would not be attending the King's banquet for Trump during his forthcoming state visit. It goes without saying that Trump wouldn't have the first clue who the Liberal Democrat leader is. (More pressingly for Davey, and perhaps more in his power to do something about, is the polling this week that showed that 35% of his own Lib Dem voters also haven't the first clue who he is when shown a photo of him.) But Davey believes boycotting dinner is the best way he can 'send a message to both Trump and Starmer' that they cannot wish the catastrophe unfolding in Gaza away. He means well, yet this gesture still feels one rung above a tweet – or, indeed, a *Guardian* newspaper column, which is how he announced it. Regrettably, neither of the above are levers in international conflict.

Being unable to plot a path to answers means a question dominates our turbulent age: is being well-meaning enough? Is it, in fact, all I can be? Have I acquitted my responsibilities in the face of historic horror by posting about it, or attacking someone else for not posting about it, or by suggesting that someone cannot care about any subject on which they have not done a post? Perhaps it's nice to think so, but I fear that far from being the most engaged, those who live like this are the most beaten. Some of the worst people in the world – at least, some of the worst people without access to state armies – run the social media companies, and the idea that spending comfortable hours policing their platforms, working for them for free, is taking a stand or showing you care in any useful way tips beyond bizarre into cultural sickness.

Social media claims to connect and empower people – a populist promise if ever you heard one – and yet what many of us hear our friends and family say all the time in conversations about the news is that they feel powerless. People have been atomised and narcotised by this supposedly unifying and uplifting technology, and when the great perspective of history is afforded to our descendants and perhaps even our future selves, we might well find that most of our present crises were catalysed by it rather than cured. This morning, I saw a much-shared cut-out of Travis Kelce kissing Taylor Swift in their engagement photo superimposed on top of a war-demolished building, above a bell hooks quote: 'All our silences in the face of racist assault are acts of complicity.' Dear me. Stick it in a time capsule, along with an apology note for the cultural rubble it'll have to be dug out of.

At operational level, however, things don't change. The path to peace still goes through politicians with power. Many of them are still terrible people. They will still have to have unpleasant and even 'toxic' conversations in which horse-trading and moral compromise are inevitable. And yet these things are still desirable, because this is the way it has always ended. This is the way the bombs go silent, the way the children stop starving, the way the hideous carnage ends. It is a long, perilous and precarious path, but history has made it familiar, because it is the only one that actually gets anywhere near where we need to go.

To anyone who thinks Trump can bring peace and equality to Iran, I've got a bridge to sell you. Going cheap

3 March 2026

If POTUS can really bomb peace, stability and women's rights into the Middle East, I'll take my hat off to him. Judging by his role in Gaza, I won't hold my breath

Donald Trump says Keir Starmer has damaged the special relationship by not helping him more in the US–Israel war on Iran. But you have to remember that when you do help, Trump pretends you didn't anyway, and also pisses on your war dead. Still, what could be more enticing than the Americans trying to sell you a timeshare on a war in the Middle East?

And so to Iran. 'War is the realm of uncertainty,' said Carl von Clausewitz, who – and not to be a bitch – I still think of as a more impressive military theorist than Pete Hegseth. Certainly, Carl had fewer Crusades tattoos than the US defence secretary. Hegseth is 100% certain about all his nailed-down positions, even the ones in apparent conflict with each other. And it feels like a great sign that he, Marco Rubio and JD Vance already seem to have different rationales for why this war was launched. This is an administration that came to power on an explicit 'no more wars' ticket – but look, as Pete keeps saying, this isn't a regime-change war. If that seems confusing, given he first said it about 10 minutes after US–Israeli strikes had cratered the ayatollah's compound, Hegseth has since been on hand to scoff that what's going down in Iran is 'no nation-building quagmire, no democracy-building exercise'.

Of course not! Trump and his guys don't even love democracy in their own country, so they're not exactly going to want it for one of the so-called 'shithole' countries. Too many moving parts. Think of this as a regime-refresh war. You're still not going to be able to spell the difference between ayatollahs, but ideally, the new guy will have more of a Venezuelan-puppet feel to him. I don't know about 'women' and 'freedom' and stuff, but I can guess that Hegseth would be extremely relaxed about them being in the old TBC file.

Alas, so stupid and binary has the standard of debate become that anyone even writing about the subject (the most irrelevant act in the world – sorry, fellow columnists) has to preface it by saying, 'Of course I believe in freedom and women's rights,' for fear of being jumped on by guys who *six calendar weeks ago* were righteously furious about Trump's threat to annex Greenland but now think he's Boudicca. Wake up. How many times do you have to get hurt by this wingnut before you start thinking yourself into positions where, actually, his way might not be the answer? More times than we're up to, apparently. I know they think this is realpolitik. But it's not. It's just real forgetful politik. There is a certain strand of our muscular politician/pundit class that actually just resembles the friend you sit in a bar with every few weeks as she explains why the latest dumping hasn't held. 'No, but he's changed. This time, he has. I really believe it. He even paid me back the money he owes me. Well, he says he's going to.'

For crystal clarity, the last ayatollah was scum, and I'll loathe his successor, too. I truly wish the Iranian people had freedom, most especially the women and girls who live under the most wicked oppression of all, and I cheer their every uprising. But to be clear-eyed about the region for two minutes, there isn't a single democracy in the Gulf, and that's the realest of the realpolitik. Furthermore, Trump lies or dissembles about absolutely everything. If he really can permanently end Iran's nuclear programme (a few months ago, he said he already had), stop Tehran funding all its revolting terrorist proxies and bring about favourable regime change in what he's said will be about 'four weeks or less', then great. But realistically, what's the betting? It is massively more likely that fog and unpredictable consequences ensue. Already in the post are the years – decades – of unintended consequences that will flow from his backing for the razing of Gaza.

Meanwhile, it's quite something to think that bombing Iran might turn out to be not even the most significant US military decision of the past five days. Consider the news that the defence department – sorry, department of war – has dramatically terminated its contract with AI firm Anthropic, after the latter refused to loosen its ethical guidelines. These prevented the use of Anthropic technology for things like mass domestic surveillance, but also for autonomous lethal weapons (that is, no humans in the loop). The Trump administration wanted this amended, and when Anthropic wouldn't do it, they binned them off, threatened madly punitive sanctions – and seem to have found an alternative provider. It is, of course, our old friend Sam Altman at OpenAI, who initially said his deal had the same red lines as Anthropic's. So why did the Pentagon threaten to destroy Anthropic if the OpenAI deal had the same guardrails? Perhaps because it has since emerged that it likely hasn't. As always with Altman, things aren't quite what they seem – and by the time you find out what they are, it's always just that bit too late. Bad with chatbots, arguably a little worse with murderbots.

Rather than getting any kind of handle on this unknowably dangerous, civilisation-altering technology, perhaps it's inevitable that

Trump should revert to something very 1.0 and bomb the Middle East. For a no-more-wars guy, his entire MO has been taking things that were once priced in and throwing them up into the air.

So there is a counterpoint to the idea that he is resetting the world in a positive way. Namely, that the most serious damage to our way of life – yes, our selfish western way of life – is being done by a certain Donald Trump. As I said, leave aside democracy in the Middle East, where it barely exists; does he truly care about it in the US, where it is under demonstrable threat by him and his proxies? Isn't he letting AI get out of control and into the most dangerous places before our very eyes? Has he not abandoned the notion that leadership is built on any kind of moral code, lying daily to his people and the world without a second thought? Has he not repeatedly undermined trust among his own international allies? Has an American president ever personally enriched himself so nakedly and so eye-wateringly while in office? When he leaves that office, gracefully and smoothly or otherwise, will the world be safer and more widely prosperous than when he found it? He can talk all he likes about our way of life. Like the call in a horror movie, the threat's coming from inside the house.

Britain's war hawks are very upset that Keir Starmer isn't personally riding a bomb all the way to Tehran

6 March 2026

Didn't you know? True British patriots are the ones who want to join an obviously disastrous war on behalf of Israel and Donald Trump

Have you heard enough pant-wetting about Britain's 'reputation' this week? Honestly, I don't think any of us can bear the social embarrassment of not getting immediately involved in an obviously disastrous war in the Middle East. The awks of it. How will good old Britannia hold her head up high if she isn't an instant ride-or-die for a US administration described by a former senior Nato commander as 'gung-ho nutters' with 'no clear understanding of how this thing is going to end'? You should be simply unable to stand it. You should have Middle East-catastrophe Fomo.

Opposition party politicians seem genuinely excruciated by the fact that Earth's pettiest man, Donald Trump, sniffed earlier this week of Keir Starmer: 'This is not Winston Churchill we're dealing with.' Boo-hoo for you, pal. We're having to deal with the Cheeto FDR, so everyone's making sacrifices.

It's often said that most things in Britain are about class, so maybe the Westminster meltdown about having at first declined our Paperless Post invitation to a war is the geopolitical version of worrying you're not keeping up with the Joneses. The Joneses in this case being a career vulgarian who addresses his nation in a baseball cap and whose defence secretary talks like a third-string capo in an AI mafia gif and is tattooed like a prison school desk.

Either way, it's interesting to find politicians going so hard on the if-you're-not-with-us-you're-against-us stuff. This is very much not the view of the people, with polls showing UK citizens opposed to US–Israeli attacks on Iran by 49% to 28%. Pressed on this data indicating that wedged halfway up Trump's colon is not actually where the British public wants to be, Nigel Farage told reporters curtly: 'I don't follow public opinion.' Weird, because the Reform UK leader has spent his entire career honking that politicians should listen to public opinion. And, indeed, has spent the past year explicitly making a case for him sweeping to power on precisely the basis that he listens to ordinary people. Maybe we are entering a new 'the voters are stupid' period, only instead of being in favour of Nigel's Brexit getting you called stupid, it's not being in favour of his American mate's dumb war.

Incidentally, the aforementioned 'gung-ho nutters' diatribe came courtesy of former general and Nato commander Richard Shirreff, whose operational experience of wars (Middle Eastern and otherwise) should arguably carry greater weight than the posturing of 20th-century commodities trader Nigel Farage, a man who would undoubtedly let down his country just to not get disinvited to his scheduled dinner with Trump at Mar-a-Lago tonight. A burnt steak, a burnt steak! His kingdom for a burnt steak.

Meanwhile, Kemi Badenoch's entire demeanour since the war was launched has been that of a teenager who discovered via social media that some of her friends got together without her at the weekend and vaporised an ayatollah. Thursday found the Conservative party leader really drilling down on the nation's most sensitive nerve, declaring: 'It's extraordinary that Bahrain and Kuwait . . . are publicly criticising us.' Criticised by Bahrain? Oh, the shame. This feeling we're having must be the same sort of awkwardness Bahrain feels when people remember they arbitrarily lock up dissidents and torture their own people. And that they are not a democracy.

Badenoch seems worried that in the rooms where it happens, all British politicians are somehow tainted by association with what she is hellbent on everyone seeing as Starmer's shame. But Kemi should, of course, be assured that the occupants of these rooms have never even heard of her, and that she will be out of a job long before they reach the advanced stage where their protocol aides have to make a call on how to correctly pronounce her surname.

As for the various available definitions of weakness this week . . . The following analogy gives the attacks on the UK a nuance and depth they have yet to achieve, but they're basically the equivalent of your child coming home from school and explaining they got involved in some stupid, dangerous trouble because some other kid told them to. Instead of deploying Correct Parenting 101 and going, 'Oh my God, and would you jump off a cliff if he told you to?!' a significant number of Britain's politicians and punditry class are now suggesting that the notional parent in this analogy should have said: 'Good boy – literally nothing is more important than your reputation in the playground. And if he tells you to jump off a cliff, you go for it.'

That said, I understand why some of our politicians thought there was a lapdog vacancy. You always need one lapdog in a madly destabilising Middle Eastern war, and historically it's been us. But this time it's Trump, whose secretary of state, Marco Rubio, let slip this week that the US tagged along with the bombing because Israel told them they were doing it anyway. Rubio making this on-camera boo-boo was just another ludicrous wartime vignette, in a week in which they have not exactly been in short supply.

Take Thursday in the Oval Office. If you haven't seen the pictures, please take a moment to zero in on Lionel Messi's million-yard stare as he realises he and the rest of the Inter Miami squad are merely the meat backdrop for a war update. Or take Trump's suggestion that he must be involved in picking Iran's next supreme leader, dismissing the proposed nepo-ayatollah as 'a lightweight'. So . . . he'd like a really heavyweight ayatollah instead? Please don't try to make sense of the president's endlessly spasming war aims; just let them wash over you like an extremely volatile liquid and hope no one brought a match.

Finally, Trump is demanding that Israel grant an immediate pardon for his mission boss, Benjamin Netanyahu, which suggests there might have been an infinitely more elegant and infinitely less bloody solution to this. Alas, none of us has a time machine to go back a few weeks, but maybe using every pressure to simply secure Bibi the pardon *before* he felt the need to launch this war would have been the more reasonably priced move. Not to call it too soon, but at this stage in the Israeli prime minister's martial journey, many observers do have the sneaking suspicion that Netanyahu will keep on finding wars he has to attend to, just to defer the day when he gets booted out of office and has to face trial for his allegedly corrupt actions.

Could we all not just have a whip-round and buy him a $200m house, with a $1bn cheque in it, and promise to guard it in perpetuity, just as long as he gives up his absolute favourite hobby? At this rate, it'll be unbelievably cheap at the price.

WHEN CELEBRITIES DO POLITICS (WHETHER THEY MEAN TO OR NOT)

The great celebrity biathlon of our times is to be both a defining figure in entertainment culture and the winner of a medal in the culture wars. Sometimes, a warrior like Sydney Sweeney is conscripted without her consent, forced to accept that her lucrative and hot jeans advert can only – only! – be read as a eugenicist's charter. Other times, a warrior like The Rock is forced to claim – unprompted – that he had previously been approached to run for president by both the Democrats and the Republicans, while the vast cavalcade of stars who came out for Kamala Harris are more likely to pass through the eye of a needle than accept that they might just have been part of the problem. And the sea change on woke left celebrities all at sea, with stars used to telling people what to think suddenly unclear which side of history was now the most professionally beneficial.

Can you smell what The Rock is cooking? Could it be the most surreal presidential bid yet?

2 April 2024

He's never wanted to be in politics, you know, but if the people keep asking, he might just have to become America's Final Boss

Where do you stand on The Rock? A question to which the answer can only be: 'Please, not on his face!' Wrestler, movie star, high-intensity interval philosopher, skincare entrepreneur, self-styled future presidential candidate . . . Personally, I believe that Mr Dwayne Johnson is a net hilarity for humanity, though the idea he could ever truly limit himself to enriching the lives of only one species – or, indeed, only one planet – feels profoundly suspect.

Last week, The Rock graced Fox News with a lengthy interview, in which he announced he will be withholding his wildly coveted endorsement in the forthcoming US presidential election, having given it to Joe Biden last time. The reason? The Rock believes that very endorsement – his specifically – 'caused an incredible amount of division in our country'. Evidently, The Rock judges himself a mega-market-mover in terms of American discord, so this time he is declaring support for neither Biden nor Donald Trump. Quite a statement from a guy who 100% seems the type to have a tattoo of the words 'If you choose not to decide, you have still made a choice.' Obviously, not in English; in either Sanskrit, Latin or Hindi, curling round some sort of calf muscle called a trizeltoid or something that he's got a cool abbreviation for. #trizos #gainzneversleepz #warriorpoet

Anyway: the path to the Oval Office. The Rock assures the public that 'My goal is to bring our country together.' As indicated, I yield to no one who says that contemporary America cannot be swiftly depolarised by men's grooming products, somewhat faltering action movies and a board seat on the company that just sold the rights to WWE's *Monday Night Raw* to Netflix for $5bn. Even so, could it be The Rock has more conventional plans for how to unify that great nation and is making his much-touted political move (call it the Heartland Chokehold, even though that sounds like what happens to troubled interns who sleep with their congressmen and think it's something more)? Could Johnson be offering citizens of the US the chance to have him as their Final Boss?

And could he even be staking out a pitch? After all, in the wide-ranging sit-down with Fox, he also attacked 'woke culture', a development that some may judge reveals the direction this is all going in. That doesn't mean he's specifically picking a side. Although listen: the Democrats and Republicans have apparently both asked him before. Last year, The Rock claimed that in late 2022, 'I got a visit from the parties asking me if I was going to run, and if I could run.' Mmm. This is for president, supposedly – and honestly, given who the American electorate has voted for and may yet vote for again, could you even call it a comedy pick? Surely once they elected Trump to the White House, it permanently demeaned the office – a bit like when Jinder Mahal became WWE champion after pinning Randy Orton at Backlash 2017. Although obviously not as bad.

As for The Rock, he also uses the Fox interview to insist that 'My goal has never been to be in politics.' Really? That seems odd, given the sheer volume of interviews in which he is on record as saying stuff like the fact that running for president is 'a realistic consideration', 'alluring' and 'if it ever happens, it'd be my honour to serve'.

I get the feeling the honour would be all ours, from day one, when Dwayne would ditch the famous Resolute desk and replace it with what he calls 'my GSD (Get Shit Done) table that's inside my trailer'. According to The Rock, this is where 'many productive meetings and big business deals have been sealed', and the table 'holds a lot of great mana (spirit/power) and energy'. In fact, it was probably at that very table that he sat down during the filming of *Fast and Furious 8* and called his co-stars 'candy asses'. Yup, this is a guy who's not afraid to go tit-to-tit with Vin Diesel (real name: Mark Sinclair) – and more importantly, not afraid to obliquely tell the world about it in a swiftly deleted social media post. 'When you watch this movie next April,' The Rock explained back then, 'and it seems like I'm not acting in some of these scenes and my blood is legit boiling – you're right.'

Ooh! Funnily enough he was saying something very similar recently, when he followed a WWE opponent out to the car park for afters. 'I can't shut my high emotions off just because a script says we're done,' claimed The Rock, even though he can. 'But . . . this is a microcosm of a larger issue I have with individuals, corporations and governments – telling us what we can or can't do. You have to do it this way, you have to say it that way, or you'll get cancelled . . . Fuck that. I say it the way I want to say it.' Totally. And you know, without having to bring it back to his most recent tag team result, he and Roman Reigns did win against Cody Rhodes and Seth Rollins last weekend. The guy is 51. How does he do it?

No, but I mean, how does he do it in a way that can be discussed in a newspaper? Over to The Rock! 'Pushing myself physically, mentally and psychologically to places I've never gone . . . Honoured to share the ring, go to war in our squared circle and entrain the fans . . . *Audaces Fortuna Iuvat*.' And if those last three words sound to you like some kind of herbal supplement to which you could never get access, I am blown away to tell you that they are indeed Latin. Fortune DOES favour the brave – though whether the American electoral system does remains as yet tantalisingly unclear.

To the stars vowing to flee Trump's America: maybe your excruciating endorsements were part of the problem

15 November 2024

The cringeworthy campaign for Harris made it clear: voters aren't simply going to do what mega-rich celebrities tell them to

I wish celebrities would learn the art of the French exit. But they can't, which is why Eva Longoria has announced she no longer lives in America. 'I get to escape and go somewhere,' she explained. 'Most Americans aren't so lucky – they're going to be stuck in this dystopian country.' What's brought this on, apart from the obvious? 'Whether it's the homelessness or the taxes . . . it just feels like this chapter in my life is done now.' Great to learn that Eva dislikes both homelessness and taxes. America's loss of this major political thinker is some other country's gain – and this highly called-for intervention reminds us why celebrities should speak their brains even more often. If only into a pillow, or an abyss.

As always in these moments of the silly voters making a silly mistake, many stars have pledged to follow her. We'll see. Either way, celebrities seem totally unaware that these high-handed statements of first-class migration are not the admonishment to the lesser orders that they are meant to be, and may even encourage them. But then, stars have always been totally unaware of how very little they bring to this particular party. The last few days of the Harris campaign were an increasingly excruciating riot of celebrity bandwagonning. Did the Kamala campaign ask man-born-in-Pennsylvania Richard Gere to make his video for her, or did the actor freelance one out of fear of not having 'used his platform'? It was certainly Richard's most critically misunderstood electoral outing since his address to the Palestinians before their 2005 elections. 'Hi, I'm Richard Gere,' that one began, 'and I'm speaking for the entire world . . .'

If anything good were to come out of the wreckage of the Harris campaign, let it be the final death of the idea that showbiz endorsements can help swing elections. They can't. Not one bit. Not even if it's Taylor Swift in the 2024 US presidential election, not even when it was Russell Brand in the 2015 British general election, and not even if they have tens of millions of followers. (It does move the dial, however, if you own the platform.) Election issues and politicians swing elections.

The minuscule amount of positive data we have on celebrity endorsements suggests they might have some effect in getting their fans to register to vote and volunteer for campaigns. I suspect these days that is more than offset by the perception of elitism that actively harmed the Harris campaign and others before it. If anything could turn you hard Maga, it's watching Lady Gaga sing 'Edge of Glory' at Kamala's eve-of-polling-day concert – the worst thing she's been in since *Joker II* – and then discovering that Oprah, who also appeared, had billed the Harris campaign $1m via her company. This week, Winfrey insisted she wasn't paid personally, with the Harris campaign simply required to pay for 'production costs' on an earlier 'townhall' featuring her, Meryl Streep, Julia Roberts, Ben Stiller, Chris Rock and Jennifer Lopez. Hmm. If only there was some billionaire – but the good kind! – or even just some mega-rich folk involved in said event who could perhaps have picked up the wage bill herself/themselves, rather than siphon it off the campaign.

Meanwhile, it is easier to leave Twitter than America, as I think Marcus Aurelius once remarked. In the week the *Guardian* exited X – though not in the French style – you couldn't move for people informing you they were herding with almost impossible dignity over to Bluesky. And it does feel slightly hilarious that huge numbers of people who have spent the past decade-plus shrieking about the evils of social media – usually on social media – have been 'liberated' from one platform, only to promptly rush and enslave themselves to another. Really? You can see it all stretching ahead of you: fun period, emergence of Blueskyocracy, the first Bluesky cancellation of someone, the exponentially intensifying purity spiral, followed by legacy titles or legacy humans announcing an exit from that one too. It's all such a predictable timesuck. Bluesky might be the new email.

Speaking of which, when people ask me for my email, I have to tell them very truthfully that I am so old-fashioned that I have only one – my *Guardian* one. I always used to follow this up by saying something along the lines of: 'I know, it's ridiculous. If I ever stopped working there, no one would be able to contact me.' But now I keep thinking: Oh my God! No one would be able to contact me via email! THE MODERN DREAM!

This has felt particularly desirable since the election, when I've been drowning in emails from the multiple liberal publications I already subscribe to, stagily rending their garments and assuring me that 'we do this for you'. It seems like every cloud has a silver lining – ideally, a gold one – with all sorts of titles dreaming of the Trump subscription bump they got last time around. Again: we'll see.

My unfashionable view is that the world would benefit from less partisan media, not more. Over in the US for the election, I mistakenly kept turning on CNN for news and was genuinely shocked at how it had degenerated since the last time I seriously paid attention to it (admittedly, some years ago now). It didn't really even have headlines on the hour, let alone coverage of 'news', and appeared to be a talking shop that saw itself purely as an active agent for the Harris campaign. To this outside observer, it didn't seem to be doing anything different from Fox News, except that it was doing it for the other side.

And it doesn't even work. Retreating into ideas of 'resistance' is a big part of how we got here. People hate on Trump for cashing in with his merchandise, but isn't rather a lot of the current liberal media convulsion just another form of Trump merchandise? Off-brand, yes. But still Trump merchandise – and as tacky, intentionally commercial and likely to lead to regret in the end as the official stuff.

It's the Oscars on a knife-edge: who'll win the award for hating *Emilia Pérez* the most?

7 February 2025

Hailed as a progressive triumph, now it's mired in scandal and acrimony. If that's not a film for our troubled times, what is?

The implosion of the awards juggernaut *Emilia Pérez* is extremely watchable. Honestly, this is a five-star controversy for a three-star film. Each day brings a new piece of hilarity, as a hurt elite entertainment community, who were simply trying to do the correct and approved thing, now struggle to navigate the possibility that, actually, they might all have been involved in a big old shitshow. Take Zoe Saldaña, whose Oscar campaign has been simply ruined by her marginalised-community co-star's historic attempts to marginalise some other communities. As she heroically put it yesterday: 'I'm allowing myself to still experience joy.' Me too, Zoe. Like many, I have given myself permission to be amused.

If you've missed this one, *Emilia Pérez* is a movie musical about a transgender Mexican drug lord, acquired after its Cannes premiere by that adorable indie-outsider-that-could, Netflix. Along with its lead star, Karla Sofía Gascón, the film has been nominated for masses of awards, and Gascón declared at the Golden Globes:

'The light always wins over darkness . . . I am who I am, not who you want.' Alas, it has since emerged via a trawl of her old tweets that she's quite a committed marginaliser herself. Muslims, George Floyd, Chinese people – they all came in for a pasting. But probably the worst thing she did in the eyes of the marginalised community she's seeking to impress – Hollywood – was criticise the Oscars. 'I didn't know if I was watching an Afro-Korean festival, a Black Lives Matter demonstration or the 8M [Women's March],' she opined of the 2021 Academy Awards. 'Apart from that, an ugly, ugly gala.' OMG. Actual sacrilege.

Emilia Pérez took $13.5m (£11m) on a budget of $25m (not including marketing), so it's fun to keep reading that it was a hit in cinemas. But as the world's TV channel, Netflix has different metrics for success, and it'll do well enough for them on the platform. What Netflix craves, though, is movie awards, so I'd love to know what the full-time *Emilia Pérez* awards team, who will have numbered in double figures, were doing instead of deleting Gascón's old tweets. That's day one, guys! You have to detonate the entire shaft before the offence miners get there. Failure to do so means Netflix is now engaged in a ludicrous rearguard attempt to firewall the movie's other awards prospects. They're even taking Emilia Pérez out of the *Emilia Pérez* posters. Amazing.

Or is it? Many people will find themselves so lost after the cultural contortions of the past few years that they might think that counts as trans erasure. But it's happening over a movie that a lot of people think was involved in some kind of Mexican erasure? Even though everyone's given it every award nomination out there, when they tipped all over the author Jeanine Cummins for her deeply researched 2020 novel *American Dirt* because she wasn't Mexican? Oh dear. What a muddle. It's almost as if things haven't been as simple as we've been told to believe for so long.

Which brings us to why the *Emilia Pérez* controversy is most interesting. It has blown up at precisely the moment when a necessary conversation is being had about the blowback from, or logical end of, the cultural politics that has defined the past decade or so. A few months ago, I was chatting to the pollster James Kanagasooriam about something, and he noted that 'the left tends to issue-bundle'. Which feels like a good way of putting it. Many people will have felt the increasingly illogical restrictiveness of this all-or-nothing deal in recent years of supposed progressive politics It's as though you can't consider each subject or cause on what you, personally, judge to be its individual merits. Instead, you must buy the entire suite of opinions off the shelf, and you have to agree with all of them, or you are 'on the wrong side of history' with the ones you don't. This was odd, James pointed out, because outside the small minority of the hyper-politically engaged, most people in the world are not actually like this. His example was that most people in the UK are extremely pro-gay rights, but a substantial proportion of this group might also support the non-progressive cause of restoring the death penalty.

Anyway: *Emilia Pérez*. A trans story! Latin actors! Big-swing cinema! It's all good, right? Except: no. Apparently Mexicans hate it. Apparently trans people hate it. Now old-skewing liberal Academy voters – who loved it – have seen these controversies and know they have to do a 180 and hate it too. For all its superficial whimsy, *Emilia Pérez* feels like an issue-bundled movie, and the implosion of its star's awards campaign feels like the absurd logical end of this prescription for looking at the world. It was pitched as a progressive triumph; now it's on 'the wrong side of history'.

On which, before we conclude, a note: I can't stand that infantilising, hectoring phrase, which has spent the past decade being the laziest but most successful way to force someone to agree with you. Ditto the idea that if you share any opinion – at all – with people on the other side of a supposed divide, then you should just consider what that makes you and fall back into line with your tribe. What bollocks.

In fact, the present political climate in the US seems to have been exacerbated by people performing their endless taxonomy of what is and isn't on the wrong side of history. It's enough to make you feel that the left, who bang on about polarisation the whole time, are actually more invested in it than the right. The movie industry could always come up with a big-swing, important movie which explores that. And maybe more people would go out and see it.

Jeans, controversy, used bathwater: Sydney Sweeney's selling it all. A showbiz masterclass, if you ask me

5 August 2025

Five years ago, she'd have been doing feminist stunts, but times change, and Sydney has captured the zeitgeist. She might flog that to you too

'SORRY FOR HAVING GREAT TITS AND CORRECT OPINIONS.' Not my words, readers (although, having said that . . .), but the words of a sweatshirt worn across the aforementioned acclaimed rack of Sydney Sweeney last year, shortly after some madly overheated controversy or other involving the *Euphoria/Anyone But You* star. I forget which controversy. Like Marvel movies, too many Sydney Sweeney controversies were made, and they all seemed to connect to each other in ways no one but the truly initiated could understand, so now only the saddos turn out for each and every one.

You might be dimly aware there's another one going on at the moment, following Sydney's participation in an American Eagle denim advert, a fashion retail event that obviously spiralled into some fatuous blue jeans/red state flame-war that has seen deranged

TikTokers claim something about 'eugenics', the president trouser-rubbingly decide he likes Sydney Sweeney, and American Eagle shares climb 23% in a week. Tell me the US will still be Earth's dominant superpower in 30 years, because I simply DON'T want to hear anything else. This is the behaviour of a culture with legs. (And a perfect ass – sorry if you can't handle it.)

Anyway, aside from the white supremacist lunacy, there is frothing disquiet about the extent of Sweeney's commercial brand partnerships, which include Miu Miu, Armani Beauty and a men's grooming product firm for which she recently did a tongue-in-cheek ad to flog soap that contained trace elements of her bathwater. It all seems quite a lot of lucrative fun, which must, of course, be stamped on, particularly when it seems to be being had by a woman.

I had to laugh at the intervention in a *New York Times* article of the fashion analyst who said: 'It seems like she's not embarrassed or ashamed by promoting all of these different projects.' Oh my God. Imagine! In fact, that explicit mention of shame reminded me of something that I read last year in the *Guardian*, which described Sydney Sweeney as 'problematic yet unashamed'. I do so enjoy these funny ways of talking, although perhaps one's not supposed to?

I certainly genuinely loved the moment last year when Sweeney offered *Vanity Fair* a temperature check on the aspirational sisterhood of . . . hang on, let me get my reading glasses on . . . the Hollywood movie business. 'This entire industry, all people say is "women empowering other women"', Sydney explained. 'None of it's happening. All of it is fake and a front for all the other shit that they say behind everyone's back.' Oof. Ladies and gentlemen, she went there. And how can you not love it? Chalk up another correct opinion and just accept that Sydney now might not get cast in a strong-female-led film based on a kids' book, inspired by a theme-park ride or commissioned by a toy company.

As for Sydney's online adversaries, what is it that clichéd enemy characters say in the movies? 'You and I, we are not so different after all.' Fact is, Sydney Sweeney is an actor. She wants attention. And – newsflash – so does some dreary TikToker making the nutty claim that American Eagle has done a white supremacist advert. They're just a million miles less good at it than Sydney.

Unless, of course, my other theory is true: that there are masses of undercover Maga agents whose sole job is to pose as woke warriors and say things so provocatively dumb that they further degrade the already cratered global reputation of the American left. Or, to couch it in their preferred language: if the vice president and Fox News seize delightedly and profitably upon the usefully idiotic things you say, then it's just possible you are in your least desirable location – 'the wrong side of history'. Or, to put it in even more basic terms: YOU ARE NOT HELPING.

Furthermore – and perhaps even more importantly – you are making the world less amusing. What you have failed to understand is something that us normies know instinctively. Namely, that this is how we want our celebrities, and most particularly our movie stars, to act. Most ordinary people want – and have always wanted – their movie stars to be gorgeous, fantastical, completely ridiculous figures in any number of ways, or else they'd be the most boring thing in the world: just like us.

We want our movie stars to be 'unashamedly' hot. We want our movie stars to tell us that they literally have to sell their own bathwater to eat, then find out that they have a property empire that includes, but is not limited to, a \$3m house in Westwood, a \$6m house in Bel Air and a \$13.5m house on a private Floridian island with a 520-bottle wine cellar, an aquarium and an infinity pool with a swim-up bar.

Of course, not everyone's a normie. It will have come to your attention that there are some people out there who want celebrities to drone on about causes, to post like it makes the blindest bit of difference and to hold fundraisers for Joe Biden till it's miles too late. But these people are strategically bankrupt, don't really have a cultural hinterland and should largely be avoided at parties.

Listen, five years ago, a commercially instinctive Sydney Sweeney would have done a feminist stunt or a tweet about mental health. Plenty of stars did, and made plenty from them. But nothing's static and vibes change, so stars are doing different starry things now. Or, to put it another way: they're all in the infinity pool, but some of them are headed for the swim-up bar. That's showbiz – try not to choke on it.

WESTMINSTER IN DECAY

Are the Houses of Parliament falling down more *literally* than they are falling down *metaphorically*? It's a tough one. About £100m a year is spent just on patching up the Palace of Westminster, with wholesale restoration estimated in the multiple billions and involving the relocation of its bubbled populace for one or two decades. But rather than get a grip on the issue, MPs couldn't face dealing with the horror and preferred to repeatedly kick it down the road, presumably waiting till parliament caves in on them or catches fire. Metaphorically, amazingly, things might have been even worse . . .

Pity the MPs who hate the London bubble and its elites – but just can't leave them behind

19 May 2023

The decaying parliament building – and the hypocrisy of those who should be fixing it – says a lot about a nation that's seen better days

Britain increasingly feels like a terribly old country. We keep hearing its pipework hasn't been properly overhauled since the Victorian age, so its own sewage laps at its shores and courses through its rivers. Earlier this month, we crowned our oldest-ever new monarch, a man who looked a picture of melancholy pretty much throughout, even if media sycophancy made it *verboten* to categorise the mood as anything other than one of joyous renewal. The country is overwhelmingly governed in the interests of older voters, at the expense of the young. And this week, the latest update on the literally crumbling Houses of Parliament warned that the building is so comprehensively knackered that it could be destroyed before renovation is agreed upon, let alone begun. This would be the only conceivable occasion on which this cohort of politicians could be described as bringing the house down.

Even the sewage crisis has been folded into the nostalgia myths that some find more comfortable than dealing with the present. 'I remember as a child in South Wales swimming in sewage,' reminisced the Conservative MP Damian Green this week. 'Jackson's Bay in Barry used to be a sewage outlet where we all went and paddled and swam . . .'

But the Palace of Westminster situation is arguably the standout for those who like their metaphors so heavy-handed as to beat them senseless. The building from which this country is governed is on the point of various collapses and existential crises, but no one can really face dealing with them. Bending reality or fleeing it altogether remain preferable. Stop me if it's all getting too excessively symbolic for you, but the Houses of Parliament have been in grave decline for decades, with dangerous wiring and endless leaks and asbestos discoveries now resulting in 4,000 maintenance issues reported every week.

Even tentative decisions on how to properly renovate it are either procrastinated over or overturned. Last-chance moments have come and gone without action. Successive generations of MPs have been paralysed by indecision and an inability to grasp the nettle. Things are now so bad that it's almost as if the MPs who hold the building's future in their hands have given up trying to fix its problems.

But this mismanaged decline is not cheap: as confirmed by the recent public accounts committee report, we are currently forking out a stunning £2m a week – A WEEK! – just on patching the Houses of Parliament up in the short term. All measures are only temporary. £140m has been spent on temporary fire safety. £8m has gone on temporary sewerage. (Failing to deal with effluent is one of the repeated features of our olden public realm.) There is a long-held sense that the serious multibillion-pound investment required to fix the building would upset the shareholders (the British public). There is no plan for what to do, so nothing gets done. Many have given up hope a plan will ever come, so simply wait fatalistically for disaster.

Those who have faced up to the problem know that the optimal solution at this advanced stage of decay is for absolutely all MPs, peers and staff to move out and go somewhere else, so that full-scale renovation can be carried out in the round and comprehensively. Various solutions have been suggested, from parliament sitting in temporary digs in London to relocating to another city for several years. Supporters of destinations outside the M25 argue that such locations would represent a breath of fresh air for our legislators, a chance to reconnect with the provinces that, they keep telling us, have been neglected.

How odd, then, to find so few such supporters among those who cheerfully force other institutions to relocate all the time – namely, the 'levelling-up' fans of the current government. Channel 4 is now headquartered in Leeds, for instance, while the Arts Council has been ordered by the government to move more of its spending out of London, resulting in the body telling the English National Opera that it needed to leave the capital or else lose all public funding. The powers that be seem to think that moving out of London is very good for you if you are a cultural institution – just the bracing shock to the system these London-bound elites could do with.

For the powers that be *themselves*, however, such a move is not proposed. But why? Why, when we have had to listen to all kinds of valid and not-so-valid criticism of the London metropolitan elite, do an extremely significant part of that elite – the lawmakers themselves – not think a breath of fresh air may be in order for them too? In fact, why was the navel-gazing and only occasionally coherent NatCon conference this week not preoccupied with this totemic idea? Given that Suella Braverman spent so much of her speech railing against experts and elites, surely the queen of the NatCons might reasonably have suggested a Khmer Rouge-lite emptying of the cities of the likes of herself, perhaps establishing some rural parliament to hasten the next stage of Britain's modern evolution. If they hate the Westminster bubble so much, why don't they burst it?

The answer, of course, is that they don't want to. At best, the ruling powers lack the skills and drive to do anything but keep patching up the past. At worst, they see the dysfunction as an opportunity for exploitation. Forgive me chucking this detail in again, just as a serial attempt to keep it on the boil, but at last count, almost 60 MPs were being investigated for sexual misconduct, while several of those already exposed still sit as MPs. That single statistic should be permanently enraging. Instead, it feels of a piece with wider decay. A rotten building houses a rotten culture that – unsurprisingly, really – is allowing the country itself to rot in all kinds of avoidable ways.

The good folk of Mid Beds appear to be missing an active MP. Where is Nadine Dorries?

25 August 2023

The former culture secretary has moved on and is now an all-round entertainer. But she is still a member of parliament

If you are a Mid Bedfordshire resident living in mould-infested rental accommodation with an asthmatic child, should you contact Nadine Dorries's theatrical agent? The question arises – theoretically speaking – after a glance at Nadine's social media profile, which reads: 'Recovering secretary of state. *Sunday Times* bestseller. TalkTV *Friday Night with Nadine* 8pm. *Daily Mail* Tuesday columnist.'

Agent details are listed. But has she missed something? Has madam, in the rush to announce herself as entertainment's hottest multi-hyphenate, omitted a string to her bow? Spokesmodel for a biodynamic shellac brand, perhaps? Creative genius behind a range of steel-capped espadrilles? Gaffepreneur? People in Mid Bedfordshire seem to think a more significant line of work has been left out, what with the fact that Nadine Dorries is still their member of parliament. Nominally, yes, but meaningfully? Unclear.

Nadine last spoke in the Commons more than a year ago, and last voted back in April. As you may know, she didn't manage to get the peerage Boris Johnson had promised her in his resignation honours back in early June. Having raged publicly in every available format about this, Nadine announced she would be resigning as Mid Beds MP 'with immediate effect', a pledge that turns out to have redefined the words 'immediate' and 'effect'. Put simply, it's been a long time since she made it, and jack shit has happened. She still draws her £86,500 MP's salary. She still reportedly employs one of her daughters as a senior parliamentary assistant, a role where the average salary is £42,000.

Dorries's next published work will be a book called *The Plot*, apparently about 'the political assassination of Boris Johnson'. Perhaps she'll finally resign as part of the promotional campaign for its September release – right before the party conference, in a way calculated to cause the most possible trouble for Rishi Sunak.

In the meantime, Nadine seems to have become a single-issue politician, that issue being: why the hell didn't I get a peerage? She was last heard of making a subject access request to try to answer this question, and getting knocked back by the Cabinet Office on the basis that information relating to honours is exempt from disclosure rules; and in any case, collecting every single piece of government correspondence in which Dorries is mentioned over recent years would be a pointlessly vast task.

And yet, the actual answer does not seem desperately opaque. Johnson was told long before the list was finally submitted that Nadine wouldn't be able to get one if she clung on to her parliamentary seat until the next election, but he either thought this rule somehow wouldn't apply to his honours picks or just forgot to tell her because it was a hassle and he doesn't really care about anybody except himself. It's really not complicated. I mean, look at the state of the House of Lords – you can hardly say there's a conspiracy to keep useless horrors out of it.

Strangely, the non-baronessing of Nadine does not appear to be an issue that's preoccupying her constituents and erstwhile colleagues. Rishi Sunak has said her constituents deserve committed representation; Keir Starmer demands that the PM somehow make that happen. When Tory MP Caroline Nokes went on air this week and said Dorries should 'crack on' and stand down, given 'her heart's not in it', opprobrium finally reached critical mass. Dorries duly emerged from the metropolitan elite circles gestured towards in her bio, issuing a statement to the *News Agents* podcast in which she claimed to be 'working daily'.

This seems to be news to many in her constituency. Dorries has not held a surgery for three and a half years, and the building in which she once did so was long ago turned into a dance studio. She lives, as you'd expect of the Mid Beds MP, somewhere in Gloucestershire.

For all her maddening escapades, though, Dorries was occasionally notably right about things. There *was* something fantastically entitled and born-to-rule about David Cameron, who did indeed run his government in a lofty, patrician way, until it bit him on the bum so badly that history might judge the defining Cameron quality to be a total absence of bum. When first elected, she *was* unfairly patronised by a certain type of Conservative colleague, being no more under-informed and inadequate than most of them – and having clawed her way up from disadvantage and horrors that almost none of them could even begin to imagine.

I've written before that it's a shame she couldn't marry up the warmth many people saw in private with her public persona. Instead, she became harder than hard, a snarling media attack dog who thought it less important to be on top of the facts of her brief than to be out there defending Johnson at all costs. But she hasn't recently gone missing in action; in fact, it's been going on a lot longer than that.

Given quite how many MPs are currently self-terminating or being terminated, the adage that all political careers end in failure is starting to feel as depressing for the public who are failed as for the failures themselves. It shouldn't be a cause for celebration that

Dorries has become everything she always said she loathed – disengaged, a media luvvie, distracted by self-advancement from helping the people MPs are elected to serve. She might be a figure of fun, but as a symbol of a necrotic government that claims not to have checked out, even though it has, the joke can only be on us.

Dear Mr Speaker, what are we to do about the honourable gentlemen for Sexpest North?

27 October 2023

Crispin Blunt has denied rape claims against him, but why are we always asked to think of the fallout for the PM, not the alleged victims?

Another week, another arrest on suspicion of sexual assault for a member of parliament, Britain's grimmest workplace. Even the nightclub bouncer community have been arrested fewer times this year. This week it's Reigate MP Crispin Blunt, who resembles an off-brand Terence Stamp and was interviewed by Surrey police for the second time this month over allegations of rape and possession of controlled substances. He denies the allegations.*

With the supremely practised efficiency of an F1 pit crew, the Conservative party is once again rolling out the suspected-scumbag protocol. Blunt has had the whip withdrawn – a piece of arcane styling that always makes it sound like the person in question has merely breached some in-group etiquette – and been told to stay away from the parliamentary estate, which is physically crumbling but otherwise increasingly feels like a fine example of a bail hostel in the Gothic style.

* The rape case against Crispin Blunt was dropped in May 2025, with police stating there was 'insufficient evidence to proceed'. In March 2026, Blunt pleaded guilty to four drugs charges.

Last week, of course, it was Wellingborough MP Peter Bone losing the whip, after parliament's independent expert panel upheld bullying accusations that had somehow taken the Conservative party years to investigate. You get the feeling its internal affairs department sees its peer group as the Mexico City police department. Motto: protect and serve yourself.

Also last week, there was a byelection in Tamworth, a seat that had been finally vacated by Tory Chris Pincher after specific groping allegations were made in July 2022. Non-specific groping allegations pre-dated those, and Boris Johnson has declined to deny he remarked 'Pincher by name, pincher by nature' around the time he cheerily promoted Chris to deputy chief whip.

Maybe Johnson was right. Chris Pincher, Peter Bone . . . there does seem to be an element of nominative misfortune at work here. You wouldn't be feeling too confident if you were Gavin Rapist MP. Then again, would you? He's probably on a collision course with a mild parliamentary dressing-down sometime around the 2037 mark.

I often wonder if part of the problem is the way the political media puts these things, which often seems to be exclusively in terms of how one powerful man has caused a 'headache' for an even more powerful man. Google the phrase 'byelection headache', and you will see how prime ministers are forever being given this twee, low-level ailment by rascals who have simply groped some office fodder a couple of decades their junior or got themselves imprisoned for sex offences.

It was paracetamol time again this week for Rishi Sunak. 'Peter Bone Gives Rishi Another Byelection Headache', honked the *Spectator*, which probably just got lost on the way to typing: 'Peter Bone Gives His Aide PTSD, Several Whacks and an Unwanted Sight of His Penis'. (Peter Bone denies he gave his aide these things.)

In the past couple of years alone, 'byelection headaches' have been brought on by the likes of David Warburton (sexual harassment allegations, denied, and cocaine use), Imran Ahmad Khan (convicted of sexual offences against a child) and Neil Parish (tractor porn). Sometimes headaches threaten but don't end up coming on. In July, it was reported that another Conservative MP had not attended parliament for more than a year after being arrested for sexual offences, misconduct in public office and more. His police bail has been extended five times, but he has not been charged and denies any wrongdoing.

Even so, given that some form of alleged sexual misconduct has been the most popular reason for forcing byelections of late, perhaps it's time to retire the 'headache' cliché. The very idea that those accused of sexual misconduct are 'giving' the prime minister anything suggests it's just a cleverly calculated means to an end. Maybe police are working on a theory that an unspecified number of men are allegedly committing sexual offences as part of an elaborate plot to erode Rishi Sunak's parliamentary majority. Maybe they're Manchurian creeps, groomed (politically speaking) by Boris Johnson, back when he was PM, with the sole aim of being activated to destroy his successor/trap Sunak's party in a byelection loop/give Rishi a light migraine.

Or maybe – maybe – time would be better spent establishing why this stuff keeps happening in our seat of democratic government. The UK parliament currently feels so degenerate, and in such a darkly farcical way, that it could easily be the subject of a *South Park* episode. The percentage of MPs accused of deeply unpleasant things is surely miles out of whack with almost any other (legal) workplace in the country. Is it that the place and its illusions of power sexually corrupt some people, or is it that sexually corrupt people are drawn to it? Or both? Pretty horrifyingly, finding out becomes more urgent with every passing week.

Rewarding failure? With David Cameron's return, it's being celebrated like never before

14 November 2023

Meet the new foreign secretary – same as the old prime minister. If you've enjoyed the years of turmoil he set in motion before whistling off, do welcome him back to the stage

Who's that walking up Downing Street? Why, it's the man who ghosted Britain! In some ways, the sight of David Cameron back in SW1 was always a possibility. Behavioural science tells us these guys often return to the scene of their crimes, either to retrieve a trophy or to show police the various burial sites in the hope of receiving a slightly more lenient sentence. In this case, from the history books.

But let's be real: the only acceptable excuse Cameron could have for being in the Downing Street area is that he has been sent back in time to terminate his past self before the moment he accidentally sets the UK on the course of permacrisis politics, in which it is still agonisingly and destructively trapped. Unfortunately, the Cameron unit has made the wrong calculations – again – and emerged through the space–time tear seven and a half years too late. He is now foreign secretary, and after his full-spectrum triumph in Libya, it will certainly be interesting to see what Mr Failed State achieves in that role. Sorry, that's unfair – Lord Failed State.

With the best will in the world, then, Rishi Sunak's big move feels most squarely pitched at the emergency podcast market. Is there such a thing as an emergency foreign secretary? Tangentially, I'm actually slightly surprised Cameron himself isn't already doing a podcast. His closest political ally, George Osborne, has got one with his own former Labour opposite number, Ed Balls, where the chat has the feel of two buddy cops shooting the breeze in their car on a stake-out outside the Treasury. If they move their vehicle to the kerb opposite the Foreign Office, Cameron can now send room service out to them, like Axel Foley in *Beverly Hills Cop*.

Inevitably, people have suggested that pulling a move to restore Cameron to the frontline is like rearranging the deckchairs on the *Titanic*, but arguably that doesn't really cover it. This is not like shifting the deckchairs in 1912, an hour after the iceberg had hit, but like doing it now, in 2023, when Cameron's form has been largely consumed by molluscs and fish have been swimming in and out of his cavities, along with the various Treasury committee members who, in 2021, probed his lucrative lobbying of ministers on behalf of the now-collapsed Greensill Capital. These days, he's arguably more reef than man.

Perhaps instead of representing the triumph of experience, as billed, Cameron's return as foreign secretary says something about our age of defeat, when some of the gurus most fetishised are the ones who already had a go and failed, in many cases absolutely disastrously. I know you learn a lot from failure, but I sometimes wonder if the United Kingdom deserves slightly more than to be a recurring plot device in these people's journeys towards personal growth. Many will feel David wouldn't even deserve a comeback as an ITV press officer, his only previous job outside politics.

In fact, speaking of ITV . . . at almost the exact same moment as Cameron was being photographed shaking hands with Sunak in the cabinet room, Nigel Farage was being photographed in Queensland for his upcoming stint on *I'm a Celebrity* (having somehow sidestepped Australia's famously strict biosecurity rules). Which of these two employment gambits will turn out to be the more significant booking in the long term? It says a lot about the deranged political culture we've been living in since Cameron do-be-do-be-dooed his way out of Downing Street in 2016 that, at the present moment, I'd call it for Farage's trip to the jungle.

For now, we might have to accept the Cameron appointment is like the moment in a much-loved family game when you realise you've played it through, and the children start wailing, 'We've HAD all these cards!' And after years of exhausting turmoil in which the only thing achieved has been decline, we have indeed had all these cards. As Andy Warhol once remarked, in the future every single Conservative MP will hold a vital UK government brief for 15 minutes, and this has surely now been so comprehensively accomplished that we are downcycling former prime ministers into vacant jobs. Fifteen people alone have been housing minister since May 2010. You have to remember that even Andrea Jenkyns, the missing link between the vegetable and mineral kingdoms, has been an education minister. At the time she held this role last year, Andrea was pictured walking into Downing Street giving the middle finger to members of the public, so it means a lot that she saw yesterday as the opportunity to announce 'enough is enough' and submit her letter of no confidence in Rishi Sunak.

At the time of writing, we are still waiting for the formal departure letter from Suella Braverman, who was very belatedly sacked by Sunak on Monday morning, apparently over an issue with tone. Which makes her sending-off sound like it was for sarcastic applause to a referee, as opposed to whipping up tensions to the point where far-right thugs stormed the police barricades round the Cenotaph on Armistice Day. While they've had a lot to say about other aspects of Saturday's march, there has been a distinct lack of condemnation of these particular scenes from the right of the Conservative party. Perhaps they found them charming? In any case, Sunak's attempts to buy them off seem unlikely to do the trick. But mildly eye-catching appointments on that front include the return of Esther McVey, who becomes a cabinet-attending minister without portfolio and whose actual brief, it has been reported, is to be the 'common sense tsar'. Something of an oxymoron there. Then again, maybe there is something of the late-stage Romanovs to this latest attempt at accommodation with a fast-advancing appointment with unpleasant reality.

Ultimately, we now have an unelected foreign secretary appointed by an unelected prime minister and are being asked to consider the mood as fresh. It was only a few weeks ago that Rishi Sunak was trying to cast himself as the change candidate and to define the rest of his prime ministership against all the mistakes made by all his recent predecessors, including Cameron. Evidently, that pose has now been abandoned, as others will be on the prime minister's inexorable journey towards the next general election. Sunak comes across as a man who has had only one good idea in his entire political career (the furlough scheme) and is forever trying and failing to have another one, convinced that he'll strike upon it if he just drills into a bit more detail/rummages deep enough in the bag of yesterday's men. There must be another one down there somewhere . . . mustn't there?

A PPE farrago, a car crash interview and a fight with the PM: Lady Mone has her foot on the gas, hasn't she?

19 December 2023

For everyone enraged by the Covid equipment scandal who can't quite find the words, try these: Michelle Mone and her husband, Doug

Draw near, readers, for these are testing times for bouncy-blow-dried plague profiteer Michelle Mone and her husband/support garment Doug Barrowman. And also, perhaps, for the Conservative figures who ennobled her ladyship, then helped her and Doug fast-track their way into providing £203m of Covid PPE, from which they cleared at least £65m in profits, even though much of the PPE was allegedly unusable.

Michelle lied repeatedly, and for years, about her involvement to the *Guardian*, which broke the story, and on Sunday insisted: 'That's not a crime.' PPE Medpro and the couple are being investigated by the National Crime Agency, which – and I'm honestly just going on the title here – does maybe have something to do with crime. The Mone-Barrowmans, obviously, deny everything.

But look, let's just get into technical terms for a second: Michelle is 5ft 9in of pure chaos, and watching Rishi Sunak whinnying feebly about 'taking all these things incredibly seriously' tees up the spectacle of the prime minister and a number of other drippy male politicians further incensing this category-five 'force of nature', who will lash out all the way down on her well-earned fall from grace. Is that as good as taxpayers getting their money back? No. But I'll watch.

Before we proceed, though, a recap. Can it really be only 11 years since Michelle was granting a mesmerisingly messy interview to the *Sunday Times*, in which she wailed rhetorically: 'Why did I want to be Michelle Mone? Why did I want to start all these businesses? Why can I never be satisfied with what I've got?' Yes. Yes, I do believe it can.

Can it really be only six years since Mone and Barrowman were granting 'their first joint interview' to *Hello!* magazine, standing in formal wear in front of their Isle of Man McMansion, a Ferrari parked with gossamer insouciance just behind them, as if to say . . . well, as if to say: 'GREETINGS, SHITHEADS – DID WE MENTION WE OWN A FERRARI?' Again, it can. Readers of various outlets have since been invited inside the property, where decorative flourishes include a paved drive (sorry, but no) and an amphitheatre (actually hysterical). 'I feel like I'm in a fairytale,' Michelle told the publication, 'a beautiful dream I don't ever want to wake up from.' Three years ago, as a belated wedding present, she gifted Doug a gelding (I bet she did).

And so to Mone and Barrowman's absolute disasterclass of an interview with the BBC's Laura Kuenssberg last Sunday, which came out not long after a YouTube documentary that turned out to have been paid for by Barrowman's firm, much to the retrospective surprise and distaste of several of the experts featured therein. Choice cuts? Too many to mention. 'There's a reason why I live in the Isle of Man,' Barrowman explained to Kuenssberg. 'I don't want anyone in the press to know of any business activity or anything that I get engaged in.' Mmm. On the basis of the current horror show, Doug is almost as skilled at this as he is at sourcing acceptable PPE.

Anyway: the Conservative fightback. On Monday, former Covid-era health minister Lord Bethell – one of the few people even less qualified to be in the House of Lords than Michelle, given he inherited his title – posted a screenshot of a message from Mone dated 4 October 2020. In this, she referred to 'they' rather than 'we' when talking about PPE Medpro.

Not sure that's enough to let the government play the innocent. Then again, Bethell's gambit means so much more from someone who previously claimed to have lost his phone 'in early 2021', then revised that to say he had the phone but it was defective, then revised that to say it had been given to a family member, most recently alighting on the position that he'd deleted the Covid contracts messages for space and telling the *Today* programme that important decisions happened via the red box system and not via WhatsApp on phones. Still, thanks for dialling in again, Lord Brains.

The summer after winning the PPE contract, Michelle posted a picture of herself abroad on a newly purchased yacht, the *Lady M*, accompanied by the observation: 'Business isn't easy. But it is rewarding.' Counterpoint: is it possible that business is sometimes way too easy? So many people in this country have looked at what has emerged about the way vastly lucrative Covid contracts were awarded in the panic of a deadly pandemic and thought: who knew it was actually so easy, if only you were shameless and grasping enough? Who knew that as long as you had a hotline to the people at the top and just a phone number for some factory, you could set yourself up as a PPE provider, having never worked in the space before, and clear millions upon millions of pounds of profits on a load of unusable crap that might end up getting flytipped next to New Forest nature reserves and the like?

The government is always saying it wants to talk about things that matter to people, yet it simply will not talk, in public and apologetically, about the grotesque profiteering that happened during Covid. Please be aware that every time you see a Conservative MP lying that they had a 'great day on the doorstep' in their constituency, what they will in fact have had is a day when people mention this issue with varying degrees of fury. The complete failure to reckon with it in any meaningful way is eroding trust in politics and political processes by the hour.

None of which is to be unrealistic about the situation the country found itself in during the Covid pandemic. Of course it was a mad scramble to get something – anything – to protect the very people trying to care for the sick and save their lives. Of course the process was imperfect – that is understood by most people. What can't be understood, and never should be in a nation that retains any level of self-respect, is why ordinary people are somehow supposed to be forelock-tuggingly grateful to those who were already multimillionaires (and, in the case of the serial tax-avoider Barrowman, reportedly a billionaire) for 'helping' in this way.

What absolute rubbish. If these white knights really were so altruistic, then they'd have waived the profits in the interests of civic duty, instead of rinsing the public purse beyond all imagining for equipment that often could not even be used. I can't believe it needs to be said out loud, but if you made £65m pure profit for 'helping' during the most acute national crisis, then you didn't help – you helped yourself.

Who would you rather see in the Lords, Post Office scandal hero Alan Bates or Michelle Mone?

12 January 2024

The PM says the campaigner should have a knighthood, but why stop there? He could show feckless peers what public service looks like

According to Downing Street, the prime minister is now backing a knighthood for Alan Bates. Bates's 20-year campaign for justice for post office operators has finally got the recognition it deserves, thanks to ITV's extraordinarily consciousness-raising drama *Mr Bates vs the Post Office*. But why not offer him a peerage? It seems odd to think he would somehow fall short of a standard apparently cleared easily by Michelle Mone.

The obvious answer would seem to be that Mr Bates is not rich or parasitic enough, has never moved in the 'right' circles, nor has he given enough money to a political party, ideally the governing Conservatives. (Boris Johnson alone appointed enough peers to account for 11% of the entire current House of Lords.) Furthermore, Bates has not taken a penny for his decades of tireless labour, somehow failing to realise that you are supposed to get very rich doing something and then receive an honour to say well done. Either that or you should assist Liz Truss in detonating the country's economic stability.

But aside from those shocking black marks against Bates's name, isn't he precisely the sort of person most people would like to have in an upper chamber worth its salt? Dogged, steely, unshowy, and unemotional by design, Bates is almost tailor-made out of the characteristics we ought to seek in public servants. (Whether or not he'd want the role is, naturally, a separate issue.)

We will be unpicking for some while the reasons why ITV's landmark drama has struck quite so deep a chord with the public at this particular moment in time. A very large part of it is, of course, the story itself, which is a tale of such staggering and long-term injustice that it should beggar belief. But crucially, it doesn't quite beggar belief. It increasingly feels as though the show has landed so well because it speaks to something people feel about the way UK society can be stacked. Many feel there is something rotten in the state of British life – and given that it has taken a TV drama to bring the most widespread miscarriage of justice in British legal history to the forefront of the national consciousness, they would surely be right. A whole host of systems, institutions and individuals have failed in order for us to reach this strange point, and in this most circuitous way (large sections of the media included).

A House of Lords riddled with cronyism and self-interest is part of that. And so it is that even after such a formidable and hitherto thankless campaign, Alan Bates is still somehow the sort of guy you'd just give a knighthood to, while Mone or Evgeny Lebedev or incredibly minor officials from Johnson's disgraced administration get to have their say on the shape of British laws for life. Or at least those who bother turning up do.

Interviewed by *The Times* last weekend at home in Colwyn Bay, Bates assured the paper that it didn't matter that he'd never been paid for his work, on top of having had his business destroyed by the Post Office, because 'you don't need a ridiculous amount of money' in life. For some reason, I am reminded of one of the many 'at home' interviews Lord Lebedev has granted newspapers and interiors publications over the years, in which it was explained that his oculus – a skylit architectural dome in one of his properties – 'is lined with shards of blue amethyst'.

That said, I must be very careful mentioning Lebedev. He tends to respond in one way or another to a run-out in these pages and is prone to accuse the *Guardian* and others of anti-Russian racist harassment. To which the only reasonable response is: lol. Peer of the realm, newspaper baron thanks to vast inherited wealth, half of Britain's more credulous great and good on speed dial . . . if this is racism, I'm sure most people in this country would love to be signed up for a dose of it. Forgive me if it's racist to say that the House of Lords has no record of Evgeny Lebedev ever voting – not even once.

None of which is meant to imply that all peers are work-shy or venal or self-aggrandising – very far from it. One of the other tireless campaigners for justice for the post office operators is the former Conservative MP James Arbuthnot, now Lord Arbuthnot, who this week gave an object lesson in self-deprecation. 'In the end, I achieved nothing,' he reflected to *The Times*. 'I'm sad to have to say that it has actually been significantly less effective than I wish it had been. As you probably deduced from the drama, however heroic I and other MPs appeared, I achieved absolutely nothing.' How markedly in contrast that stands to the crazed bandwagonning of some MPs and ministers this week, who have fallen over themselves to look retrospectively heroic now that the scandal has gone radioactive.

As for Arbuthnot's views on Alan Bates, with whom he remains in touch most days, they reflect the idiosyncratic inscrutability of the former post office operator, which the actor Toby Jones identified when trying to work out how to play him. 'It's hard to say what Alan makes of things,' Arbuthnot told *The Times*. 'He just ploughs on. He's much more stubborn than I am, working away at his unpaid work.'

It would be nice to think the honours committee would at least offer Bates the chance to become a formal House of Lords colleague of Arbuthnot. Maybe the trouble with Mr Bates is that he would feel a sense of responsibility to turn up and do the job.

Look at the political hellscape of Sunak, Anderson, even Starmer and ask: are they making my life any better?

27 February 2024

When politicians compete in a race to the bottom, is it any wonder that the public are not far behind?

Four weeks ago, Rishi Sunak was hoping he could find a way to return Lee Anderson to his job as the deputy chair of the Conservative party after Anderson's resignation over the Rwanda bill, with the prime minister's spokesperson letting it be known the PM still had 'a lot of time for Lee'. He's certainly spending a lot of time on him. A mere month on, Sunak seems to be hoping he can find a way to persuade Anderson to return to the Conservative party. Meanwhile, much of public life seems to be moving in a fast and febrile way at the moment, and a lot of people are rightly worried about where it will all end.

While the de-whipped Anderson flirts with joining Reform, Sunak's appeasing position is that this celebrated 'red wall' whisperer's comments about Sadiq Khan were 'wrong' but not Islamophobic. By way of a reminder, Anderson used a GB News appearance to assert that 'Islamists' had control of London and the London mayor had given the capital to 'his mates'. No politician should speak like this. But by being utterly unable to say why the remarks were 'wrong', the electorally desperate Sunak gives the impression he'd like to have Lee back, not speaking exactly like this, but a bit like this, in fact, quite like this, not that we'd all say it in the same way, and, you know . . . Lee is Lee!

Not that what we might politely call incendiary carelessness is limited to this 'side'. After supporters of Donald Trump notoriously overwhelmed security at the Capitol on 6 January 2021, you'd think anyone thoughtful who was organising protests outside seats of government would give extra care to their rallying cries. Yet Ben Jamal, the director of the Palestine Solidarity Campaign, who convened the protest in Westminster on the night of last week's Gaza ceasefire vote, reportedly declared: 'We want so many of you to come that they will have to lock the doors of parliament itself.' Jamal has now said: 'For the record, when I called for people to come to parliament in such large numbers they would have to lock the door, I was calling for mass participation in the cornerstone of democratic accountability.' Yet why would one need to 'lock the doors' against that? Many thousands of protests have occurred outside parliament down the years, without explicitly creating the impression that it needed to lock its doors. It is a shame that Jamal is as unable to acknowledge the dangerous stupidity of his words any more than Anderson is.

But then this is what populism looks like, wherever in the spectrum it rears its head. It is aggressive, it is artless, it prefers a verbal boot to a measured argument – and it always ends in failure or worse. This week, it emerged that three female MPs (both Conservative and Labour) have been issued with bodyguards and cars out of rising fears for their safety. Hardline activists who sneer that this 'comes with the territory' lack foresight and humanity, in a way that is not totally different to the way in which Anderson does.

After blow-ups like these, MPs often hotly defend the time-honoured 'cut and thrust' of our politics, and I suppose there is a weak argument that parliamentarians throughout history were never happier than when bandying the unforgivable insults of their own eras around. But the thing is, very few people heard or saw them. Now, the low points of Commons 'debate' and talkshow punditry are clipped within moments and go endlessly viral on social media. Parliament and its members have never been as seen as they are now. And when the standards of leadership degenerate, why should the standards of the people be far behind?

By way of illustration, in as even-handed a way as possible, let's track one motif in the 'cut and thrust'. Almost exactly two years ago, Boris Johnson bizarrely sought to defend himself against a new raft of Partygate stories by telling the House of Commons that Keir Starmer had failed to prosecute Jimmy Savile when he was director of public prosecutions. Starmer blamed this disgraceful slur by the then prime minister for the angry mob that accosted him outside parliament just days later. Yet the next year, Labour ran a social media ad that demanded: 'Do you think adults convicted of sexually assaulting children should go to prison? Rishi Sunak doesn't.' After the mob incident, Starmer had given an interview saying he'd never been called a 'paedophile protector' before in public and that 'the PM knew exactly what he was doing' – suggesting he himself knew exactly what he was doing when his own ad in effect called Sunak a paedophile protector a year later.

All these sorcerer's apprentices know what they're doing, until they suddenly don't and something very bad indeed happens. Time and again I think back to standing on College Green, outside the Houses of Parliament, in the light of the very early morning of 24 June 2016 and watching Nigel Farage meet the triumph of his political life not with eloquence and magnanimity, but with a provocative and sniping speech that, barely a week after the murder of Jo Cox, memorably included a pat on the back for the fact we'd got there 'without a single bullet being fired'.

In the immediate wake of Cox's murder, MPs from all sides briefly paid tribute to the late MP's conviction that we have 'more in common than that which divides us'. Yet so many politicians who probably thought they meant it at the time have spent the subsequent years dividing us even further. Why? Because it's easier, because it's a habit, because they can't think of anything more constructive to do, and because it gets them instant attention. Every day they indulge in it is a day they are not solving any of the problems making people's lives in the UK worse – and another sign that the era of displacement populism is upon us.

Here's the real 'enigma' about Charlotte Owen: why do we still take sexist gossip so seriously?

17 September 2024

OK, it's not great to put a 29-year-old in the Lords, but trouser-rubbing 'journalists' spreading innuendo can't back it up with a shred of evidence

Hello there. Today I would like to talk about Charlotte Owen. If you've heard of Charlotte Owen, it's probably because you've read someone – unquestionably one of the 'good guys' of the discourse – saying some creepy, innuendo-laden thing about the 'riddle', 'mystery' or 'enigma' of her relationship with Boris Johnson. Before we go on, a word on vocab: all those words are journalese for 'I can't stand up this cobblers, but I just want to publish it anyway'.

If you haven't heard of Charlotte Owen, then (a) you may be the last pure human, and (b) you will need a primer. So here goes: she worked for Johnson's No. 10 operation and was unexpectedly given a peerage in his resignation honours list. Alongside her House of Lords work, she has recently taken a position in a business Johnson has set up with a uranium entrepreneur. Any more background? I should also say I have never met Owen, who is now 31, nor had the remotest of dealings with her. However, I have watched the absolute deluge of sexism disguised as gossip that has beset her since Johnson chucked her the poisoned chalice. Though entirely fact-free, most of it has been frothingly circulated by the sort of person who imagines themselves to be on the side of the angels. So allow me to offer a counterpoint: they're not.

Listen, I'm sure it's not great to give a peerage to a 29-year-old. But let's get real: even if she were totally useless, Owen would still be only about the 200th-worst person in the House of Lords. There's no way she'd even make the cut of the true monsters, about whom we don't get any articles because they're not youngish and blonde. Do imagine if all the good guys casting twice-weekly aspersions at Owen were chucking even half that number at fellow Johnson peer Evgeny Lebedev – a serious piece of work who has somehow garnered fewer bad headlines this past year than Charlotte has this past fortnight. Records and accounts by colleagues suggest Owen is a diligent peer, turning up very frequently and offering contributions that some estimate would put her in the top 10% of speakers. (Lebedev has never even bothered voting and has asked only four written questions in four years.)

As for being unqualified for her latest job, countless 31-year-olds in this country have jobs that I'm sure their elders and betters think they're not good enough for, and they were often hired for them by people they met through previous jobs. You're going to need more than that. Yet not one person has produced a single nano-particle of evidence for their theories, while indications that they're nonsense pile up. Consider the pictures of Owen at Carrie Johnson's soirées. Seriously, Carrie's the final boss of this game. She saw off master strategist Dominic Cummings (Carl von Clownewitz). Pretty sure she'd make light work of Charlotte if there were anything to worry about.

Some people will say it was ever thus. Funnily enough, I think I was Owen's age when I started reading stories about my own affair with the former editor of the *Guardian*. Not true stories, as it goes, and I'm just trying to think back to it all. *Private Eye* ran some of them, so I contacted the magazine to tell it that they were completely untrue and asked it to correct them. Alas, corrections were not a *Private Eye* thing, I was told, but I was offered the option of writing a letter to its letters page, under my name, to counter the story. I remember sitting and wondering what such a bizarre and inherently unedifying missive would even look like. I pictured a letter reading: 'Dear Sir, Sorry to trouble you, but this is just to say I'm not actually having an affair with my boss. Yours ever so gratefully, Marina Hyde.'

I concluded that would be rather adding insult to injury, so declined to send it, and instead had to come up with a sort of renegade campaign to get the record corrected, much of which now seems excruciatingly ridiculous in retrospect. I can't remember all the stupid stuff I did, but I do remember, for example, agreeing to appear on a hideously dreary media panel, purely because the then editor of *Popbitch* was also doing it. They'd run the story too, you see, so I sat through the discussion and waited for an opportunity to confront her in public about what I think I called 'my non-affair'. This was no one's finest hour, but I couldn't think of a better way. In the end, you realise you just have to ignore people and work hard, and maybe that work will displace people's current view of you in, like, a couple of decades?

Now I am a much older lady, I wouldn't say I can say exactly what I like, but I can certainly say a lot more of what I like. And I say all this now not because I want to spare Charlotte Owen the ball-ache of having to do some dire panel on climate lies at the next COP conference, purely to tee herself up for introducing a leaden non sequitur beginning with the words, 'Hey – you know what else is a lie . . . ?' No, I am doing this because I honestly can't believe that almost 20 years later, fact-free faux journalism like this has got worse.

Much of it is down to social media being a place where people very much like to look as though they're insiders (again, they're not). The other corrosive practice, popular on social media but also with some very online journalists, is that thing of putting two pictures or stories together and saying with some kind of flourish: 'You join the dots!' To which the only acceptable response is: 'No. Would YOU mind joining the dots? You are, after all, supposed to be the professional here. The fact that you can't confirms that you're not "doing journalism", you're doing sexism, you're doing conspiracism and you're doing indolence.' Still: lovely clicks.

Allow me to end by offering a competition prize: the next person to publish any fact-free innuendo about Charlotte Owen shall be crowned the biggest trouser-rubbing weirdo in Fleet Street – and that's a tough field. Guys, that actually means something! If anyone has any evidence of the thing at which they have hinted so remorselessly, then let them produce it. Otherwise, maybe they have had their fun, and it's finally time to shut up and leave her alone. Instead, please tell us more about the uranium entrepreneur. You see, this is the other thing about getting older: you start wanting to know more about the uranium entrepreneurs. But we always look the wrong way in this country, so don't hold your breath.

Make a political hero of Zack Polanski if you want. Just don't forget to engage your brain

9 December 2025

The Green party leader is riding high in the polls. But across the political spectrum, uncritical adulation leads nowhere fast

Shortly after Donald Trump launched his first White House run in 2015, television's Kelly Osbourne made one of her regular appearances on *The View*, which is basically the American version of *Loose Women* but doesn't feel the need to have a cringey title. Trump had made some extremely nasty comments about Mexican immigrants, and Kelly had a rhetorical question for the other ladies gathered round the wood-effect dining table that morning. 'You kick every Latino out of this country,' she sassed, 'then WHO is going to be cleaning your toilet, Donald Trump?'

Oooooof. The reaction from fellow panellist Rosie Perez was instantaneously negative, to the point that even Kelly realised in the moment that this needed a clean-up. Apparently, there weren't any willing rubber-gloved Latinos on hand, so madam was going to have to do it herself. 'I didn't mean it like that,' Osbourne shot back. 'Come on! You know I would never mean it like that! I'm not part of this argument.' A media firestorm nonetheless ensued, though Kelly declined to apologise for even the appearance of racism, I think on the basis that people like her simply are not capable of subconsciously holding unpleasant views that they accidentally reveal while making important TV appearances.

I must say I thought of Kelly's faux pas when I saw Green party leader Zack Polanski appearing on *Question Time* last week. If you missed this moment, or are trying to avoid it because you quite want to vote for him and are already trying to avoid the boob-hypnosis video (more on that later!), Zack took the opportunity of the show's immigration special to explain to the audience: 'One in five care workers are foreign nationals. I don't know about you, but I don't particularly want to wipe someone's bum, and I'm very grateful for the people who do this work.'

Again: oooooof. So *that's* what they're there for – and, indeed, *that's* what care work is. Still, what a standup guy for being grateful.

And thank goodness for the anti-woke vibe shift, right? After all, Zack metaphorically showing his arse while talking about elderly and disabled people's 'bums' is precisely the sort of thing that the cancellers would have cancelled you for as recently as a year ago. Imagine my synthetic shock, then, to note so many of the great witch-hunters of the past decade finding absolutely nothing to see here. Imagine my synthetic wonderment at all the Green party devotees who are able to defend this moment as coming from a good place. I guess that like Kelly, people like Zack simply are not capable of subconsciously holding unpleasant views that they accidentally reveal while making important TV appearances.

Indeed, Polanski's reflexive supporters point to the fact that his partner works in palliative care, a line of reasoning that feels not entirely unrelated to that old rhetorical masterstroke: 'How can I hate women? My mum's one.' But the Greens are currently polling almost equal with the Tories and Labour, meaning any criticism of them is conveniently dismissed by their more vocal supporters as evidence that the party's critics are 'rattled'. If only Kelly Osbourne had been polling at 16% 10 years ago – it would have saved her a lot of flak.

And in many ways, there can be no more sobering comment on the utter failures of this century's various governments than the fact that 16% of the country is currently intending to vote for a guy who once told a woman he could make her breasts bigger by hypnosis. 'This is an extremely new approach,' Polanski claimed in a video of the 2013 session, which he knew upfront was for an article for the *Sun*, 'but I can see it becoming popular very quickly, because it's so safe and a lot cheaper than a boob job.' Oh dear.

Yet so tribal is our politics these days that Zack's 'extremely new approach' in this department is routinely defended as an adorable form of altruism by people who would literally never stop decrying it, had the boob hypnosis been performed by any other male party leader. 'His crime?' explained a hilarious pro-Polanski opinion article in the *Evening Standard*. 'Remaining professional while being bated [*sic*] and volunteering his time and skills to help a woman feel at ease with her body . . . A Prime Minister who could boost cup sizes would boost the national mood and inspire more patriotism than the current competitive flag loving.' Okaaay!

Listen, nobody's perfect. People have always held their nose at aspects of politicians' characters in order to be able to put a cross in one box or another. But across the political spectrum in recent years, that sort of realistic clear-sightedness has evaporated in favour of something much more like stan culture, where your idol has to be ferociously defended even when they're in the wrong, simply because they're your idol. In fact, because they're your idol, they are axiomatically incapable of being in the wrong. This tendency is most definitely not limited to the left of that spectrum; you get it with Donald Trump or Nigel Farage or anyone whose supporters frequently refuse to be honest with themselves in the face of inconvenient revelations. But these are dangerous waters for a political culture. Wilful blindness enables bad politics.

Many people who never stop talking about red flags might be able to look past Polanski's weird boob hypnosis or the mindset he accidentally revealed on *Question Time* last week. But surely it would be better if they could admit they are looking past their guy's flaws, ideally somewhat disenchantedly, rather than shutting their eyes utterly to them. All blindly tribal politics leads to disappointment at best – but much more typically, to something worse.

THE LEAGUE OF SEMI-CANCELLED GENTLEMEN

Another difficult few years for 'difficult' men, with female TV stars and beloved female authors still lagging vanishingly far behind in the sexual misconduct stakes. Come on, gals – harassing, grooming or assaulting much younger juniors is an absolutely essential part of the artistic/retail mogul process! Hemmed in for lucrative decades by a BBC that simply failed to recognise his behaviour was some kind of disability, Gregg Wallace finally released himself back into the wild. Some got away with posthumous exposure; Russell Brand simply rebirthed himself as a messiah figure in a Thames baptism. And all the many, many hangers-on and enablers who stood discreetly by notorious men for years simply melted back into the world, presumably waiting for the next situation vacant.

It's the nation's favourite cocktail – Phil and Holly on the rocks. Sickly sweet at first and then quite sour

16 May 2023

Of course there are other matters for our country to address, but this is the one that really matters. They are us, we are them

Phillip Schofield's *This Morning* career is lying in state on a catafalque, and the queue to view it currently runs to 10 miles. Yet still they come. What a testament to the guy's particular qualities. Then again, when the loathed Hollywood executive Harry Cohn died back in the 1950s and 2,000 people attended his funeral, a comedian remarked: 'It only proves what they always say – give the public what they want to see and they'll come out for it.'

To the perennial snakepit of daytime television, then, with ITV's morning magazine drawing the rubberneckers on Monday, as former bezzies and co-presenters Phil and Holly Willoughby 'battled on' despite reports of a serious rift. Schofield has done hilariously mad things over the past week, like hire a crisis management team and issue a statement about their amazing friendship and professional partnership. Holly . . . hasn't.

Are they really on the rocks? Yes, would seem to be the obvious answer, with many viewers convinced they could feel the tension on Monday's programme. That said, these daytime shows often have the feel of a hostage video. I can't see how you would possibly be able to act like you believed in segueing from an item warning about Alzheimer's to a chicken traybake recipe unless there was some guy standing just off camera drawing a scimitar menacingly across his throat. But we'll come to show editor Martin Frizell in a minute. The one thing we can all live without hearing any more about is Holly and Phil's 'professionalism' for carrying on. FYI, commentators: most of the country works every day with people they can't stand, so spare us the medal ceremony for a pair who pull in £730,000 each for doing it only four days a week.

As for why Phil and Holly are on the rocks, who can say? Or rather, who can say in print? For now, a recap of only the barest bones of this saga. Despite being watched by an average of about a million viewers, the stewardship of the *This Morning* sofa is being written about 30 times more feverishly than the stewardship of less important places like the Foreign Office, and 50 times more feverishly than the fact that a former cabinet minister is now on record openly saying that the Conservatives sought to 'gerrymander' by insisting on voter ID for elections. Yup, *This Morning* matters – *really* matters – and the fact that a story about Holly and Phil was the most read bit of news on the *Guardian* website for a large part of Monday can only be a testament to that significance. (Needless to say, I have read every word.)

But the plotlines are byzantine and, in some cases, still obscure. Take just one knotty strand of it all. Friday's *This Morning* used to be presented by Eamonn Holmes and his wife Ruth Langsford. Back in December 2019, it was reported that Ruth had made an official complaint about Phil, a stand she was supported in by Phil's former occasional co-host Amanda Holden, who stated: 'I admire anyone who sticks up for themselves as it's not an easy thing to do. There is a tin opener and a can somewhere, and other people have found the opener.'

It's unclear what happened to Ruth's complaint, but when, soon after, Phil suddenly decided to come out as gay, he did so on a *This Morning* presented by Ruth and Eamonn, who were then shown hugging him and holding his hand. Holly was in supportive attendance. Yet Holmes now seems quite pleased to see the pair under the hammer. Eamonn presents a breakfast show on GB News and is not remotely bitter – never is, missy, never is – though Monday found him twinkling: 'I think there should have been a special award for Phillip Schofield and Holly Willoughby for best actors.' Well now, I don't think we can even begin to get our head round all the angles of that timeline. Forget it, Jake – it's daytime.

Further highly called-for perspective came courtesy of olden days polo-neck-of-shame wearer Dapper Laughs, who on Monday tweeted a photo of himself staring pensively out of a train window, with the caption: 'Sat thinking about how ITV dropped me over a joke and Schofield's still on there.' And a field day, too, for my favourite future Royal Society fellow, 'body language expert' Judi James, who comes straight off a coronation rentaquote bonanza to parse Monday's *This Morning* and declare that one moment 'gave Phil the body language advantage in what looked like a bravado fight-back, because by the time he turned to Holly her signals of self-diminishing were making her look anxious and sad'. God love Judi. I always order the word salad and am never disappointed.

Backstage gossip from the show also tends towards the scenery-chewing, with editor Martin Frizell reportedly observed forgoing his usual spot in the gallery while the show was on air to instead sit in the canteen with 'a face like thunder'. The Boswell of all this seems to be former breakfast TV side table Dan Wootton, now a GB News presenter and committed prose stylist, who currently starts a new article about Holly and Phil four minutes after finishing the last one. He ended his MailOnline column on Monday with a thunderous verdict on the latest edition of *This Morning*: 'This felt like the daytime TV equivalent of the last days of Rome.'

Mmm. Like Dan himself, that line works better as a joke. And, of course, as a passionate student of history, Professor Wootton will know that by some estimates, the last days of Rome dragged on for 200 years. Two whole centuries of corruption and catamites and caving in to the barbarians at the border. Luckily, ITV doesn't face such grave problems.

The brave victims of Russell Brand's misogyny deserve our full support. This time, let's get it right

19 September 2023

The new claims made me think about the media's treatment of the woman he so famously humiliated on Radio 2. I hope we all know better now

Contemplating the notion of crossing the line, Russell Brand once remarked: 'As I always say, there is no line. People draw that line in afterwards to fuck you up.' Anyway, here we all are in the afterwards.

Back in the day, though, a lot of people were thrilled to be on what they thought was Russell's side of the line. For a certain type of mournfully uncool man on the left, Russell Brand was quite the excitement. You only had to watch their little faces in his presence, lit up at being fleetingly indulged by the kind of guy who would probably have bullied them at school. He was a sports columnist at the *Guardian* (often also writing opinion columns), he guest-edited the *New Statesman*, while the apogee of this particular stage of Brand's inevitable journey towards alt-right-frotting wingnut was surely the ludicrously feverish speculation over whether he'd endorse Labour in the 2015 general election. Keen to be awarded his royal warrant, the then Labour leader, Ed Miliband, traipsed to Brand's London flat during the final stages of the campaign for a filmed interview, in which committed non-voter Russell inquired rhetorically: 'Since suffrage, since the right to vote, what has meaningfully occurred?' Nothing much, he reckoned. Somehow, this disqualifyingly moronic assumption did not deter his political acolytes.

I had no truck with any of this bollocks, but I don't think it will quite do for me to spend even a nanosecond on self-congratulation, because I got other things wrong. Today, I want to talk about something that at the time was called Sachsgate, because it seems quite a useful way round the current insider debates on 'who knew what, when' as far as Brand is concerned. This is because Sachsgate wasn't a comedy circuit rumour, or backstage telly whispers, or anything else that you or I never heard, being out of those loops. It happened on air, then played out in the full glare of the media spotlight. So total was this story's Fleet Street dominance for weeks that it knocked a certain other little story – the 2008 financial crisis – off the front pages day after day.

Somewhat like the out-of-control bankers, Brand was a master of his universe, and one October evening found him pre-recording his Radio 2 show with guest co-host Jonathan Ross. Andrew Sachs – Manuel from *Fawlty Towers* – had been due to be a phone guest. Brand had had a fling with Sachs's granddaughter, who is called Georgina Baillie, and when the then 78-year-old Sachs didn't pick up, the pair began leaving messages on his voicemail. In the first one, Ross shouted, 'He fucked your granddaughter,' and three more messages to Sachs later, the pair had added grimness to horror, including singing songs. 'It was consensual and she wasn't menstrual,' warbled Brand at one point. He subsequently revealed that Ross had tried to make him cut the calls from the broadcast, but he had refused. The BBC aired it. From here, I'll assume you have access to Wikipedia.

As for the wider backdrop, explaining 'the culture' for women during the 2000s is quite hard if you weren't there. (I am very much looking forward to *Toxic*, a forthcoming book by the writer Sarah Ditum, which promises to enlighten those who swerved the decade and bring back shudder-inducing memories for those who didn't.) When it wasn't unremittingly vicious (Britney), it was weird and gross, top to bottom. And 2008 was also the year in which even the then Lib Dem leader, Nick Clegg, felt moved to tell *GQ* that he had slept with up to 30 women.

What is completely bizarre, with the benefit of 2023 hindsight, is how the Sachsgate story was framed, both by those who were reflexive defenders of the BBC and 'comedy' and free speech (then a somewhat lefty preoccupation, funnily enough), AND by those who wished their destruction. Fleet Street quickly settled into tribes and covered it as a story in which each assumed the other was acting out of vested interests. This was back when our only culture wars were about things that happened on the BBC. (My, how we've grown.) *Mail* vox pops were incandescent; some *Guardian* ones found it an 'overreaction'.

When the Brand exposé broke last weekend, I found myself transported back to that time. And with my 2023 head on, rather sickening alarm bells began to ring, because I knew – I knew – that I wouldn't have centred anything I wrote about it on Georgina Baillie. I had this shaming suspicion that I had treated it as a sort of media story, and so it proved. My mentions of it say Ross and Brand were total scumbags, but they chiefly ridicule the fact that people complained to Ofcom because of the *Mail* titles' coverage, despite never having heard the original broadcast. I mean . . . so what? Speaking of moronic points, LOOK NO FURTHER. Dear 2008 Marina, you think you're being clever, but you're being horribly obtuse. Get your head out of your arse. It doesn't matter whether or not they heard it, it's still hideous, and they have every right to think it's absolutely unacceptable for the BBC to have aired it.

Yet despite getting it right on the vileness of the broadcast, the tabloids pursuing the BBC got it wrong by endlessly and ferociously slut-shaming Baillie (even though 'slut-shaming' wasn't a term people used at the time). They cast the entire affair as an insult to Andrew Sachs, instead of to Baillie as well. She was roundly blamed. I'm sorry if the *Guardian*'s cuttings archive is incomplete and I've missed something, but I couldn't find a single column centred on defending Baillie in any contemporaneous newspaper. A year later, Baillie sold an interview and underwear photoshoot to the *Sun*, in which she said the media maelstrom had sent her 'insane', subsequently telling the *Guardian* she was 'a tart with a heart, a nice girl'. I am mortified to see I reacted to this by saying she should stop banging on about the whole thing.

In fact, Baillie sank into addiction and out of the public eye (barring the fact that for the rest of her life, the Brand story will probably be all anyone sees when they google her). But last weekend, she gave an interview to the *Mirror*, in which she reiterated that her relationship with Brand had been consensual, though the radio prank and its nuclear fallout had obviously been anything but. Brand made millions with a standup tour in which he mined the incident and further humiliated her, while – among other desolations – her grandfather didn't speak to her for eight years. She revealed that Brand had got in touch apologetically a few years ago and paid for her stint in rehab. Georgina's reflections were so without fury and blame as to be utterly heartbreaking. 'For about 10 years after Sachsgate it was very hard,' she said, 'because I didn't know whether I was in the wrong, so when he apologised it was a huge weight lifted off me.' That quote floored me. She spent a decade thinking it was all her fault. That's 'the culture' right there.

I'm just one of the many people who got many different things wrong about how that story should have been covered and framed. If we have learned anything – and I'm not entirely convinced we've learned nearly as much as we think we have – then it is vital we all treat these newly uncovered stories better, as the *Sunday Times*, *The Times* and *Dispatches* most certainly have with their painstaking investigation. And as I hope I have done with other stories, as I got older and a bit wiser. Tribalism is the enemy of truth and justice – even more so now than then – and the victims must always be put at the heart of the stories, which are, after all, theirs. However belatedly, that's the right side of that line.

So Russell Brand was baptised in the Thames and all his sins were washed away. Cheaper than a lawyer, I suppose

14 May 2024

His journey to Christianity was very moving, and infinitely more spiritual than his trip to the police station to deny criminal allegations

A hazmat dredger, please, to the stretch of the River Thames in which Russell Brand was recently baptised, in an event apparently conducted by TV adventurer and chief scout Bear Grylls. I know, it's incredible: Thames Water is no longer responsible for the biggest piece of shit in the river.

In his mystical biography of the Thames, Peter Ackroyd observed: 'There are some parts of the river that create or harbour distinct properties that are not susceptible to rational analysis.' And I think we might be dealing with one of those properties right here. Rational analysis deserts me as I survey a recently released photo of a topless Brand, a topless Bear and the unidentified owner of what appears to be an S-reg Japanese *hannya*-mask back tattoo embracing in the waist-deep current. Then again, it's possible the third figure is actually identified. The Brand-penned caption on this Insta-trocity runs: 'Me, Bear Grylls, The River Thames and of course, The Holy Spirit.' Sorry, but does the Holy Spirit now have a back tattoo? Game's gone.

Theodicy is an attempt to reconcile a just God with a world of suffering, but in this case the problem is having to explain how on earth this lot weren't made to suffer far more, with at least *E. coli*, for this ludicrous spectacle. But before we go any further, a reminder that Brand has been accused of rape, sexual assault and emotional abuse by at least four women after a joint investigation last year by Channel 4's *Dispatches* and the *Sunday Times*. He has been questioned twice under caution by the Metropolitan police and denies all the allegations. On the other hand, the Sachsgate alumnus will always retain goodwill for his endorsement swinging the 2015 general election for Labour.

It's fair to say this was not explicitly touched on by Grylls in his stated reflection on the baptism, which simply declared: 'Faith and spiritual moments in our lives are really personal, but it is a privilege to stand beside anyone when they express a humble need for forgiveness and strength from above.' Righto. Has Brand asked for forgiveness from the 16-year-old schoolgirl who alleges he sent cars to her school to bring her to his house (he denies it all), or is he focusing on 'from above' as a useful generalised covering-off device – the Notes-app apology of taking responsibility? Or indeed, speaking of tattoos, the 'Only God Can Judge Me' tattoo of taking responsibility? (I very much enjoyed the intro to a news story last year that ran: 'A man whose many tattoos include Tupac Shakur's "Only God Can Judge Me" appeared before Miami-Dade judges on Thursday and Friday in bond court.')

Anyway, back to the Grylls statement on the Brand baptism, which concludes: 'Friendships when we go through tough times are worth so much.' What twee twattery is this? Please picture it cross-stitched into a sampler and wall-mounted in whatever five-star Costa Rican hotel room Bear's staying in during the filming of upcoming Netflix series *Bear Hunt*, presented by former *This Morning* co-host Holly Willoughby. Poor Holly. You travel half the way across the world to escape brand contamination, then your co-star comes down with Brand contamination.

As for Bear, his decision to yoke himself to Brand is intriguing. Their friendship seems to have begun last year, when Russell filmed an episode of Bear's Apple show *Running Wild with Bear Grylls* in the Hebrides, although that was before The Unpleasantness emerged. To see it persist afterwards has raised a number of eyebrows. But, of course, Grylls is, famously, a great advocate for embracing risk in life. And with this latest buddyship, he definitely runs the risk of troubling his employers at the Scout Association, who, for obvious historic reasons, probably don't feel an immense need for their chief scout to be creep-adjacent.

Yet the question of what really draws the two men to each other is arguably less obscure than it seems. Certainly, neither is held back by self-doubt. Both are prone to emanating a certain sense that the rules that apply to lesser mortals are an affront to themselves. Discussing his financial affairs, Grylls once told an interviewer: 'I find it demoralising to pay income tax at 40 per cent when I work really hard and spend a lot of time away from my family.' Mmm. Can't help feeling he should toughen up a bit.

There's not a whole lot less appealing than someone now worth an estimated £20m whining about paying his fair share like everyone else, from nurses to teachers. That said, I'm a huge fan of people who talk about making extremely lucrative TV shows like it's a tour of duty in Afghanistan. Appallingly, Bear's got only an OBE. Where's his George Cross for taking down Una from the Saturdays in the Central American jungle?

Concluding with Brand, his spiritual journey has been what you might expect of a bog-standard sex-case-turned-wingnut. He was previously a Buddhist, then earlier this year began endorsing a Roman Catholic prayer app called Hallow, and seems to have settled for now on whichever branch of the Anglican faith permits telly survivalists to rebirth you. 'Week one as a Christian has been amazing,' Brand said the other day, adding that he felt 'changed, transitioned'. Onlookers are unlikely to spot the difference. He still has a conspiracist TV portal, in which viewers are treated to material on the deep state/Bill Gates/'the plandemic' – in short, all the usual suspects of the usual suspects. It's hard to know how long his conversion will last, but you can't help thinking there will be room for only one messiah in that relationship – and unfortunately, it won't be Jesus.

Behind every Al Fayed or Diddy, there is a small army of enablers. This column is dedicated to them

24 September 2024

'Entourage' is too wan a word for this motley crew of enforcers, concealers, NDA experts and crisis PRs

I'm afraid I shrieked when I read that Michael Cole, long-term publicist for the late former Harrods owner Mohamed Al Fayed, cannot come to the phone these days. If you covered a certain phase of British public life, you would know that Michael Cole could always come to the phone. Coming to the phone was what Michael Cole did, always to emit some hugely pompous shitblast in defence of his master, who is now the subject of multiple rape and sexual assault allegations. Alas, Michael is currently so shocked that no emission has been forthcoming. Instead, his wife was deployed to inform the press that Michael 'is not giving any interviews or talking at the moment'. However, she did claim that he found the women's allegations 'terribly distressing' and that 'of course' he had been unaware of all of it.

From spokesman to sending out your spokeswife . . . I would say life comes at you fast, but of course it doesn't. Fayed ran his entire race without his years of alleged sexual crimes catching up with him, and though he is not entombed in a pyramid on the roof of Harrods, as he wished, he certainly got away with it all. When he died, Cole rushed out to inform Radio 4's *Today* programme that his former boss was 'fascinating . . . larger than life . . . full of great humanity'. Yeah – not the third one.

According to the spokeswife, Cole is now in seclusion, dealing with the incredible shock of the mounting allegations that Fayed was a prolific sex offender. Since the BBC documentary based on the testimony of 20 women aired, another 100 approaches have been made to the legal team who were already representing 37 women, and it is safe to assume there are many still too traumatised to make that call. I shall leave it to readers to decide whether Michael, a former journalist, has somehow forgotten about all the allegations of sexual impropriety made during Fayed's lifetime that he personally batted away, or whether he is simply the worst publicist ever for having zero clue about any of his client's alleged . . . what is the word? . . . 'vülnerabilities'. Given that Tom Bower's unauthorised biography, which detailed several allegations of sexual assault, came out while Cole was specifically charged with handling Fayed's publicity, his lack of curiosity/memory seems sensationally remarkable.

But then, it isn't remarkable, and it is unfair to single out Michael. *The Times* yesterday published a useful rundown of Fayed's people, from the mouthpieces, lawyers and security henchmen to the doctors who performed 'purity examinations' on young female PAs. When you see the vast scale of it all, 'entourage' sounds too wan a word for this motley crew of enablers, enforcers and concealers, and for all the other motley crews that surrounded 'larger than life' men, from Michael Jackson to Harvey Weinstein to Jimmy Savile. I prefer to think of such set-ups as the sex-case industrial complex.

Fayed's isn't even the only one in the current news cycle. Much has been and will be written about the charges of sex trafficking, racketeering and transportation to engage in prostitution laid against the music mogul Diddy, real name Sean Combs. But due to space constraints, I want to focus on a 2016 surveillance video that surfaced back in May, in which a towel-clad Combs is shown throwing his former girlfriend, Cassie Ventura, to the floor in a hotel corridor, then repeatedly kicking her, before dragging her motionless body back towards the room she has just escaped.

I wasn't surprised that Cassie had long been telling the truth, despite Diddy's serial denials. What took my breath away was what the location implied: the sheer number of people who must have been involved in justice not being served. What, exactly, is the process for covering up a filmed incident of serious assault by an international star in the corridor of a hotel owned by a major international chain? Let's just say I imagine Diddy's lot are quite familiar with it. But think of the hotel's side. There are CCTV images; it is a whole department's job to monitor the CCTV. Were the management informed? Where were the police? Quite the mystery.

In Combs's camp, you can only guess at how many of the sex-case industrial complex were called upon to do their special designated job and make it go away. Lawyers, NDA experts, crisis PRs . . . who knows the precise combination of moving parts, but they were presumably all working in perfect symphony to ensure that this ghastly footage never went anywhere, until CNN published it in May, a staggering *eight years* after it occurred. Diddy's powers were beginning to desert him, but even weeks before, a raid as he was about to board his private jet had resulted in the arrest of only one individual for possession of drugs. Not Diddy, you understand, but a former college basketball star player who was part of his entourage. 'How Did a College Hooper Become Diddy's Alleged Drug Mule?' ran a *New York* magazine headline.

The sex-case industrial complex is a place where everyone has their job, a whole interconnected corrupt society that regularly comes into contact with actual society, a boring place of rules and boundaries, but only in order to take what it wants and spin off back into the lawless ether again. Mohamed Al Fayed's Harrods was also like this, according to multiple allegations. As far back as 1998, Henry Porter wrote in the *Guardian* of some investigative run-ins with Fayed's people, stating that he had been 'left with the eerie sense that we had been dealing with a foreign power: a fiefdom, which despite its real location in Knightsbridge, operated quite independently from the rest of Britain, with a security service of its own, an armed police force and a tyrant in command'. He was right, as all those shut down by the Diddy machine in recent years were too. We still live in a world of powerful men's Neverlands.

Gregg Wallace is in trouble. I would tell him to put a sock on it, but isn't that what caused the problem?

29 November 2024

As the MasterChef *host 'steps away' from the show amid claims of inappropriate sexual banter, might he reflect on his approach to women and work?*

One of Gregg Wallace's wives used to be charged with compiling his daily to-do list. As the *MasterChef* host once explained, in words he somehow said out loud: 'It starts off every morning with "yoghurt", then "leg band", then it'll be "teeth", then it'll say "tablets" because I've got to take my cholesterol tablets and vitamin C, then "check BBC News". Those are all the things I must do before I leave the flat. Then it'll say "Twitter" because I want to tweet twice a day, then it'll say "H" for Heidi because of all the things I need to discuss with her.'

As you can see, at no stage does this list say 'remove all clothes and walk around workplace with sock over penis', so it's a mystery why, in a period possibly contemporaneous with this list running his life, Gregg is alleged to have done that. And, indeed, alleged to have joshed in a whole host of other inappropriate ways, over a period of 17 years, presumably under the aegis of other lists. Certainly while married to other wives. I'm sure Gregg would say that the idea that any list could schedule and micromanage his critically acclaimed banter would be absolutely ludicrous, and yet I'm looking at the words 'check BBC News' and thinking that perhaps he would not be the best arbiter of what is ludicrous.

Nor is he allegedly the best arbiter of what constitutes suitable workplace conduct, according to – oh dear – BBC News. Evidence reportedly provided by 13 people and counting, including the broadcaster Kirsty Wark, casts Gregg as a serial indulger in 'sexualised' jokes and inappropriate behaviour. His lawyers deny that he engaged in any sexual harassment. *MasterChef* is made by the production company Banijay UK, which is conducting an immediate review of the allegations and has announced that Gregg will be 'stepping away' from the show while it investigates. 'Stepping away' is rather a twee way of putting it. Then again, I always feel the words 'historical allegations' also create a misleadingly quaint impression. Reading them, it's hard not to think of Gregg allegedly behaving inappropriately at work while wearing a doublet and hose. Or, on this evidence, while not wearing them. Ye olde penis socke, perhaps.

Before we go on, I should say that no one has alleged Gregg is some serious sex criminal – certainly not his lawyers. Indeed, there are already defenders out there, posting along the lines of 'Oh my God the BBC is so woke for suspending him, I actually love being spoken to like this.' Remarkably, they will also be the same people who frequently rage that the BBC is absolutely riddled with sex cases. Go figure. Actually, don't bother.

Meanwhile, Gregg has posted yet another Instagram video inspired by the allegations, videos that primarily have me asking: who on earth is Gregg Wallace's agent? What are you doing, mate? Maybe cut his internet? Tether him to his cross trainer? Because it is the videos that reveal far more about the whole business than

Gregg presumably intends. Consider one from October, made after this story first started breaking, in which he hotly denies saying anything 'sexual' on the basis that 'I have ALWAYS been true to my wife Anna, and have NEVER flirted or hit on anybody in the 12 years that I met her and fell in love with her'. (Anna is wife number four, following Gregg's sundering with Heidi.)

And there it is. You will note that Gregg seems to see all women as divided into two categories: the ones he would consider flirting with and hitting on (a category containing only his wife), and then all other ones, who just have to soak up the banter like they're a really absorbent kitchen towel. I can't help feeling that Gregg's mistake is not to have realised that there is actually a third category of women, which is by far and away the biggest category. In fact, it genuinely contains multitudes, and comprises the ones who honestly don't want to hear any of this boringly gross stuff, who make that abundantly clear by not 'getting into the spirit' of it, and whose cues deserve to be read and respected rather than repeatedly, endlessly ignored because you want to tell them you aren't wearing any pants.

Amazing, really, that all Gregg seems to care about is the idea that people would think he had in some way disrespected his wife. The notion that there are multiple junior women who found his behaviour unpleasant to the point of complaint does not warrant acknowledgment in any of his video output thus far, not even a 'sorry if I made anyone feel uncomfortable'. Whatever he's serving, it certainly isn't humble pie.

As I say, perhaps the agent should by now have delivered a primer? But if it falls to me to break it down for you, Gregg: *this is literally nothing to do with your wife*. Nothing. I'm sure she's great, and that's great. This is about how you made *women other than your wife* feel. Mad that such creatures exist – and yet, they do. Some of them are probably even other people's wives. One of them seems to be Rod Stewart's wife. The point is, it is possible to repeatedly, serially be a dick to people you work with, and for it to be nothing at all to do with cheating. Other transgressions are very much available.

Women's claims of sexual abuse must be heard – unless they're about master storyteller Neil Gaiman, apparently

17 January 2025

It's easy to process allegations against textbook scumbags like Harvey Weinstein. When it is beloved authors and 'allies', less so

Draw near, allies, for these are dark days for 'kink-shaming'. At best, this is one of the whiniest, most pathetic and least helpful phrases to have entered the parlance of modern times, and at worst, it's just another guy's excuse for sexual abuse. It's confusing. You try to be modern and post-conventional, and you end up enabling the most old-fashioned and conventional nastinesses of all.

Still, thank heavens for the parade of embattled famous men fighting kink-shaming's corner. I have just one thing to say to all the lady authors, lady pop stars and lady actors out there, and that is: if you haven't had an eye-wateringly expensive lawyer draft a statement about how consensual your sex with a tormented junior was, then are you really properly creative at all?

Fighting out of a Brooklyn detention centre, we have the rapper Sean 'Diddy' Combs, who is on remand, facing sex trafficking charges and about 120 lawsuits alleging drugging and sexual abuse, including of teenagers and minors. He denies the charges, some of which relate to his so-called 'freak-off' parties. This week, Diddy's lawyer's take on the multiple federal charges was that the US government was trying 'to police non-conforming sexual activity . . .

The prosecution of Mr Combs is both sexist,' this lawyer hazarded, 'and puritanical.' Righto.

Elsewhere, we have actor and oil scion Armie Hammer, #MeTooed back in the day over a number of sexual abuse and coercion allegations, plus a little light cannibalism talk, which he says was like being 'left standing there naked in front of the world with all of your proclivities or kinks being judged by the world'. Despite police reports, no charges were brought, and Armie now observes of his downfall that 'people were my bags of dope with skin on it'. Ah, ye olde sex addict, hoovering up his chosen substance – women – that just happens to have 'skin on it'.

Meanwhile, Channel 4 is currently showing a documentary on the rock star Marilyn Manson, who has successfully ridden out years of grim abuse allegations, including by his much younger former partner, Evan Rachel Wood. The documentary contains some previously unaired interview footage, in which Manson declares: 'I'm not into rape whatsoever . . . I prefer to break a woman down to the point where they have no choice but to submit to me. Rape is for cowards, for lazy people.' Certainly for other people.

But arguably the newsiest one this week concerns the author Neil Gaiman, subject of what might have been last summer's dam-breaking Tortoise podcast, *Master*. Except there are some dams that people – and fandoms – are hugely invested in keeping intact. It has taken till now for the follow-up, courtesy of *New York* magazine, in the form of an investigation entitled 'There Is No Safe Word', which features eight young women who allege sexual assault, coercion and misconduct by Gaiman, six of them on the record.

Gaiman denies anything was non-consensual and says that the claims contain 'descriptions of things that happened sitting beside things that emphatically did not happen'. He has remained largely hidden behind lawyers since the allegations surfaced last year, with one of these legal eagles telling Tortoise that 'sexual degradation, bondage, domination, sadism, and masochism may not be to everyone's taste, but between consenting adults, BDSM is lawful'. Was boundaried BDSM what was going on? The alleged victims say no, and they say it at complex length in the *New York* investigation.

Take the story told by Scarlett Pavlovich. Even unconventional people end up needing conventional things such as childcare, which Gaiman and his ex-wife Amanda Palmer seem to have decided was best obtained by hiring women who were also fans. Aged 24, Pavlovich has arrived for her first day of work at Gaiman's – he is 61 – to discover the child is in fact on a play date. She has known the author for only a couple of hours when he suggests she takes a bath in his outdoor tub while he's on a work call. Minutes after, he appears, naked, and joins her, swiftly beginning to stroke her feet. According to the *New York* magazine report, she tells him that 'she was gay, she'd never had sex, she had been sexually abused by a 45-year-old man when she was 15. Gaiman continued to press.' Indeed, he does so to the point of anal penetration. 'Then he asked if he could come on my face, and I said "no" but he did anyway. He said, "Call me 'master', and I'll come." He said, "Be a good girl. You're a good little girl."' She goes home to google '#MeToo' and 'Neil Gaiman'. Yet in time, she also goes back to Gaiman and Palmer's houses. And months later, a vulnerable young adult without a home and estranged from her own family, she is still stuck in this toxic cycle. And has still never been paid for all the childcare.

In our era, people have righteously debunked the myth of the perfect victim, but less so the myth of the perfect perpetrator. The perfect perpetrator is an evil stranger, yet sexual abuse is overwhelmingly likely to be carried out by someone you know, whom you may be related to or in a relationship with, and who is pretty nice to you some of the time. These are complex and inconvenient truths, but they are truths.

Furthermore, there are perfect perpetrators in the public imagination. Harvey Weinstein, once he was exposed, was the perfect perpetrator. Physically repulsive – hey, it is what it is – and not actually famous in the world outside his professional community, he was the kind of 2D scumbag no civilian could possibly be invested in. People in the normal world will always be incalculably more relaxed about the exposure of a movie producer, a job they instinctively regard as commoditised, than they will be about losing any kind of artist, a job whose works have affected them over the course of many years. Perhaps this is why many fans of the master storyteller Neil Gaiman are refusing to listen to the less appealing, less magical accounts of those women who allege he took advantage of them.

As for Neil himself, I see he still can't let go of the allyship argot, which frequently feels performative and knackered, but in the circumstances of this case comes off as actively ludicrous. Finally breaking the silence on Thursday, Gaiman said that he hadn't commented thus far on the multiple, months-long stream of allegations, some of which he had allegedly sought to silence via NDAs, 'out of respect for the people that were sharing their stories'.

'Sharing their stories', if you please! Neil, some of them have 'shared their stories' with police forces. Are you attempting to be an 'ally' of your own alleged victims? Either way, great to find you holding space/checking your privilege for them. You'll note that people like Neil even react to sexual abuse allegations in a superior way. Honestly, I'm feeling somewhat lesser here. I've literally never given $60,000 or $275,000 to people I haven't sexually assaulted so that I can – hang on, let me get my reading glasses on – help them get therapy/'make up some of the damage'. Having said that, I have always paid my nanny via PAYE and have never attempted to have sex with her. I recommend it.

Huw Edwards hates the TV dramatisation of his life. Maybe he should have thought of that before . . . you know

24 March 2026

He's done it again. The convicted sex offender, creator of victims, has gone and created another one – himself

I see Huw Edwards is still not the subject of any of his verbs. The BBC's former iconic newsreader (trademark: Huw Edwards) has emerged from a minibreak in the wilderness to excoriate Channel 5's forthcoming dramatisation of his downfall. 'Mental illness is misunderstood by many but can never be an excuse for criminality,' Huw informed the public, the overwhelming majority of whom are already well across this particular point. 'It can, however, at least help explain why people sometimes behave in shocking and reprehensible ways, and why things fell apart for me in the way they did.' Fell apart because of you, I think you'll find.

Anyway, there was a lot more of Edwards's lengthy statement. 'I have been open about my struggle with persistent mental illness over a period of 25 years,' he continued. 'What is less well known is the severity of that condition, which was managed successfully until the downward spiral which led to an appalling outcome.' Again, note the tragic passivity of 'an appalling outcome', as though a flow chart and not a person has led us somewhere we'd very much rather not be.

Failing to apologise for your interactions with a teenager and instead deploying mental illness as an explanation in the year 2026 would be more understandable if Edwards had spent the last 18 months in solitary, or been cryogenically frozen, instead of passing the time as a free man in some nice Welsh village or other.

Ironically, he seems not to have kept up with the news, in this case the development that this stuff doesn't work like magic any more. Edwards first trotted this explanation out at the fag end of the Peak Woke era, when casting various things as mental illness was still – just – an axiomatically unassailable form of victimhood. It's why his defence was initially taken up with such mad enthusiasm by elements of the reflexively wrong Good Guys of the media when the *Sun* first started running stories about him secretly paying huge amounts of money to a teenager. First it was a private matter. Then it was a vile witch hunt by the tabloids. Then it was a witch hunt that had driven a vulnerable man into the protective care of medical professionals.

In the end, of course, it was a conviction for possessing multiple indecent images of children, including category-A images, a crime that feeds on and perpetuates the suffering and sexual exploitation of children and traumatises those victims for life.

Edwards still hasn't paid back a penny of the £200k of licence fee payers' money he was happy to keep taking while on suspension from the BBC, awaiting trial for a crime he would plead guilty to. He'd much rather talk about a different media organisation to the BBC – Channel 5, whose production values he has taken issue with. He doesn't think the new drama is likely 'to convey the reality of what happened'. Furthermore, he suggests producers 'also refused to disclose whether any of those making allegations had been paid for their contributions'. Hifalutin words, particularly coming from someone who forked out over £35k to one teen who'd become homeless, before allegedly asking if there was something he could get in return (police said they found no evidence of criminality). Then again, most sex offenders have got some kind of screw loose, haven't they? I've got a feeling 'having a screw loose' is no longer deemed an acceptable term for talking about this stuff – and yet, it describes the mindset of all sorts of sex offenders so much better than 'mental illness'.

At this point I should say I haven't seen anything other than the trailer for Channel 5's show, so have no idea what it's like. I do have deep reservations about 'true story' dramas, which have become a genre of their own and scripted TV's most runaway success in recent years. However, making shows about real-life criminals is hardly a new thing, and you can argue the Edwards drama sits more traditionally in that basket. It's not a point Huw argues, inevitably, preferring instead to lambast Channel 5 for not checking its narrative with him at script stage. Again, TV producers tend not to bother asking criminals to give script notes. But Huw could definitely pitch the jump from sex offender to story consultant as one of those unfair barriers-to-entry in the creative industries if he's after a new avenue for his victimhood.

That said, I can picture Huw handing down a lot of the classic executive notes that all writers love to hate. 'Can we make the character more likable?' 'I don't get the "why now?" of it all. Why not never?' 'I'm not really feeling the stakes, because at the moment the character returns inside of two years explaining he essentially didn't have any agency at all.'

According to some very chatty publicist, Edwards plans to speak out further in the future. 'I am making an effort,' Edwards himself declares, 'to produce my own account of these terrible events.' No rush. 'This is a slow process' – finally, some good news – 'given the fragile state of my health.' There it is. A reminder that, for Huw, and indeed so many of the difficult men of television who have been forcibly resigned from our screens in recent years, their issues are much better clinicalised than owned. Yet are they all just victims of illness? Or are they, infinitely more pertinently, creators of victims?

THIS SEPTIC ISLE

And did those feet in modern times walk upon England's mountains green? No, would seem to be the obvious answer, with our green, unpleasant land afflicted by everything from riots stoked from Ayia Napa sunbeds to the perception of two-tier justice and a festering problem with free speech. Politicians conveniently judged it all to be mostly the fault of social media, which is, ironically, a hot take so malevolently wrong that it properly belongs only on social media. Elsewhere, his part in the handling of a horrific child abuse investigation claimed the mitre of the Archbishop of Canterbury, who opted to make his House of Lords resignation speech an ecclesiastical shot at a Netflix comedy special. Good times? Not really. But times, certainly.

Where are the brave inciters of Britain's race riots? From Tommy to Elon, they're far, far away

6 August 2024

Thugs may be rampaging in the streets, but their leaders-from-behind are more likely to be found sipping cocktails by the pool

'My kids are crying. We come here so I could spend some quality time with them. Now they are scared people are coming here to get them.' Thus bleated Tommy Robinson from the five-star, all-inclusive Ayia Napa hotel from which he is currently influencing sustained violent disorder on Britain's streets.

And yet, multiple paparazzi photos from the resort show Daddy either floating like a lonesome turd in the pool or splayed out on a four-poster sun lounger glued to his phone, with not even a pixelated Sproginson to be seen. Perhaps they were fomenting looting in the kids' club? If not, Pops has certainly broken with the form book by not co-opting them into his war games. Robinson's previous stunts have included filming his disturbingly tearful children on the day he emerged from one of his prison sentences (it was the attempting-to-collapse-a-rape-trial one, I think, as opposed to the massive-mortgage-fraud one).

The EDL founder immediately packaged and publicised what should surely have been a private family moment as a donation-driving propaganda video. Kerching! Robinson's current means of funding five-star holidays remain opaque – although I think most of us have zeroed in on one particular theory – but they clearly far outstrip the days when he was merely a Luton tanning salonista.

As does his virtual social set. Elon Musk, Tommy Robinson, Nigel Farage, Laurence Fox: you don't have to have taken a divorce well to be currently leading from behind on UK thuggery and race riots. But let's be honest, it helps! Think of this gaggle of would-be civil warfluencers as a loose collective, on which we'll slap the working title Fathers4Injustice.

Barely a day goes by without the shitposter's shitposter, Elon Musk, informing the world that in the UK, 'civil war is inevitable'. Sorry, but he doesn't even go here? Surely a better use of the X proprietor's time would be persuading various of his 12 children to even talk to him, instead of continuing with his sadsack experiment of paying $44bn to act like the world's disinformer-in-chief.

Meanwhile, that even shiter inciter Laurence Fox was pictured leaving the UK on a flight for Cork on Sunday, also welded to his phone. Ah, the old thought leader's grindset. 'I cannot believe this traitor,' thundered Laurence of a Keir Starmer statement on the riots (dateline: Stansted airport). 'For decades British girls have been raped by immigrant barbarians and now he's finally come out. On their side. Fine. Then it's war.'

Oh dear. Laurence's Aryan looks once made him a shoo-in for playing Nazis; these days, he just has to issue statements like them. He actually once played Charles de Gaulle, but has now gone full Pétain, if you can imagine the marshal wearing Nike hi-tops at literally the age of 46, like some ghastly old sex case from a boutique advertising agency. (For the record, I think I probably can.)

As for Nigel Farage, the Clacton MP and owner of Britain's largest collection of dog whistles is presently blowing the one marked 'two-tier policing'. Righto. What about two-tier MPing – that thing where you record an insanely irresponsible video in the wake of the most appalling child murders, suggesting 'the truth is being withheld from us', then a few days later emerge from your hidey-hole with a statement affecting to condemn the riots fuelled by just this sort of crap?

Then again, we saw that same nervy clamming-up from Nigel after the far-right murder of Jo Cox in the final days of the EU referendum campaign. Farage suddenly went very quiet indeed for a few days, before emerging on the morning after the vote with that historically distasteful speech, in which he declared victory had been achieved 'without a single bullet being fired'. Within a year, he was saying he'd 'pick up a rifle' if Brexit wasn't delivered – and now he's in Westminster, issuing portentous statements that I note he signs off as 'Nigel F'. Why not simply 'NF'? It would arguably make his key points more concisely.

Perhaps his Reform party will soon be joined by Suella Braverman, who has had precisely nothing at all to say on the current violence, would you believe. Her most notable recent public statement concerned her withdrawal from the Conservative leadership stakes and was headlined 'I've Been Branded Mad, Bad and Dangerous by My Own Party'. Which, again on the form book, means a lot.

Finally, no hymn to leaders-from-behind would be complete without a mention of the MailOnline, whose comment section I have in recent years read more obsessively and in greater volume than the contents of many newspapers. It is currently quite the window on to the fruits of a long-term strand of its coverage, and I can only implore the readers who have been deliberately fed a diet of it to urgently catch up with its metropolitan elite editors, who are now hastily decrying the disorder. Alas, there seems no sign of this happening. Presumably, those editors have noticed that every one of their articles condemning the current horror show is followed by absolute torrents of overwhelmingly positive comments in support of the thugs. Even Tommy Robinson's five-star Ayia Napa war room has been saluted in maudlin terms by that section of the British public that is never happier than when some blatant grifter is making a fool out of them.

Quite how large that section is remains to be seen, but it is not short of blatant grifters to be right behind them. Sometimes thousands of miles behind them, huffing another complimentary frozen margarita – but truly, it's the thought that counts.

Social media is a problem, Keir, but so is life for too many in Britain. I'd deal with that first

9 August 2024

Elon Musk may be a useful villain, but that should not distract politicians from the basic facts about inequality and poverty

Is Keir Starmer eyeing Elon Musk as a useful villain for his season one? If so, I can't help feeling the prime minister's chances of getting a season two will diminish. 'Let me also say to large social media companies and those who run them,' Starmer intoned this week, 'violent disorder clearly whipped up online: that is also a crime. It's happening on your premises, and the law must be upheld everywhere.'

Something big happened in the UK over the past fortnight, even if aspects of precisely what remain unclear. But we know the thing that happened doesn't happen in countries that are functioning well or are – how to put this? – fit for purpose. It feels a mixture of inadequate and tangential, then, to be hearing various senior political figures indicate that the thing that isn't fit for purpose is . . . the Online Safety Act. 'I think very swiftly the government has realised there needs to be amendments to the Online Safety Act,' London mayor Sadiq Khan says. 'I think it's not fit for purpose.' Starmer has since suggested he agrees.

Since arriving in this industry back in the late Triassic period, one of fewer than three professional opinions I've come to hold is that journalists covering something mostly as a media story is mostly because they don't quite know what to do with the real story, or perhaps are even unaware of what the real story is. (And no doubt I've done it plenty of times myself.) In keeping with technological advances, journalists covering something mostly as a social media story indicates the same.

But politicians doing something similar is of a different order of magnitude, albeit one with a tradition stretching back to when tweets were wax tablets. Plato – a true poster – called the type of myth the elite propagated to maintain social harmony a 'noble lie'. Nightmares have power, and leaders currently seem to be coalescing around the notion of X (formerly Twitter) as a sort of rogue state. The technology secretary, Peter Kyle, has declared relations with some social media companies to be 'much more akin to the negotiations with fellow secretaries of state in other countries'.

I note that newly returned Venezuelan president Nicolás Maduro has just broken off diplomatic relations with Musk and is currently blocking access to X in his country for 10 days for 'inciting hatred'. Hmm. Is Musk really the main problem with the Venezuelan election? Or is it, perhaps, something deeper? X has been banned in China, Russia, North Korea, Iran, Myanmar, Pakistan, Uzbekistan and Turkmenistan. Which is something for the good guys calling for it to be banned in the UK to consider.

Another inconvenient reality is that organising for real-world violence tends to happen on apps such as Telegram. Speaking to *Politico*, one UK government official asked, apparently rhetorically: 'What are we meant to do about an app headquartered in Dubai and used by the Russians for disinformation?'

How about: address ever-increasing wealth inequality? If that seems a weird answer, then maybe the wrong questions are being asked. Britain has just witnessed the worst far-right street violence since the 1970s. As the *FT* reports, seven out of 10 of the most deprived areas in the UK saw riots this past fortnight. Placing asylum hotels in these areas was the decision of the previous Conservative government. Who has this profited, other than the private companies that have raked in huge sums?

It's not clear at all that the unrest is over, or whether further flare-ups are in the post. But they likely will be if people treat this as a social media story. Nor does it bode too well to find the chancellor forever sounding like her predecessors. 'When household budgets are stretched, families have to make difficult choices,' Rachel Reeves explained recently. 'And government needs to do the same.' And yet, it's just possible that the answer to entrenched problems is not continuity solutions.

Meanwhile, it must be said that Musk – X's King Lear – could really use a villain too. Elon increasingly comes off as yet another twattish media figure whining that X isn't as good as it used to be. Hilariously, having less than a year ago told advertisers to 'go fuck yourself' if they didn't want to advertise on his platform, Musk this week started suing those same companies for not advertising on his platform. 'Now it is war,' he thundered. In which case, I hope he likes losing. As the entrepreneur and professor Scott Galloway recently remarked: 'No company with over $1bn in revenue has ever lost 60% of its revenues in a 12-month period, in a non-war period. I don't think that's ever happened. Twitter is literally the worst-performing business in history since a change in ownership.'

Poignantly, it might have been different had Musk persuaded just a single user to return to the platform. Yet despite, presumably, the most ardent back-channel approaches, Donald Trump has not done so, remaining in comparative seclusion on his Truth Social platform, with analysts predicting it will make him billions in the event of a win in November. For my money, Musk now feels he has to go online as understudy. Witness how painfully hard and frequently he has tried to push the line that 'civil war' in the UK is inevitable. Witness the very Trumpian nickname he pushed out this week – 'two-tier Keir'.

Ultimately, Musk is a crisis-hit businessman in need of an enemy. If he has alighted on the prime minister of a declining medium-sized country, then that perhaps tells its own story. But it would tell a much, much more depressing story about this country's prospects for real improvement if our leadership found it convenient to return the favour.

Farewell, then, Justin Welby. Good to see that you have already forgiven yourself

6 December 2024

The Archbishop of Banterbury could have used his speech to express remorse to the victims of abuse. But then there wouldn't have been any room for lolz

I imagine the outgoing Archbishop of Canterbury doesn't have a tattoo. But if he did, he'd have that one beloved of so many insouciant people: 'ONLY GOD CAN JUDGE ME'. As it goes, people with this tattoo frequently appear in court. In fact, sentencing guidelines for people with auto-satirical body art is one of only about three subjects that Justin Welby didn't make some public comment about during his tenure as the Archbishop of Canterbury.

But the great pontificator is now turning in his badge and mitre, and yesterday could be found delivering a quite staggeringly tone-deaf final speech as the Archbishop of Canterbury in the House of Lords. As a reminder, Welby's resignation was called for because he definitely knew about the victims of John Smyth, a sadistic monster whom he had once hugely admired. Smyth's victims, groomed and horrifically beaten, begged repeatedly – and for years – for an investigation, which the Church of England did not instigate. Many of them now state the Church's ignoring of their trauma was equal to the abuse itself.

And so to Welby's final speech to the Lords. 'If you pity anyone,' he twinkled of his unexpected departure, 'pity my poor diary secretary.' Sorry . . . WHAT? But I'm afraid the Archbishop of Banterbury had officially logged on. 'My Lords,' ran another gambit. 'It is often said, and it is a cliché to say it – but hey, I am the archbishop still – that if you want to make God laugh, make plans.

On that basis, next year, I will be causing God more hilarity than anyone else for many years.' I mean, if he was looking for the perfect tone for a farewell that in essence derives from failing to investigate grotesque child abuse . . . this ain't it. And tone was all there was; there wasn't a single expression of sorrow or remorse for the huge number of Smyth's victims, several of whom are known to have tried to take their own lives down the years.

On Friday afternoon, something – perhaps the anguished reaction of survivors? – prompted Welby to issue an apology statement. As well he might. That particular context certainly added something to another bit about a head needing to roll, 'whether one is personally responsible or not . . . There is only, in this case,' Welby expanded, 'one head that rolls well enough.' How convenient for the wider institution. 'Smyth survivors want all those responsible to stand down,' one of the victims was forced to reiterate in the wake of this speech. As for that 'whether one is personally responsible' . . . To clarify: one IS personally responsible. One massively messed up. One's 'distinct lack of curiosity' – not my words, but the verdict on Welby and other senior Church figures that was reached by the official independent review into the Church's handling of Smyth – is the terrible sin of omission here. The allegations against Smyth were first investigated and publicly aired not by the Church of England, but by *Channel 4 News*, from whose 2017 report the precious-little-justice in this case has flowed.

To pick one date, speaking of diary secretaries, it really is mad to think that Welby spent 1 October 2014 blogging about the importance of listening to victims of abuse and declaring them never to blame, when he could have spent it talking to victims of Smyth's abuse and telling the authorities about the man to blame. During the years he knew about the many British victims of Smyth, Welby found time to address a vast range of topics. The legitimacy of fear in the Brexit debate, *Bake Off*, the gig economy, usury, reality TV, credit unions, the iniquities of the global trade system, airstrikes against Islamic State, the broken economic model . . . all of these things – and so many more – over which Welby had no operational control were given a hose-down of his reflections, while Smyth moved on to abuse at least 85 more boys (at current estimate) in African nations. This was a horror that Welby could have actually directly prevented. Smyth eventually died in South Africa in 2018 as a free man, despite finally being under investigation by Hampshire police. For all his evil suggestions to boys that his torturous beatings were a way of avoiding brimstone, I assume Smyth never even actually believed there was a hell, or he wouldn't have spent a lifetime booking his spot in it.

Ultimately, the live story since Welby's resignation should be the speed with which this entire archbishop-felling affair is already being swept under the Church's vast carpet, despite victims working desperately to stop that. Yet why should victims have to keep pushing in order to keep the matter prominent? Why should it be up to people who have already been through the most hideous things to have to somehow find the strength to push for a huge, powerful and evidently self-interested institution to make serious changes?

Before he tendered his resignation, allies of Welby defended him with the jaw-dropping argument that other senior Church figures knew far more about Smyth's abuse than Welby, and for a lot longer. In which case: who are they? What are their names? What is being done to hold them to account? Every one of those supposedly godly figures should be facing consequences, but won't be, because the Church of England is somehow still in charge of its own safeguarding arrangements.

Institutional cover-up of abuse so reliably follows the same patterns that I have come to think that all who fail to inform the proper authorities once abuse has been reported to them should be liable to criminal charges of aiding and abetting. Perhaps that would sharpen their thinking as to the right thing to do. Until then, the entire way in which this business has played out, and is still playing out, confirms not just that 'justice cannot be replaced by religious observance or pious comment', but that 'the justice of the powerful is not justice at all'. A supposedly wise man once made those declarations. I shan't insult you by saying who.

The internet's nastiest gossipmonger has been exposed and guess what – he wants his privacy

20 June 2025

If you're not familiar with Tattle Life, congratulations. It's a site that subjects women to relentless scrutiny, and lo and behold, it's run by a spineless man

With as much as two weeks to kill before nuclear winter sets in, many of you will be looking to road-test your new fallout suits. In which case, can I interest you in the sensational unmasking of the founder of Tattle Life? It turns out that the guy who operates the radioactively toxic gossip forum is a 'vegan influencer' – I think it's one of those new types of job, dear – and his name is Sebastian Bond. From that professional description, Sebastian would never hurt a living creature – unless it's a mummy blogger, in which case he would gut her like a pig. Metaphorically, of course! Sorry, but that is simply the price you pay for not declaring that the nappies you're unboxing on Instagram are actually sponsored.

But I'm racing ahead. If you're not familiar with Tattle Life, it's an online forum that claims to be 'a commentary website on public business social media accounts', much in the way the torpedoing of the *Lusitania* was a commentary on the commercial cruise business. At one point, Tattle Life was said to have 12 million monthly visitors. Which, to put it into context, is more than *The Times* and *Sunday Times* website gets, and considerably surpasses the visitor numbers of something like GB News. The other thing Tattle Life says about itself on its homepage is: 'We have a zero-tolerance policy to any content that is abusive, hateful or harmful.' This is a little bit like the *Racing Post* saying it has a zero-tolerance policy for stories about horses, greyhounds or sports betting.

In effect, Tattle Life comprises a pulsating collection of live threads, in which anonymous users spend their lengthy wine time ignoring their own kids in order to obsessively tear down Stacey Solomon for some infinitesimal perceived mistake she's made with hers that day. That's it, Tattlers – you crack open another chilled box of rosé and remorselessly slag off, dox or expose this or that influencer/Instagrammer/minor rando for infringements of a code of which you're the self-appointed enforcers. And if you don't like that description of yourselves, boohoo. What, NOW you want accuracy and restraint?

Anyway, the site has been positively thriving like this for some years, despite regular petitions to take it down and frequent outpourings of distress from celebrities, sublebrities and whatever the class of recognition below even that is, many of whom believe it has either destroyed their professional lives and/or mental health or had an incredibly good go at trying to. Two such victims were Neil and Donna Sands, a Northern Irish couple with a clothing line and various other small businesses. Donna discovered that she had been targeted by site users in 2021, when a friend alerted her to the fact that people in her office were laughing over a 45-page thread about her. Forty-five pages! I guess no snowflake in an avalanche feels responsible.

The deranged interest/abuse continued, to the point of posting her whereabouts at any given time, and drove Donna to the verge of a nervous breakdown. The pair sued Tattle Life for defamation and, after a long and complex battle, won. They were awarded a combined £300,000 in damages, as well as costs, now estimated to total about £2m. But who was to pay? Tattle Life was run anonymously, and it was only a week ago that the high court of justice in Northern Ireland lifted various reporting restrictions and orders, leading to one Sebastian Bond being exposed as the operator of the site.

Many think the floodgates to further legal action will now open, but whatever Tattle Life's fate, it's interesting as a period piece. The site sprang up in an era when fame came to be regarded as a grasping business decision and not a cultural accolade. Anyone who made money in the public eye was fair game for anything. And look, no one likes a grift, we can all have sympathy for people who feel they're being mis-sold something or other, and most of us would fear the Faustian bargain of explicitly monetising our personal lives, let alone our children. But the elevation of even tiny bits of poetic licence by individuals most people have never heard of to the level of massive consumer fraud is mad, and says so much more about the self-styled cops of our age than the robbers.

In the end, investigators got Bond via his own site's preferred methods: obsessively tracking his public digital footprint, piecing together bits of often contradictory information, searching for chinks in his armour. The biter was bit. And, would you believe, Sebastian had pretended to be a woman on Tattle. Went by the name of Helen McDougal. 'I was just not surprised that it was a man pretending to be a woman,' Donna Sands told the *Mail* this week, 'and pitting these women against each other – driving them to their darkest places.'

So where is Sebastian Bond now? Some reports place him in Thailand, while others ran pictures of his parents' nice house in Somerset. As for who he is . . . he's a man posing as a woman in the course of drawing profit, an individual dedicated to exposure who didn't have the nuts to reveal himself, a grifter who'd rather vanish than face his own music. In fact, so vast is the disconnect between who Sebastian really is and who he presented as for his money-making activities that there really ought to be hundreds of skin-flayingly vicious threads about him on Tattle Life. And yet, needless to say, there aren't.

Glastonbury chanters or the Southport hate-tweeter – throw the book at one, you must throw it at them all

1 July 2025

There are many nasty, big-mouthed idiots in the world, but whether the offence was at a music festival or online, none of these people should be in jail

News that Avon and Somerset police have launched criminal investigations into the bands Bob Vylan and Kneecap for their Glastonbury sets reminds me that we have a severe prisons crisis in the UK, and that we need to build more of them. Perhaps we should build a special one for all the people we keep criminally investigating for saying, rather than doing, bad things. I'm pretty sure they have a few of those types of prisons in other countries. Although it must be said that those are normally countries that are run by people we consider bad. Confusing! But look, maybe we're becoming the sort of country where we imprison lots of people for saying awful things. I don't . . . love this look for us, I have to say. But no doubt someone has thought it all through very, very carefully.

If so, they could put the two nasty idiots from Bob Vylan in this special prison. Obviously, all of Kneecap too. Maybe those guys would have their cell on the same landing as Lucy Connolly, the woman who was imprisoned for two years and seven months for a repulsive tweet in the wake of the Southport child killings. They could be joined by whoever at the BBC didn't pull the Glastonbury live stream on Saturday after Bob Vylan started their repulsive chants, given that Conservative frontbencher Chris Philp is now officially calling for the corporation to be 'urgently' investigated. I see Chris is also calling for the BBC to be prosecuted, so I guess he's already done the police investigation for them, and all at the same time as absolutely acing his brief as shadow home secretary for where-are-they-now political outfit the Conservative party.

In terms of Spewing Hate into the Nation's Living Rooms™, it must be said that the footage of Bob Vylan's offending set is still embedded into multiple stories on the MailOnline website, all containing an exhortation to 'watch the full video'. Should whoever is leaving the videos up on MailOnline also be investigated and prosecuted? Perhaps Chris Philp could adjudicate. Either way, let's keep a cell or five for them in the special new prison. After all, why on earth shouldn't we imprison a few journalists too? In for a penny, and so on.

Needless to say, embattled prime minister Keir Starmer has made time to spout plenty of official views not just on the behaviour of the two bands, but on any future decisions to book them. If all you have is a hammer, everything is a nail – and if your big job before politics was being director of public prosecutions, then I'm sure everything looks like a prosecutable offence.

It certainly did to the prime minister after last summer's riots in the wake of the Southport murders, when Starmer seemed to relish responding in the best way he knew how: by rushing it through the courts. Connolly was one of those prosecuted, in her case for a manifestly revolting and racist but also clearly tossed-off post responding to a false rumour that the killer was an asylum seeker, saying people could set fire to asylum hotels 'for all I care'. She admitted inciting racial hatred in court, but has since become something of a cause célèbre for the fact that she is a mother with an otherwise clean record (and one who had lost a young child herself), and that she has received a harsher sentence for this tweet, which she later deleted, than some convicted rapists.

I wrote in the immediate wake of the riots that it was clear that something big had happened in the UK, though it wasn't yet precisely clear what. Unfortunately, the prime minister seemed to think it was fairly simple. 'Let me also say to large social media companies and those who run them,' he said, albeit to some reporters instead, 'violent disorder clearly whipped up online: that is also a crime. It's happening on your premises, and the law must be upheld everywhere.' Sadiq Khan seemed to think it was something to do with the Online Safety Act not being 'fit for purpose'.

In more successful hot takes, it was also the moment when Elon Musk test-drove his epithet 'two-tier Keir'. That one has stuck, and it will stick even harder if, for example, sublebrity band Bob Vylan don't get the book thrown at them in the same way that no-mark Lucy Connolly did. To be clear, I don't think any of the aforementioned lot ought to be in prison, however vile and unacceptable their behaviour was. But if you don't deal with them in pretty much the same way, then people are going to be talking far more loudly about two-tier justice again.

This type of talk has already reached all the way into the Oval Office, where, in February, vice president JD Vance suggested to Starmer that the UK had a free speech problem. You might have seen that Bob Vylan have promptly had their US visas revoked for what the deputy secretary of state called 'their hateful tirade'. But we can't expect consistency from the Trump administration.

What we expect of our own country is infinitely more important. I used to think masses of legislation around what horrible things people could or couldn't say was a niche-application civilisational advance, but I have changed my view and now fear we are sleepwalking towards a society where half the people will think certain incarcerated miscreants are political prisoners, and the other half will think a different bunch of incarcerated miscreants are political prisoners. I am very much for living in a country where we don't think we have political prisoners at all. Getting there isn't simple – but stopping travelling in the wrong direction would be a good start.

GOOD SPORTS, BAD SPORTS

The political-sporting complex seemed to have reached its final form with the Qatar World Cup, but it turned out that Fifa boss Gianni Infantino has so much more to give – specifically, the inaugural Fifa Peace Prize, which went to a tireless American pacifist by the name of Donald Trump. The rise in popularity of women's sports continued to delight all but a gazillion guys who insisted it must be some kind of conspiracy, despite the fact that England's women footballers do actually win tournaments. (Although England's men nearly did too.) And we reached peak sport-o-tainment in the advertorial documentary space, as F1's Christian Horner experiences the downside of getting into bed with . . . hang on, where are my records . . . with Netflix. Getting into bed with Netflix.

Beer ban, Beckham and a vagina stadium: the World Cup in inglorious Technicolor

18 November 2022

In some ways, it's a shame not to be in Qatar to see how this all pans out; in others, not so much

Some of my greatest regrets in life are things I've declined on principle. So, in many ways, I'm sorry not to be in Qatar for the World Cup. On reflection, I'd have liked to have taken a detailed look at the horror show *in situ*. I was once extremely close to travelling with Donald Trump's presidential party and some bad boys of Brexit to Mississippi, where the fash-Wotsit was guest of honour at the opening of a civil rights museum, of all things. Insulting? Disgusting? Grotesque? Obviously. But let me tell you, there would have been plenty to write about. I'd have got 5,000 words out of the plane flight alone.

Fast forward to the present day, then, and I am nearly disappointed not to be seeing one of the great horrors of the sporting/geopolitical age in inglorious Technicolor. Then again, how many words are honestly available? It's possible Fifa has finally contrived to pull off the genuinely unprecedented: a World Cup where, two days out from kick-off, there is only one thing to say about it all.

Even someone as electrifyingly articulate as David Beckham is reduced to promoting Doha by claiming it has 'one of the best spice markets I've ever been to'. Surely not better than the 'Say You'll Be There' video, the spice market where he chose his wife? (And which, coincidentally, was also desert-based.) Unfortunately, the only thing anyone now wants to hear from Beckham is an answer to the question: 'How much money is enough?' Some estimates place his Qatar promotional fee at £150m over 10 years, which is about £12m for every hour he did earning PR points in the queue for the late Queen's lying-in-state. Cynical? Hey, it's not me who's a self-marketed metrosexual whose family wealth was recently estimated at £425m, yet who somehow wants even more cash from a regime that imprisons and brutalises gay people.

Given the choice of addressing this or the modern slavery deaths, I see Gianni Infantino has instead taken refuge in some mad diversity-and-inclusion message. The Fifa president recently released a snippy little open letter to national football associations. 'At Fifa,' this ran, 'we [try not] to hand out moral lessons to the rest of the world.' Very wise. It would be like Charles Bronson drawing himself up to his full height and explaining that at HMP Woodhill, he tries not to hand out moral lessons to the rest of the world.

The Fifa boss went on to tell fans to shut up about Qatar and love the World Cup, because 'No one people or culture or nation is "better" than any other . . . this is also one of the core values of football.' To which the only decent reply is: what are you talking about, you grasping shitmuncher? The entire point of your tournament is for one nation to be better than any other! That is literally what international sport is! And guess what, the nation that ends up being better at football is not going to be Qatar, who are (a) crap, and (b) treat people like crap.

Honestly, can someone mint a participation medal for Gianni, preferably one that weighs 250 kilos to keep him rooted to the spot for the entire tournament and able only to contemplate the radioactively sarcastic words of its engraving: 'WELL DONE FOR TRYING'? If not, we're going to be subjected to weeks of him offering variants of his recent exhortation: 'Please do not allow football to be dragged into every ideological or political battle that exists!' OMG, likewise. Can YOU stop also allowing it to be? Fifa voted for the two most recent World Cups to go to Russia and Qatar, which is about as non-political and non-ideological as things screamed off various European balconies during the first half of the 20th century.

Anyway: is there anything to love about the imminent World Cup? Certainly not the sensational last-minute beer ban. (Although let's face it, serving only Budweiser was already a de facto beer ban.) I'm told the tiny geographic scale offers itinerant fans some 'logistical relief'. It takes longer to get from Infantino's eyebrows to his hairline than it does to travel between the various host cities. And I like the fact that as part of their attempts to create some kind of fan Stasi, the hosts have reportedly paid for some of the England Band to attend. That means that every time you hear possibly the nation's most annoying sound (including a reversing Securicor vehicle), you'll forever know that some of its purveyors have shown their arses for coins. Arguably, a valuable public service.

But, hand on heart, my favourite thing so far is the Qatar World Cup stadium that looks like a vagina. I feel it says everything about what we're dealing with. Consider this: at no point in the design sign-off process did one of the guys on the organising committee – and it will have been all guys – have the balls to say: 'Look, lads, I might end up taking a lot of stick, but doesn't this . . . doesn't this look like a vagina?' I mean, come on – they must have seen one.

More to the point, in a country where you can be arrested for being gay, you'd have thought it a social imperative for these men to publicly show an easy familiarity with the intimate parts of the female anatomy. Yet every single one of them appears to have been too fearful of something to say anything, which means that they've ended up with THE biggest self-own of a stadium in world sport. And so it is that, game after game, 'dignitaries' from this vicious, censorious, homicidal, women-hating regime will turn out to sit in a giant fanny. It doesn't remotely make up for the rest of it, obviously. But I am here for that spectacle, at least.

So, what is it about the brilliant, victorious sportswoman Mary Earps that bovine men just can't abide?

22 December 2023

The England keeper won BBC Sports Personality of the Year – and bitter old farts hated it. But they are losing ground, and they know it

UN election monitors to the BBC Sports Personality of the Year ballot, please, as a load of guys simply cannot accept that England goalkeeper Mary Earps won the prize in a public vote. Did these guys vote in the poll? Don't be stupid. Did they pass comment about the chaotic general election taking place this very week in the Democratic Republic of the Congo, where millions are starving and lead lives under permanent threat of extreme violence? One of the candidates, the Nobel peace laureate Denis Mukwege, declared that the 'electoral fraud of the century' was currently taking place. In which case, I guess Denis didn't hear about what went down at Spoty on Tuesday night.

In terms of what did actually happen, it wasn't hugely complicated, so you'd hope the election monitors would be done and dusted in time to proceed to the DRC. Mary Earps, England and Manchester United keeper, was voted Sports Personality of the Year in the annual BBC contest. That 'personality' in the title is often misunderstood: it's the old-fashioned word for a well-known person. The award is not an award for personality – Nigel Mansell won it twice. Notably, though, Earps does actually have a personality in that modern sense: she has become hugely popular, despite England's agonising loss to Spain in the World Cup final, with a big TikTok presence and a whole generation of young girl players looking up to her. Furthermore, a number of women of all ages felt her on-pitch persona simply spoke to them, specifically the famous bit where she saved a penalty kick to keep England in the final and glossed the moment with an eminently lip-readable 'FUCKING YES! FUCK OFF!'

So, for a lot of us at least half of that quote has played on the lips when observing the widespread wetting of pants in the manosphere that has attended Earps's win. No sooner had she lifted the trophy than the victory was subjected to denigration and ridicule by Joey Barton, Piers Morgan and countless angry keyboard warriors. I think if you'd have asked them what was wrong, they would probably have zoned in on 'everything'. The vote was wrong, the BBC was wrong, Earps's dress was somehow wrong. And a selection of male sports stars who probably don't give a toss . . . well, they were the people wronged by all this wrongness.

I think – I think? – the suggestion is that the 'woke' BBC has somehow rigged the poll. That is genuinely mad; the BBC fiddling the ballot for one of its most high-profile shows would be a huge scandal. If prominent media figures and outlets do think the BBC did it, then they should certainly get working on that scoop, as it would be one for the ages and would win them awards of their own. But if they don't really think the BBC did it and are simply having a pop at it because it gets them attention and the corporation would never sue them . . . then please ask Santa for some self-respect.

By way of a little plot echo, that spot kick Earps saved in the fateful World Cup final had, in fact, been taken by Spain's Jenni Hermoso, another top player plunged into a much bigger nightmare right at her moment of triumph. In the immediate aftermath of Spain's win, you will recall, Hermoso was grabbed and kissed forcibly on the mouth by Luis Rubiales, president of the Spanish Football Federation, who had been seen minutes before pointing at the victorious Spain players and grabbing his crotch. This set off a chain of events that would lead to the depressing overshadowing of the women's triumph, the Spanish Federation's open harassment of

Hermoso, multiple death threats for her, and Rubiales's incredibly delayed forced resignation the next month.

Four months on, it's depressing that many girls who have idolised and been amused by Earps will have clocked the backlash against her doing something as innocent as winning a trophy, led by bitter men older than their dads who would somehow regard themselves as more enlightened than palaeosexists such as the defenestrated former Sky pundits Richard Keys and Andy Gray (but aren't). However, there is much to be positive about. Tomorrow, Rebecca Welch will become the first woman to referee a Premier League game, as she takes the whistle for Fulham v. Burnley. Welch has spent years working her way up from the ground on the referee programme, which for some will count for absolutely nothing – but what a landmark.

In fact, speaking of landmarks, the whole Earps/Spoty controversy this week reminded me of Taylor Swift's mega-interview with *Time* magazine this month, having been named its Person of the Year. In this chat, after a year of undisputed global domination, Swift served an ice-cold dish of revenge to Kanye West, who had famously grabbed the mic off her 19-year-old self during an awards acceptance speech and declared she shouldn't have won. Fourteen years later, in an article in which *Time* described Swift as 'the master storyteller of the modern era', she finally spoke of the extremely long and unpleasant saga that followed, but from a position of total triumph.

A useful time to be reminded that there will always be some Kanye who wants to literally or metaphorically grab the mic off you in your big moment and tell you that, actually, you are shit and undeserving. Women shouldn't have to get past that, but every day plenty are showing that you can. It's the sad men and their dwindling audiences who can't, but they will end up self-limited and part of yesterday. As Taylor put it so very quotably in her *Time* interview victory lap: 'Trash takes itself out every single time.'

It's the Christian Horner paradox: F1 is now hideously dull, but the drama has never been better

5 March 2024

Who cares if the races lack competition, you can tune into the Red Bull boss's personal life in the latest episode of Keeping Up with the Carkrashians

Episode two of the new season of *Drive to Survive* begins with an at-home scene of Father Christmas visiting Red Bull team principal Christian Horner's house. It's a charming vignette from the Netflix show, literally just Horner, his wife, Geri Halliwell, his two young children and a TV crew with at least two cameras so they can get both wide and cutaway shots. Those childhood opportunities to be part of father's content farm are so precious, and Santa begins by asking the children: 'Has Dad been good this year?' No, would now seem to be the answer.

Not to break out the journalese or anything, but the boss of Formula One's entirely dominant team is currently embroiled in the headlines for all the wrong reasons, thanks to a mushrooming scandal that I have very little legal leeway in terms of being able to discuss fully here. It's all very *Keeping Up with the Carkrashians*. Let's just say that Horner was accused of controlling behaviour by a female Red Bull employee and cleared last week by a resolutely opaque internal probe,* only for a cache of messages, said to be between the two, to be leaked.

At last weekend's grand prix, the season opener in Bahrain, footage emerged of Horner having an intense discussion with

* Christian Horner's accuser later challenged this decision, but her appeal was not upheld.

the arguably even ghastlier father of his unbeatable driver, world champion Max Verstappen, while his Spice Girl wife private-jetted in to kiss him for the cameras with the 1,000-newton jaw clench of a wronged Tory wife. F1 is heading to the next human-rights-abusing petrostate – Saudi Arabia – this weekend.

Before we go on, don't worry remotely if you don't watch either Formula One or *Drive to Survive*, because they're incredibly easily explained (obviously, I never miss either). Formula One is a sport in which the chief propulsive force is provided by something other than a human, to the point that alongside the competition for the individual drivers' trophy, it runs a team contest, which it calls the 'constructors' championship'. Races happen around the world, ideally in grim autocracies, and the same guy has won pretty much all of them for quite a long time now, and will probably win all of them this season too. Formula One has never been more boring or more popular. Which brings us to *Drive to Survive*.

Drive to Survive is a lavishly edited behind-the-scenes look at the F1 season a year prior to the one taking place at any given time, and is such a monster hit for the sport that over the past few years, up to 53% of new fans have said it was mainly or partly why they began watching F1. It is the apotheosis of what we in modern sport are obliged to call 'plotlines', and if Leni Riefenstahl were still alive, I imagine she'd be shooting second unit on it. Huge numbers of those most exotic demographics – women, young people and Americans – have been drawn by *Drive to Survive* into becoming emotionally invested in a sport in which you can't even see the faces of the competitors while they're participating. Listen, I take my hat off to it.

You'd think one of the drivers would be the de facto star of *Drive to Survive*, but I have to tell you it is Horner. With the possible exception of about three 19-year-old footballers, no one in world sport has wanted to be famous quite as much as Christian Horner. He came to the realisation of this ambition comparatively late in life (he is 50), and consequently has yet to settle into his 'easy charm' years. A hilariously unbearable short king, Horner is forever organising cursed clay pigeon shooting events and playing to the cameras on the pit wall, or inviting them to capture him and Geri trotting along on their horses in the Cotswolds, or being filmed asking his children leading questions about what they most wish for. 'What about Max winning the world championship?' As his small daughter once put it somewhat brutally on camera: 'That's your wish.'

The current drama is not believed to be Horner's wish, but it does showcase the Faustian downside of sports actively treating themselves like a soap opera. As previously happened with football, where managers have become main characters, the F1 money guys have realised that the actual sport happens for only about 90 minutes, while big bits of its aspired-to global audience are asleep. And in the case of F1, is incomprehensible unless you're watching the on-screen clocks and stats. But the plotlines can happen the entire time, making it sensible to foreground managerial non-athletes as 'characters' and hope they create drama. The matches/races/whatevers can then just be something that happens between episodes of the soap opera.

In terms of those brief punctuation marks, F1 has been at a particular disadvantage because it is currently the most boring motorsport series on Earth, with its governing body either unwilling or incapable of coming up with ways of making it less so. It's not really great for a sport if its very first fixture of the season is marked by one of Red Bull's so-called rivals being asked if it's effectively over already. 'Unfortunately, yes,' judged Mercedes team principal Toto Wolff, after Verstappen's different-galaxy 22-second margin over the rest of the field last weekend.

Consequently, what people are now left to talk about is mostly things that aren't the sport, with the Christian Horner scandal being the absolute motherlode. Asked last year if he wished Formula One were more competitive, Horner scoffed: 'There's not one ounce of me that wishes that.' Hmm. I wonder if there is now?

A weekend of deranged hope, dread and stockpiling flares – it's the Euro 2024 final

12 July 2024

Gareth Southgate's side have made the hardest possible work of this – such is the only script our national psychodrama permits

Light the touchpaper on your flares, because England stands on the threshold of two days of giddy possibility. There is, quite simply, no greater weekend available to an England football supporter than the one leading up to the climax of a major tournament in which the national side has made the final. Truth be told, there is not a whole lot more English than trying to sound insouciantly au fait with that type of weekend. Let's face it, we barely know what we're talking about on this front (also very English). The reality is that England have previously made precisely two of those finals in the entire history of the game, and one of those was on a Saturday, not a Sunday. But listen, three of anything makes a trend.

Just as the long buildup to Christmas can be infinitely more joyful and infinitely less stressful than the day itself, so this is a weekend to be intensely savoured before the inevitable tip over into mindless something-or-other when the whistle blows for the end of play on Sunday night. To be clear: I am hoping for mindless euphoria but also preparing for one of the other mindless options available. Expect anything and everything other than mindfulness. With a dedicated breathing coach and movement therapist, there is a definite holistic approach to Gareth Southgate's team bubble, but it's fair to say English fandom remains wholly untouched by wellness. Unless you count sticking a flare up your arse – arguably the England fan's equivalent of Gwyneth Paltrow sticking a jade egg up her vagina.

You might recall that particular act of self-care took place in Leicester Square in the buildup to England's last Euros final in 2021. The chaos of that day latterly became the subject of a Netflix documentary, which has helpfully managed to share our local magic to all the streamer's global territories. We invented this game, doncha know – and then we invented putting flares up your bum as part of the buildup. You're welcome, world! I can't remember if we think we invented policing too, but do please recall that despite that day's absolute disasterclass in it, the then Met chief was not relieved of her job, but instead found herself at Buckingham Palace within days, being made a Dame Commander. Again: that's how we do it. If you have to ask, you'll never know.

The one change this time round is that the new government is not currently setting its arse on fire by stoking culture wars over the football. Ahead of the Euros final in 2021, there had been whole weeks of excruciating discourse about England players taking the knee, including from the then prime minister, Boris Johnson, and his ministers. But once they got to the final, even second-toughest-at-Rada Laurence Fox was issuing formal tweet-thread apologies. 'I have always been behind England in any sport and any English team in any competition,' bleated Laurence, who, not four weeks previously, had stated he felt 'embarrassed to be British' and declared: 'I hope any team but ours wins in any future sporting endeavour.' He probably did another U-turn when England eventually lost that final on penalties, but then many people of greater consequence did too.

Once Southgate's young side failed to clinch that 2021 final and a tide of racist abuse for the penalty-missing black players came in, even the prime minister was walking away from his farts. 'I always said it was wrong to boo the England players,' lied Johnson, live on air. But all that, let's be honest, is very England too: being a dick, and then either pretending you didn't do it or being tearfully apologetic about it the morning after. Hating people but loving them really but also hating them.

Some travelling fans in Germany are probably right now not simply explaining that the beer they threw at Southgate earlier in the tournament was in fact a sign of gratitude and respect, but explaining it and honestly believing it. The Pope famously accused Elizabeth Taylor and Richard Burton of 'erotic vagrancy' after their carrying-on in Rome, and there is something of that chaotic sensuality to the England support's relationship with the national side in pretty much any city in which they've mawkishly failed to break up with each other again. Certainly, as a fandom, we can put the booze away like Burton and Taylor.

Spain have come the hardest way to this final and look clearly the best side at the tournament. England have come the easiest way, got lost in the woods, had a crisis, recovered, had another crisis, come together, come apart, dodged cup missiles – and that's just the team. The fans have been on more journeys than Marco Polo. Take penalty shootouts. Spent my life dreading them, after bitter experience. But now? After this tournament? Extremely keen for Sunday night to go to penalties. I've said – I've ALWAYS said – that they are England's happy place.

This, then, is us: a country where the switchback ride sometimes feels it is the destination. Maybe that will change with this final, and maybe it won't. Maybe the England fan who got Gareth Southgate's face tattooed on his arse in 2018, above the slogan 'It's coming home', has since had it lasered, then re-inked, then lasered again, then re-inked. But if England do win on Sunday, you can assume he will enhance this eternal gluteal trauma site by adding a vast banner bearing what must, by now, be the unofficial England motto. All together now: 'NEVER IN DOUBT!'

Welcome to the 2026 World Cup shakedown! The price of a ticket: the integrity of the game

12 December 2025

In World Cup parlance, Qatar was Fifa president Gianni Infantino's qualifier. Now, it's the big time for Trump's dictator-curious protégé

I used to think Fifa's recent practice of holding the World Cup in autocracies was because it made it easier for world football's governing body to do the things it loved: spend untold billions of other people's money and siphon off the profits without having to worry about boring little things like human rights or public opinion. Which, let's face it, really piss around with your bottom line.

But for a while now, that view has seemed ridiculously naive, a bit like assuming Recep Erdoğan followed Vladimir Putin's election-hollowing game plan just because, hey, he's an interested guy who likes to read around a lot of subjects. So, no, Fifa president Gianni Infantino hasn't spent recent tournaments cosying up to authoritarians because it made his life easier. He's done it to learn from the best. And his latest decree this week simply confirms Fifa is now a fully operational autocracy in the classic populace-rinsing style. Do just absorb yesterday's news that the *cheapest* ticket for next year's World Cup final in the US will cost £3,120 – seven times more than the cheapest ticket for the last World Cup final in Qatar. (Admittedly, still marginally cheaper than an off-peak single from London to Manchester.)

Like all dictator-curious populists, Fifa loathes its people – the fans. Thinking back, I've even been at tournaments where the governing body has sponsored show trials. In South Africa in 2010, we had something called the Fifa World Cup Courts: 56 courts where Fifa indicated it had finally outgrown fast-food tie-ins and slapped its branding on justice itself. Or rather, on summary justice, which became an unofficial tournament partner as cases were rushed through to appease the governing body. A group of Dutch women who'd worn orange mini dresses to a game as stunt-marketing for Bavaria beer were arrested. Fifa filed criminal charges against the company.

Again, in retrospect that all seems rather small beer (sorry). Orange-coated faux fans are positively encouraged these days, but only if they come in the sole form of US president Donald Trump, whose bromance with Infantino has been one of the more mesmerisingly weird developments of his presidency. But then, just as power-playing moguls place themselves on each other's company boards, so autocrats love other autocrats. Back in January, many of us were still vaguely startled to see Gianni given a great seat at Trump's inauguration, barely two rows behind the tech oligarchs, where he was able to laugh uproariously at the bit of the speech where Trump announced he'd be renaming the Gulf of Mexico the Gulf of America. (Just a little niggle between Fifa co-hosts.) But now that we've seen Infantino pop up everywhere from Gaza peace conferences to regular turns in the Oval Office, it almost feels strange when he isn't part of Trump's malarial travelling court – the Dontourage, if you will.

Whether Infantino will at some point end up in the woodchipper, just like everyone does with Trump, is unclear. For now, the president is enjoying having his tummies tickled. A week ago, at the World Cup draw, Trump obligingly suggested the NFL give up the rights to calling its sport 'football' in the United States. 'But when you think about it, shouldn't it really be called . . . *this* is football,' Trump waffled. 'There's no question about it. We have to come up with another name for the NFL. It really doesn't make sense when you think about it.' This is what happens when the president gets booed at the Super Bowl, instead of being given an inaugural award, like he was at Infantino's fever dream of a draw.

Yes, even though you couldn't believe the shamelessness until you actually saw it with your own eyes, it was incredibly credible that Infantino would indeed confect some nutty Fifa Peace Prize and award it to Trump.

In recent history, both the Olympics and the World Cup have shown that they are always able to covertly or overtly override the local laws of the host country for the duration of their sporting event. Fortunately, though, this is unnecessary in the US, where being ripped off for sports tickets is effectively the 28th amendment. Furthermore, this World Cup is already shaping up to be the sort of reciprocally abusive arrangement we've seen when the tournament previously tipped up in non-democracies. Trump can use it to threaten Democrat mayors with loss of city hosting rights, while Infantino can charge genuinely crazy money and have Fifa run the entire secondary ticketing/scalping market without interference. Everyone's a winner, as long as they hold all the cards.

And the peasants – the fans – just have to suck it up. Fifa elections have effectively been hollowed out by the strong-arm practice of buying off the votes of smaller nations via disproportionately large grants. The dictator makes sure countries know what's good for them. The gravy train rolls on. So if you fancy getting rid of Gianni and everything he represents, I'd love to know the mechanism you have in mind. Maybe one day football will have some kind of revolution, in which hordes of endlessly oppressed people who actually like the sport will storm Infantino's Zurich palace and loot all the valuable gifts of obscure provenance. But it won't be soon, unless one or more of the big football markets gets it together and pulls out.

Until then, we'll just have to accept that there is simply no one who cares less than Infantino, and simply no sport that hates its fans quite as much as football. In fact, if only those fans could afford the tickets, they'd have the receipts to prove it.

ARE WE ALL GOING TO REFORM SCHOOL?

In June 2024, Nigel Farage unresigned for the umpteenth time as a party leader, and this time it was serious. The party, which has had more previous aliases than a rogue double-glazing salesman, was now called Reform. Luckily, commentators had been explaining for years that it was inconceivable anyone could ever break the two-party stranglehold on the British political system, and inconceivable that an insurgent party of the right could ever garner more than 12 or 13% support. Absolutely inconceivable. And now? As Inigo Montoya is forced to remark at one point in *The Princess Bride*: 'You keep using that word. I do not think it means what you think it means.'

Is Farage's win a new dawn? We could ask Labour, but they're still fast asleep

2 May 2025

The local election results tell us one clear thing: the 'two main parties' offer a change that actually changes nothing – and voters know it

It's been a funny old decade. Just over 10 years ago, the comedian Russell Brand was lionised in some quarters for appearing on a *Question Time* panel with Nigel Farage and producing what was widely, if bafflingly, interpreted as a brilliant zinger about the then Ukip leader. 'He is a pound-shop Enoch Powell,' honked Brand, 'and we gotta watch him.' Well now. Perhaps it takes someone who needs to be watched to know someone who needs to be watched. Mr Brand returned to the UK this week from the Florida base of his conspiracist Christian media outlet, appearing in court today on rape and sexual assault charges, which he denies.

Anyway: the local elections, where the big thing that people said could never happen seems to be happening. Farage now leads Reform UK, which even last year used to be bundled in the 'other' category by political pollsters; now, its standalone poll results frequently top the charts, with the fabled two parties of The Two-Party System doing not much more than simply wailing that it isn't supposed to be this way. In terms of last night's byelection, Reform has taken Runcorn and Helsby, one of Labour's safest seats in the general election you might dimly recall it won by a massive landslide 10 months ago.

Reform might have nicked it in record-breaking fashion by only six votes, but the word you rightly keep hearing is 'seismic'. Speaking of the mineral kingdom, the missing link between that and the vegetable kingdom – former Conservative Andrea Jenkyns – was victorious in the Greater Lincolnshire mayoral election and is now the most questionably gifted entity ever to hold the position of mayor, including Mayor Humdinger in *PAW Patrol* and that goat that was once elected somewhere in Texas. She holds a majority of 40,000.

The Runcorn byelection may have been forced by the former Labour MP literally punching one of his constituents, but people's metaphorical sense of having been mugged by politics-as-usual was surely a big part of Reform's surge. Keir Starmer didn't even bother to go to Runcorn during the entire campaign. Hearing repeatedly this morning from the Labour party chair, Ellie Reeves, that 'traditionally prime ministers don't campaign in byelections' felt like just another way of falling back on weird conventions that no one normal has ever heard of and expecting the old results. The old results are gone. Hearing people talk politician-speak has tipped over from being annoying, passed through being exhausting, and has now become actively enraging.

Yet as the Runcorn result was confirmed early this morning, Labour issued a statement that in many ways epitomises the sense that the old guard won't – or perhaps can't – see that they are going to have to find completely different ways of talking to people, let alone work out how to do it. 'Voters are still rightly furious with the state of the country after 14 years of failure and clearly expect the government to move faster with the Plan for Change,' it droned robotically. 'While Labour has suffered an extremely narrow defeat, the shock is that the Conservative vote has collapsed. Moderate voters are clearly appalled by the talk of a Tory–Reform pact.' Leaving aside the amusingly questionable analysis, who talks like this? People in politics, I suppose. It's starting to feel incredibly bizarre, in an age that supposedly prizes authenticity over all things, that most political parties are still communicating in a weird, desiccated way that has all the welcoming charm and accessibility of a panic room.

Ditto the idea that a series of small precision pivots is the answer to what is happening with Reform. In the wake of the results, Labour figures were already briefing that the government might make little concessions this way or that. But which way? Going right loses you votes to the Lib Dems and Greens. Going left leaches more to Reform – with the same bind holding for the Conservatives. And in any case, the people in question quite clearly aren't voting for tinkering. They are voting for destruction – creative or otherwise – of the old ways, which haven't worked for them. How on earth do you respond?

Not like Kemi Badenoch, is one of various answers on offer. The Tory leader was in seclusion at the time of writing, but her party's co-chair did emerge to explain: 'Kemi has said this is a marathon, not a sprint.' I'm sure whoever used to finish fourth to Usain Bolt liked to claim the same. At this rate, the stadium will have been knocked down and redeveloped before Badenoch has a full policy platform, let alone reaches the finish line.

As for Reform, a huge amount of tearful wank was expended over the past few years about people 'normalising' Farage, by extension suggesting that any voter who had time for his messages couldn't really be normal. This is what I think of as the 'People's Vote Fallacy', so-called after the equally wanky second referendum movement, which was named in such a way as to suggest that its leaders were either unaware that there had already been a people's vote or didn't really consider those who had won it to be people at all.

Even now, you have the general secretary of the TUC, Paul Nowak, this week informing people via the pages of the *Guardian* that Farage is 'a political fraud and hypocrite' and a 'public school-educated ex-metals trader cosplaying as a champion of the working class'. Paul must know plenty of trade unionists voted for Farage. Is he saying they're too dumb to see through him, or just conceding that more of the working class might end up drawn to Farage's movement than his? Across the conventional political spectrum you can find bigwigs lining up to say Farage is appalling and a chancer, apparently without realising what that then makes them. Namely, someone people find less appealing than *that* guy.

Whichever way you slice it, we're living in a time of flux, and though it is unclear what new order is coming down the line, it is increasingly possible to see that the old one has been fractured. There's a good line in a Martin Amis novel about a man who begins to crave a cigarette even while he is smoking a cigarette, and on initial inspection it might seem like there is something of that to England, where, less than a year after a 'change' election, people are fervently voting for change. But that would presuppose Labour had contrived to effect any sort of change at all, if it ever even had a plan for it. It hasn't. Instead, politics is beginning to feel ineluctably tidal – like change is happening to this government, not because of it.

Britain's voters can't resist a messy drama. How fortunate for Nigel Farage and Reform

10 June 2025

Former Reform party chair Zia Yusuf was out, then he was back in. But the chaos won't dent the party's poll ratings one tiny bit

It was a busy week for on-again, off-again Reform chair Zia Yusuf, whose job over the past 11 months had been to reform Reform. (I know.) Zia quit on Thursday. Had his job split on Friday. Returned on Saturday. Chilled on Sunday. The job split seems to have endured, though, as Yusuf will now run a UK version of Doge – as we know, the perfect role for highly emotional men – while this very morning, Nigel Farage was unveiling a new chair: Dr David Bull. David brings extensive experience in witchcraft, ghosts, spirits and beasts from his time as presenter of paranormal reality TV show *Most Haunted Live*, where he packaged the wailings of reekingly obvious charlatan/compelling spirit medium Derek Acorah for a studio audience. I can't imagine what this CV could do for Reform, but Nigel Farage must have seen something in it.

Acorah crossed permanently to the spirit world in January 2020, but it would be nice to think that shouldn't be a bar to his selection as one of those Reform candidates credited with being able to make deep connections with a public that is desperately searching for something beyond the ordinary. It would certainly be a less mad development than some of the party's other activities this week. On Monday, Farage could be found in Wales, promising to reopen Port Talbot steelworks, a plan so nutso that it could only really be believed by conspiracy theorists. Jet fuel can't melt steel beams – and Nigel Farage *can* re-melt steel furnaces that have cooled solid. Sure thing! Also, he might very well win the next election, so make of that what you will.

From the messy expulsion of their former MP Rupert Lowe to the Yusuf hokey-cokey last weekend, it has to be said that the endless drama in Reform this year hasn't dented the poll ratings of Farage's party one tiny bit. In fact, up they climb. My theory is that at some level, people actively like it. They liked Boris Johnson's fecklessness and chaos too – until, admittedly, they really didn't. Still, what a run. As discussed here previously, Britain is a majority nutter nation, and in recent history our deepest and most long-lasting political affections have been reserved for figures across the spectrum who had something of the nutter to them. Thatcher, Blair, Johnson . . . all nutters. Even Corbyn did miles better than he should have, simply by virtue of being a nutter, though he ultimately failed for not being a kindred nutter. Reform give the impression of being long and strong in nutters. 'He crawled out under the wire,' twinkled Farage this morning of Yusuf's 'bid for freedom', 'but we got him back in!'

'Sorry to put you all through that!' said Yusuf with a slightly strangulated smile. 'I did realise the only way I was going to get a couple of days off was to resign and then come back again . . . I can't thank Nigel enough for having me back. I regret those tweets, I was exhausted.' As Farage implied, this is just the sort of thing that happens when passionate people care almost too much.

For decades, the deepest analysis afforded to the England football side was that they needed to play with more 'passion', and there is now a huge amount of this in the way we assess politicians. Keir Starmer, a sterile lawyer who communicates with all the vim of a recorded 'See it, say it, sorted' message, does not reach the parts that need reaching. Farage speaks a more natural language, and consequently gets away with dismissing with one joke a row that would have consumed other parties' PR machines for weeks. 'Reform hit a speed bump last week,' he said in Wales of Yusuf's resignation and unresignation. 'Maybe it's because we were driving above the recommended 20mph . . .'

Arguably, it was ever thus. Reform keeps refreshing its moniker, but in many ways it's still the same, like a bankrupt who changes his name each time he moves town and starts another double-glazing business. Ukip, the Brexit party, Reform . . . every time Nigel leads another one you hear a lot about professional revolution, but at some level they're still the same outfit in which one MEP had some altercation with another one, after which the latter collapsed in the European parliament. As Neil Hamilton insisted at the time, this is simply the sort of thing that happens when 'passions run high'.

But by far the most important part is, it doesn't seem to matter. What's changed in a post-Trump world is that chaos and drama can be repolished as political assets. As I say, I think the lack of discipline is part of the appeal. Discipline – what, really, is there to love about that word for most people? It smacks of being told off, which many have had quite enough of over the past decade of elite cultural policing. Politicians who value rigidly conventional discipline above almost anything else have become regarded as robotic, while prodigals like Farage are polling like they're worth laying on a fatted takeaway for.

Instead of trying to counter Farage with the very conventions to which he is an adverse reaction, the two main parties should consider how unbelievably badly they've cocked things up for Nigel's rolling drama to seem like a good idea. 'Can we do it?' wondered Dr David Bull rhetorically this morning of making Farage prime minister. 'Well, to quote Bob the Builder: YES WE CAN.' Can't help thinking it was someone other than Bob the Builder who made 'Yes we can' into an iconic political slogan . . . but, to use words which may function equally well as a Reform slogan, let's not get bogged down in details.

Dear Britain, do you worry that Team Farage will be just a hot mess in power? Or is everyone too angry to care?

21 October 2025

Footage of Reform councillors fighting is further proof that uselessness abounds, but that's almost moot. To voters, they are very useful idiots

'I'm meant to be on bloody holiday this week, Paul! I don't want to be having this meeting!' There is much to enjoy about the patriotic revolution in government promised by the leaked footage obtained by the *Guardian* of the Reform UK group of councillors running Kent county council. Take council leader Linden Kemkaran, speaking for all free-speech absolutists when she declares: 'Paul! Paul! I'm going to mute you in a minute!' Or consider her repeatedly stated vision of the imperfections of representative democracy: 'You're just going to have to fucking suck it up, OK?'

Even so, I think the standout bit is when Kemkaran, who acknowledged Kent council's 'flagship' status for the party and its leader Nigel Farage, says: 'If we can avoid putting up council tax by the full 5%, that is going to be the best thing that we can do to show that Reform can run something as big as Kent council.'

'As big as Kent council'? The thing about Reform is that it could fairly soon be running something as big as the United Kingdom, with the most recent MRP poll suggesting that if a general election were run right now, with tactical voting, Reform would win a majority, with 367 seats. Without it, they could be on for 445 – the largest majority since the franchise was extended in 1918. (Not to refuse to get swept up in the moment, but I do think we might have to allow for a bit of tactical voting.)

Either way, there are currently two broad schools of thought around Reform. The first one is summed up by Dominic Cummings, who this week emerged to give a full interview in which he explained that he had absolutely no desire to return to politics, while observing that Farage will be prime minister, if he builds the right team around him. The second school of thought suggests that displays such as Kent Reform's Teams meltdown will be the thing that eventually halts Farage's march towards Downing Street, with people ultimately thinking his party is a too-risky crew of not-gifted amateurs.

For my money, a third way is currently most likely. Namely, that Reform will win, and that beyond a few golden blazers at the top, the Kent councillors – think of them as the loony lightweight tendency – *are* broadly representative of the team that will run Britain. But enough people will have had enough – have already had enough – that they just won't care about that bit enough not to vote them in.

When David Cameron blithely called the referendum on Britain's EU membership, the then Conservative prime minister may have thought he was offering a sensible we-know-best choice that could be swayed by the remain campaign's hilarious strategy of organising letters to *The Times* from 100 big business leaders or coordinating letters to *The Times* from 100 medium business leaders. But what Cameron was actually doing was giving the British public a fuck-you button and asking: 'Do you want to press it?' Personally, I didn't at the time, but it has since become abundantly clear why a lot of people did. Pressing it has not, it must be conceded, made anything any better, although many espouse the view that it is only not better *yet*.

In any case, things have developed significantly since then. Fuck-you has become the fastest-growing and, currently, biggest tribe in British politics. And instead of being simply adjacent to the fuck-you button, Farage has now fused himself with it. Go on, press him. You know you want to. A lot of people have been wanting to for really quite some time. It's just possible this method isn't psephologically scientific, but I've long spent a lot of time reading the comments beneath MailOnline articles. A few years ago now, I was struck by just how many upvoted comments, beneath a huge range of different stories, would simply be one word: 'Reform'. This was back when Reform was polling at 2%, Farage wasn't even the party leader, and the popular perception still held that under the first past the post system, you could never really break the two-party stranglehold on British politics. The story could be about potholes or small boats or the BBC or phone theft or whatever, but the comment was as frequent as it was monolithically stark: 'Reform'.

Flash forward to today, and in Reform's dry run for running the world's sixth-largest economy, the party's councils are finding it a lot harder than they made out. In Nottinghamshire, the Reform county council leader banned party engagement with the *Nottingham Post* after completely wetting his pants over an article in the paper about . . . local government reorganisation. Elsewhere, Reform have frequently shown themselves to be the free-speech warriors who love the mute button, the anti-snowflake crew who somehow constantly make complaints about bullying – and do so top to bottom. There have reportedly been eight official complaints of bullying made to Reform's south-east regional director in the past three months, while Reform's top brass actually called the police about the mean words of Rupert Lowe (previously one of their five MPs but now suspended and independent). Meanwhile, having honked endlessly about their Doge knock-off and all the millions in savings they would find just lying on the table when they took control, multiple Reform councils have found that there aren't any and they're all probably going to have to raise the council tax by the maximum amount allowed.

It's all chaos and hypocrisy and drama, all of the time – but so what? Could they honestly be any worse than what people have weathered for the past decade or more? 'Yes' has been the lesson of almost every single successive prime ministership in what's felt like a very long time indeed – but again, so what? Once people have gone fuck-you, it's quite hard to get them back, and it certainly feels far beyond the limited political gifts of either Keir Starmer or Kemi Badenoch.

There is a surprisingly common affective disorder known as the 'high place phenomenon', which is the irrational impulse to jump when on top of a tall building or precipice or suchlike, despite having absolutely no urge to die. A lot of people get it, and there is, by most accounts, a certain mad thrill to it. The phenomenon arises, apparently, when the brain misinterprets a survival signal and the instinctive fear of the height is somehow mangled into the momentary possibility of 'What if I jumped?' It is sometimes known as the 'call of the void'. Typically, the call of the void lasts only a split second, but it's hard not to feel the UK is going to be experiencing it constantly for the next few years.

Mystic Nigel has seen the future: a country run by his cabinet of taxidermied Tories

16 January 2026

By welcoming 'Honest Bob' Jenrick into the fold, the Reform seer is embracing the uniparty chaos he claimed to be seeing off

Like a 1970s Rust Belt serial killer, Nigel Farage is painstakingly assembling around him the political corpses of Boris Johnson's final, terrible cabinet. Think about it. You never see Reform's defectors after the initial press conference for their unveiling, and I'm beginning to wonder what happens to them. I think Nigel amateurishly embalms them or stuffs them with horsehair and sackcloth, then seats them round a 'cabinet' table in his cellar, where they all silently agree with him at all times and never interrupt him.

But look, I'm prepared to consider more outlandish fan theories, too, particularly after the sheer farce of Robert Jenrick's defection on Thursday. If Nigel's sloppy-seconding carries on at this rate, the Reform/Conservative party differentiation is going to feel a lot like it did when Bucks Fizz factionalised and split, then mounted rival tours of the UK. Neither music nor the United Kingdom was the beneficiary.

For now, Farage is really leaning into the enemies-to-lovers trope. On Monday, he cosied up to a man who'd previously said of him: 'Yr comments r offensive&racist. I wld b frightened 2live in country run by U.' On Thursday, he did it with a guy whom he'd incredibly recently negged as 'a fraud'. Personally, I have found both these episodes of *Heated Rivalry* the least appealing.

Hopefully, though, one day someone will write an interior-fiction novella that takes place in the five hours of limbo on Thursday when Jenrick was whereabouts unknown. During this period, he had been stripped of his home in the Conservative party, yet not granted citizenship of Reform – kind of an SW1 version of Shamima Begum. For these limbo hours, something had to fill the vacuum, and there was much to enjoy in all the staged fretting from Reform about the threat of cultural pollution from outsiders. 'The worries I get from within Reform,' confessed Farage of all these defections, 'are . . . will they bring Tory infighting with them?' Listen, someone's got to say it: if you allow these people in, they do bring their primitive, vicious culture with them.

Although this was not how Kemi Badenoch framed it in her viral video message. Incidentally, one of the multiple problems with Kemi is that she seems to have stolen her act off Dolores Umbridge. Even the voice, with that treacly-steely delivery, is straight out of the Ministry of Magic's supply teacher department. Or, even worse, the shadow Ministry of Magic's supply teacher department.

Anyway, in both off- and on-the-record briefings, the Conservatives have been keen to play this as a double-agent plotline, casting Jenrick as maybe the Ozempic Guy Burgess. As revealed by *The Times*, Badenoch had been informed by a mole that Jenrick was planning to imminently do one, and was furious that he 'came to shadow cabinet and behaved as if nothing was going on'. I hope you love the idea that anything is going on at shadow cabinet. And are even more intrigued by reports that, the week before, Jenrick had 'sat through a shadow cabinet awayday taking copious notes' about strategy. Wait – the Tories have a strategy? If so, Farage is very keen to tell them how it ends up panning out, constantly making reference to what happens 'after the May 7th catastrophe'. A catastrophe which, given it happens on 7 May, can technically not yet be called, but in Nigel's telling has already occurred. Then again, Farage undoubtedly has political gravity and momentum working for him, so there's no reason to think he can't master time as well.

Given the reputation of 'Honest Bob', it remains unclear whether Reform will ever really trust Jenrick, or if he will have to live under constant oppressive surveillance by the party's security services/a disgruntled Richard Tice. A bit like when Lee Harvey Oswald went to the Soviets and just got a load of monitoring and a factory job in Minsk. You get the feeling Jenrick wants more than a factory job in Minsk. Or, as he put it yesterday: 'I've put aside my personal ambition.' (Genuinely the most hilarious thing that was said yesterday.)

As for the upshot of it all outside the Westminster dramasphere, you hear a lot from Reform about the uniparty, the epithet meant to embody the necrotic consensus between the failed Conservative and Labour parties. But yesterday risked shifting the vibe to unichaos, in which Reform joined the big tent, too. Certainly, the lesson of the past 18 months of British decline is how easily the feeling of 'same shit, different clown show' sets in, with even Farage now offering repeated variations on how short his notional period of grace with the British public will be.

But why should anyone feel patient? To pick just one example, it is stunningly appalling that thousands of people cursed with living under South East Water have now been without water in their homes for a week, having already suffered repeated outages since November. The government has asked the regulator to 'review' South East Water's licence, but it has emerged that even if they did want to terminate it, they would have to give the firm 25 years' notice. You read that right: TWENTY-FIVE YEARS. This is one of many, many reasons why people have had it with the current system, and why many will give Farage a chance. It doesn't, however, make him the answer. I am sure Farage has the will and possibly the ability to tear dysfunctional things down. It's the fixing them or building them back up I just cannot see, no matter how many 'gamechanging' press conferences he calls. After all, if Nigel's allowed to report back from the future, so are we.

The greatest challenge Farage has ever faced: convincing the world he was never besties with Donald Trump

20 March 2026

The Reform UK leader has belatedly clocked that most British people really don't like the US president on whose coat-tails he has spent the past decade riding

At last, the culture has thrown up a split more nauseatingly up itself than Gwyneth Paltrow's from Chris Martin. It is Nigel Farage's attempt to consciously uncouple from Donald Trump, a man up whose backside he's spent the past decade most firmly lodged. Nigel's made such a massive, self-satisfied show of his real estate in the presidential large intestine for 10 years now that I actually don't think non-surgical extraction is possible at this stage. He doesn't just get to walk away whistling. The only way out is a full Faragectomy. I'll give the president a piece of drone fuselage to bite down on.

Anyway: conscious uncoupling. Back in the day, you'll remember, Gwyneth and the Coldplay singer deployed this particular phrase when announcing their marital split. Did the public love it? They did not. The general vibe – as with so much of Her Vajesty's output – was that she would do even marriage failure more smugly and unachievably than mere plebs ever could. The pivot from gushing about her perfect marriage to gushing about her perfect divorce felt like mere days.

There's a lot of this preposterously compressed timeline to Farage's attempt to distance himself from Trump, as Operation Epic Facepalm rapidly unspools. He's not alone out there, of course. As discussed here at the time, a whole posse from Britain's political and pundit classes greeted Keir Starmer's failure to jump two-footed into Israel and the US's Iran operation as a truly calamitous error. Yet these days, you can't move for the spectacle of the initial cheerleaders' reverse-ferreting. 'I don't like to see our prime minister be berated by foreign leaders,' was Wednesday's emanation from Reform UK's Robert Jenrick, who, little more than two weeks ago, absolutely loved to see it. Starmer, Jenrick explained back in the first week of March 2026, was handling the Iran crisis 'just about as badly as you could possibly go about it'.

Most of these turncoats now seem to be deploying the Josey Wales thousand-yard stare and hoping everyone forgets how any of us lived before this damn war, let alone what any of us said. The trouble is, that was ONLY THREE WEEKS AGO. I've had health kicks that have lasted longer than their foreign policy positions. In a month or so, when we're reduced to bartering screenshots for fuel, I'll have enough social media receipts to open a petrol station.

But let's focus on Farage, both on the basis that he is constantly treated as Britain's prime-minister-in-waiting and because no one in British politics has sucked up as long or as hard to Donald Trump as Nigel has. He was still at it two weeks ago. At the end of the first week of the war, Farage announced he was flying out to dinner at Mar-a-Lago and would be making various foreign policy points to Trump, who, we were led to believe, would be available to Nigel in the communal areas of his Palm Beach home. (I will genuinely never get over the fact that the US president willingly lives in a golf club.) Hilariously, though, Trump decided against going to Mar-a-Lago that night, preferring to hole up in one of his alternative Florida resorts.

So how did Farage play the embarrassment? Fascinatingly, if ludicrously, he seems to have decided to use the moment as a pivot point. The Reform leader's close aides immediately let it be known to the *Financial Times* that 'the relationship between the two populist politicians has cooled since 2024'. And look, I always fly to Florida on the off-chance of having dinner with someone with whom my relationship has cooled. In fact, transatlantic-visit-wise, Farage's Mar-a-Lago dash came with the most bogus excuse since Mister Andrew flew to New York to 'break off' his friendship with Jeffrey Epstein.

Now Farage does, very, very belatedly, appear to have grasped what the polls have long indicated: that most British people really don't like Donald Trump. And that was before he screwed their energy, food and mortgage bills and threatened to start the third world war. Yet we are now being asked to forget that Farage really, really did like Donald Trump. Hero-worshipped him, in fact. What a hostage he made himself to a very predictable fortune.

But then Farage is, and always will be, absolutely clueless on all this stuff. It was only one month ago that he was making a huge play of appointing his 'shadow cabinet'. Incredibly, this shadow cabinet didn't even bother having anyone handling the defence or foreign affairs briefs. I guess that stuff never comes up or something. Even more incredibly, now it very much has come up, Farage still hasn't bothered announcing either a 'shadow' defence or foreign secretary. Come on, dude – Lee Anderson's right there. Actually, hang on – Lee's only partly there, what with spending some of his parliamentary office time filming Cameo videos.

The reality is, this lot are total and utter chancers, and you can smell it off them, unless you're unwisely holding your nose and toying with giving them a go. In fact, Nigel would make a perfect Strait of Hormuz Guy, my breakout social type of 2026. Who is Strait of Hormuz Guy? Be honest, we all know one. He's the guy who couldn't find it on a map a month ago, has since mainlined 12 hours of political podcasts and now can be found honking: 'I don't think anyone understands what's going to happen if oil hits one-ninety a barrel!' Be sure not to get stuck with him at a party this weekend.

But also, and arguably more importantly, be sure not to get stuck with him as prime minister in three years' time.

When does Nigel Farage 'speak for the nation'? When it suits him

5 June 2026

Compare his responses – or lack thereof – to three murders over the past decade: those of Jo Cox, Sarah Everard and Henry Nowak

Which murder victim's ambulance does the would-be statesman chase? Can you be said to 'speak for England' if there are other times when you wimp out on speaking at all, either out of self-preservation or moral smallness, or out of actually just not giving much of a toss? The questions have arisen after Nigel Farage moved himself into pole position with an explicitly incendiary speech in the wake of the appalling murder of Henry Nowak.

The good news for Nigel is that he has struck political gold: increased numbers of people saying, 'I don't like him, but I agree with him on this.' The less good news for the nation he'd like to lead is that when dealing with murders that rightly horrify and outrage the country, you can't be sure which Nigel Farage will turn up. If, indeed, he turns up at all. Today, I'd like to look at three murders spread evenly over the past decade – all of which caused national outrage – and how Farage conducted himself in the wake of each.

The first murder is that of Jo Cox, the Labour MP for Batley and Spen, who was murdered outside her constituency surgery during the 2016 EU referendum campaign by a far-right terrorist who shouted 'Britain first' as he shot and stabbed her. She was 41. While other political leaders met the moment, Farage vanished from it entirely. He did not, as he did this week, hire a last-minute Airbnb and use its idyllic rural scenery as the backdrop for an address to the nation. In fact, Farage went to ground for days. When he resurfaced, his deepest thoughts appeared to be with the momentum of his campaign. 'I think we had momentum before this terrible tragedy,' he reflected wanly. 'When you are taking on the establishment you need to have momentum.' Will no one think of the momentum? Eight days after Cox's murder, Farage's referendum victory speech crowed about doing it 'without a single bullet being fired'.

The second murder was that of Sarah Everard, who was kidnapped in London in 2021 by a serving police officer. He drove her to Kent, where he raped and strangled her, before burning her body. She was 33. On this occasion, Farage did have something to say. And that was: 'We must not allow the tragic murder of a young woman to turn into attacks on men and attacks on the police.' Why did he not feel moved to coin a phrase like 'Women's lives matter'? As they were crying out to tell people during that febrile time, women had good reason to have lost faith in policing and justice. Less than 1% of reported rapes in England and Wales led to a conviction. Five years on, only 2.8% of recorded rapes even lead to a charge or summons within a year. When police broke up a peaceful vigil for Everard, arresting and cuffing attenders, Farage does not seem to have made a statement at all. Later, he would say: 'When we saw the [Wayne] Couzens case, I thought it was horrific, but you know what, you're going to get one bad person in any large group of people.'

Even two weeks ago, when three teenage boys were spared custodial sentences for raping two girls, Nigel doesn't seem to have emerged from the silence that followed the discovery of his £5m gift from a crypto billionaire to make a statement about no-tier justice for women. These days, his slogan is: 'Only Reform will protect women and girls.' Will they? Feels like quite a punt.

The third murder is that of Henry Nowak, the student who was stabbed by a Sikh man in Southampton, and to whose final moments the police were summoned by the murderer, on the false pretext that he had been racially abused. Henry died in handcuffs, telling police he couldn't breathe. He was 18. In the wake of the murderer's conviction, Henry's father explicitly asked that his death should not 'be used to create further division, hatred or tension'. Yet here, at last, is a murder that Farage seems to have decided he could go all in on. He hired the Airbnb. He told us what it said about our country.

But the thing about these three murders is that they ALL told us something about the state of the nation. Separately, they told us things about radicalisation, misogyny, institutional failure, women's sense of their safety within society, toxic political culture, race, policing, the folly of imagining our problems to be the same as the US's, the misuse of the law – and so much more. So many things. And when you are prime minister, you are prime minister of all the things. Not just the ones you happen to truly care about or think will give you a leg-up.

This week, Farage explicitly summoned anger, and many suspect we'll be seeing more of it on our streets this summer. Nigel is the sorcerer's apprentice, and anger is the magic he thinks he can control. Yet he isn't a courageous statesman, and he never has been. A lot of people don't care about that now, when they're righteously angry, which is understandable. But a lot of them will end up caring about the fallout from that lack of courage and statesmanship in the end, if he makes it to Downing Street. If you want to speak for a nation, you should speak consistently, even when it is hard. You should listen to people, even if they're not your natural constituency. And you should turn up, always – not just when it suits or moves you. Otherwise, what are you? Nothing but a two-tier politician.

Reform's genius plan is finally coming into view: field terrible candidates, then lose

19 June 2026

The unstoppable Nigel Farage is looking increasingly stoppable in the wake of Makerfield. The actual prime minister, meanwhile, has gone into hiding

You'll note that Keir Starmer is in full bunker mode – and we'll get to him – but after the Makerfield result, why isn't Nigel Farage? Why isn't Nigel ranting madly at his generals and refusing to admit that actually, everything that went wrong for Reform here flowed directly from his personal character, and is going to keep happening in one way or another because people don't change? Nigel's gonna Nigel.

Nobody fetishises plain speaking like Farage, so we owe it to him to honour that and observe that Reform really shat the bed. Makerfield is among the party's top 10 target seats in a general election, and Reform strategists' decision to field yet another inadequate liability, whose past social media activity they simply couldn't be arsed to check, seems to have proved something of a turn-off – for example, for women, who strangely didn't feel minded to vote for someone who had said: 'I'm sexist, sorry but I am.' Rob Kenyon will no doubt be back on his plumbing rounds next week. So, Makerfield ladies, make sure your husband's at home to be consulted about whether you really want your sink unblocked. It'll honestly be cheaper to replace it.

Meanwhile, it would take a heart of stone not to cackle at the fact that Reform is now losing votes to an insurgent party to its right. The thing to remember about Restore is that it is a party that genuinely exists only because Nigel couldn't handle some light strategic criticism from Rupert Lowe. Why? Because Nigel is, and always has been, a diva who has huge fallouts with colleagues and allies. Just can't help himself. When Reform removed the whip from Lowe last year, some party mook too wet to put their name to the comment gibbered: 'This is what happens when you mess with Nigel.' Counterpoint: the Makerfield result is what happens when you mess with Nigel. Try to think of it as a flow chart, where taking the 'yes' fork on the box that reads 'Did you fail to bend the knee?' always, always leads to Nigel having a meltdown.

Furthermore, the vanishingly small combined tally for the Conservatives, Greens and Lib Dems suggests that the Makerfield byelection was a truly great night for Anyone-But-Reform. Just as Own Goal inevitably became England's top scorer, so Tactical Voting could become the leading political preference in the UK. God knows we don't have a perfect electoral system, but it's *our* electoral system. And despite masses of insultingly mendacious campaign leaflets from a number of the Makerfield players, voters who don't love anyone are perfectly capable of working out who to vote for to keep out the ones they really hate. Who, rather often, are marching under Farage's Reform banner. In some ways, it's poignant that Nigel sneers at people who lament polarisation, because as these results show, he's getting really screwed by it. Unfortunately, he's very polarising.

The other increasingly noticeable thing about Farage is that he is incredibly thin-skinned and can't help showing it. Remember, he spent the first part of this campaign in sulky seclusion, after people found out about him taking a totally normal personal gift of £5m from a Thailand-based crypto billionaire. When he finally emerged to talk about it, he couldn't keep his nuclear irritation and affront under wraps. This is very Nigel. The commentator Dominic Lawson recently recalled Farage's reaction to a mild joke at some *Spectator* awards last winter, describing his face turning white before he shouted: 'Why don't you go fuck yourself?' Why do you keep fucking yourself? feels like the more salient question for Farage.

Anyway, let's leave him there for now and consider that the atmosphere in Starmer's Downing Street bunker feels faintly delulu. A few days ago, the prime minister graciously indicated that he was minded to give Andy Burnham a cabinet job. This felt a bit like Lord Cardigan saying he'd be happy to bestow the rank of half-colonel on the Russian commander 10 minutes before the charge of the Light Brigade. A very flattering offer, your lordship – but we have decided, on balance, to wait and see how your interesting military gambit plays out.

The sheer strength of Burnham's victory suggests that options have evolved, as it were, and this morning you could hear several Burnham outriders breaking the glass on the fateful phrase 'orderly and managed transition'. Oh God – PLEASE not 'orderly transition'. How many times in the past decade have we heard the phrase 'orderly transition'? I do not think these words mean what they think they mean. There's absolutely nothing orderly about being on the brink of our seventh prime minister in 10 years. Let's not kid ourselves: the mad bastards of our political class are at it again, and we are once more being assured that we will get not just a different prime minister, but a different *kind* of prime minister.

A word on that dream. Well, more of a roll call, really. Back in 2019, Boris Johnson promised to be 'a different sort of prime minister'. A few years on, Rishi Sunak was explaining that he, too, would be a different kind of prime minister: 'It doesn't have to be this way. I won't be this way.' Next up was Starmer's regular declaration that he was 'doing government differently'. So, yes – we've been hurt before. But chalk up another one, because this morning allies of Burnham are explaining that he, too, will be a very different kind of prime minister. One that people don't blame for the problems in their lives that are not being solved by politics? Good luck, as they say, with that.

ACKNOWLEDGMENTS

My first thanks go to everyone at the *Guardian* who has been involved in desking, subbing and legalling the columns in this book – most particularly, all those at Opinion who catch my mistakes and quite often let me be that pushy little madam who insists the joke stays in, even if, yes, some people might find it to be in quite poor taste. It takes a village to lower the tone like that – thanks to you all.

At Faber, I am indebted to my wonderful editor, Laura Hassan, who made our second tour round this block even more of a pleasure than it was last time. Thank you so much, Laura, for all of it – and we both know none of it happens without Sara Cheraghlou in editorial. Jess Kim and Sophie Clarke made marketing fun by tailoring it to my specific areas of interest – 'Why yes, of course I can do a quickfire video related to gay ice-hockey romances' – while Josh Smith and Hannah Turner in publicity gave me many laughs (and a lot of media placement, obviously, but laughs count most). Pre-press all-stars were Kate Ward, indefatigable copy-editor Ian Bahrami and proofreader/indexer Mark Bolland, with Rebecca Hydon acing it on production. I love and worship the Faber sales team, from Sara Talbot to Sarah Davison-Aitkins to Mallory Ladd and beyond. Pete Adlington and Matt Crockett yet again collaborated on a hugely jolly cover for times which sometimes feel anything but, while I thank Sean McTernan for his beady legal eye.

A dedicated paragraph of its own must go to my amazing agent, Karolina Sutton at CAA, who is both the queen of everything and also its most fearsome general. Never change, you gorgeous apex predator.

As always, my most intense thanks go to my family, especially my three children, who have heard the words 'What am I going to write about today?' even more often than they've heard me say, 'I will literally puncture that ball if you play with it in the house ever again.' Which is a lot. Guys, I know you want me to name you here, but unfortunately, there are a whole load of weirdos out there. Another point I believe I have made quite annoyingly to you on a number of occasions. As for my husband, Kieran, I could never know where to start . . . Thanking him for all the things he has done for me would require more pages than there are in this book.

INDEX